# IT TAKES A FOOL TO LEARN

**Copyright © 2024**

All rights are reserved, and no part of this publication may be reproduced, distributed, or transmitted in any manner, whether through photocopying, recording, or any other electronic or mechanical methods, without the explicit prior written permission of the publisher. This restriction applies to any form or means of reproduction or distribution.

Exceptions to this rule include brief quotations that may be incorporated into critical reviews, as well as certain other noncommercial uses that are allowed by copyright law. Any such usage must adhere to the specified conditions and permissions outlined by the copyright holder.

Book Design by HMDPUBLISHING

**DISCLAIMER**

This book is a work of creative nonfiction. All the events in this collection are true to the best of the author's memory. Some names and identifying features may have been changed to protect the identity of certain parties. The author in no way represents any company, corporation, brand, or song, mentioned herein.

In certain instances, names and identities may have been altered to protect the privacy and confidentiality of individuals. This includes some deceased characters whose names have been retained in their original form. Any resemblance to actual persons, living or dead, events, or locales is entirely coincidental.

Furthermore, while every effort has been made to ensure accuracy and authenticity, the author makes no representations or warranties regarding the completeness, reliability, or suitability of the information contained within. Any reliance on the information provided in this book is at the reader's own risk.

Additionally, in the event that this book is adapted into a film, television series, or any other form of media, the author retains the right to make creative decisions and adaptations as deemed necessary. Any similarities between the book and subsequent adaptations are purely coincidental.

By reading this book, the reader acknowledges and accepts the terms of this disclaimer.

# ACKNOWLEDGEMENTS

I would first like to thank my Heavenly Father, The Almighty Creator, for giving me the strength to make it through all I've been through and to have the courage to write this book. Lord knows, I spent many nights crying as I reminisced through some of these painful memories.

I would also like to thank my husband, Anthony Brown, for going on this journey with me. He has been there every step of the way.

I want to thank my National Louis University crew for their unwavering support and teachings. My Chair, Dr. Bradley Olson, my committee, Dr. Judah Viola and Dr. Ericka Mingo, and many others, as well as my strong, supportive, powerful, intelligent, wonderful, and beautiful Cohort 22.

To the characters in this book, so many memories and lessons learned that will never be forgotten. I will hold dear to my heart as I proceed in the works of the life direction in which the Lord has laid before me.

To my children, I hope this book gives you all a better understanding of your mother. I pray that you continue to be strong and see all of the sacrifices that I made for you. Please know all those hours I worked were to keep you all in decent communities, food on the table, and clothes on your back. I tried my best as a single mother to give you all a decent and deserving life. One that you could be proud of. I taught you all everything I knew, how to trust and believe in God, how to pray, to be strong and independent. And so much more. Education was always a must in our house. From the good times to the bad times, I can rest well today knowing that I've been there in every type of way for you all. Whether it was physically, financially, emotionally, a phone call, a visit, getting you out of trouble, making calls on your behalf, buying furniture for your new apartments, coming to your school events, inviting your friends over and decorating your birthday parties, for every Christmas, holiday, or special achievement, I was there and I will ALWAYS love each and every one of you. For you all are pieces of me.

To my bonus children, I also hope you all have a better understanding of me as well. Know that I'm here for you all, and I love you too.

To Sabrina, thank you for being such an amazing mother to my grandchildren. For believing in me and encouraging me as I was writing this book.

To Brenda, My A-1 from Day-1, thank you for being my best friend throughout these years. I appreciate all the times we spent together. We made it through some tough times together. And I don't know how I would've made it without your friendship.

To my big cousin Lilly, thank you for always defending me, when I wasn't strong enough to defend myself. I love you, girl.

To Cynthia Brown, you have no idea how much you helped me and my mom during our times of serious struggles. I would never forget you being there for me like a big sister. Also, thank you for taking me to the show to see Purple Rain and to the Museum of Science and Industry as a kid; you were the big sister I never had there for me.

To my Siblings, May God continue to watch over you all.

To My Little brother JR, I pray that this book gives you peace in your mind, and in your heart. I pray God gives you the strength to know who you really are and that you can overcome anything. I will always love you.

To LaDetra, thank you for being the best mentor in the world to me.

To Dr. Dulaney, thank you for your trust and belief in me! I appreciate you so much!

To Sammy, thank you for simply being you and having my back!

Thank you, Pastor White, for being there for me through my hard times. I appreciate your encouraging words and Spiritual guidance.

To my cousin Tyrone and his wife Jackie; thank you all for being there for me and coming to my special events and graduations.

To my nieces and nephews. Please know I love you all dearly and I pray you have a better vision and understanding of some of the life of your grandmother and family. I pray y'all to find motivation, encouragement and strength in this book.

To my best friend Nicole Miceli. Love you girlie

To my grandchildren and generations to come; This book is really for you all. This is your legacy. Not only to understand me as the Matriarch of this family but to understand your parents and your family history. I wished my grandmother would have left a book for me to read about our family. I pray that you find strength to push through any and every obstacle that life presents to you. And have the confidence in knowing you have what it takes inside your bloodline to make it through any and everything with the help of the Lord. Let this book be a beacon of light so that it would shine in your darkest moments leading you, guiding you, encouraging you, motivating you through it all. Let it be your strength when you are weak. Let this book encourage you to reach the highest levels in life.

To all of my readers, followers and fans, thank you for taking the time to go on this journey with me. I pray that it gives you strength, encouragement and wisdom as well, I hope you find peace and solace in areas that no one else can understand what you are going through. I wrote this book for you also, to show you that if I made it through it so can you! Please know that I love and appreciate you all as well.

# CONTENTS

### PART ONE
01. One Determined Woman...................9
02. A Match Made in Different Worldviews.................12
03. Little Angie Beginnings.................14
04. Dysfunctional Siblings Love.................24
05. From Sugar to Shit.................37

### PART TWO
06. Here Comes the Calvary.................57
07. A Twisted Family.................65
08. Child Sexual Exploitation.................77

### PART THREE
09. Trying To Find My Way.................88
10. Caught In the Closet.................101
11. The Fruit of My Womb.................115

### PART FOUR
12. Surprise!!! - Surprised???.................136
13. Ridiculous Excuses.................160
14. It's Time to Take Control of My Life.................166
15. What Happens in Vegas, Stays in Vegas.................173
16. New Love, New Lies & New Growing Pains.................176

## PART FIVE

**17.** Defiant Disorder......................................198
**18.** Devil, You Won't Defeat Me!!! .......................201
**19.** I Can Show You - Better Than I Can Tell You ..........210
**20.** A Tinder Scam........................................218
**21.** From 18 Years To 18 Wheels..........................222
**22.** Ant & Angie's, Real Good Azz Sandwiches ............232
**23.** More Than a Conquer.................................238
ABOUT THE AUTHOR........................................244

# PART ONE

# CHAPTER 1
# ONE DETERMINED WOMAN

*"This is a man's world, but it wouldn't be nothing, nothing without a woman or a girl."*
**James Brown (It's A Man's, Man's, Man's World)**

Growing up nestled amidst the vibrant, yet often gritty streets of Chicago's Englewood community is where I first began to weave the tapestry of my story. This story, like the ever-shifting shades of the sky above, is one of resilience, hardship, and the unwavering spirit of a woman named Angela Brown.

My mother, Odie Mae Bolton, was born in 1943, entering the world in the suffocating grip of the Jim Crow era. Her birthplace was Millington, Tennessee, marking her arrival as the eldest of five children born to Jane Redic, affectionately known as "Madea." In many Black families, "Madea" signifies the esteemed matriarch who guides and upholds the family structure. Tragically, my mother's father, Otis Bolton, died in World War II, leaving an irreparable void in her life.

As my mother matured, the family dynamic shifted with the arrival of her brother, James, and later, three additional siblings from her mother's marriage to C.W. My mother shared many stories about her early life, describing how she helped her mother raise her younger siblings while their mother toiled in the cotton fields. Her labor fueled the American economy, leaving my mother largely self-taught. She was forced to stay home to cook, clean, wash, iron, and tend to the needs of her younger siblings, which prevented her from receiving an adequate education. In fact, she did not receive much of a formal education at all. I remember being reminded of my mother's painful childhood experiences; there was of a huge hunk of skin missing from the back of her foot. She told me it happened when she was chopping wood with a sharp axe for the stove, missed the wood, and hit the back of her foot with the axe. Despite the pain, she persevered and tended to her family.

Sadly, my mother's childhood innocence was further shattered by her stepfather's alleged abuse. C.W, described as a heavy drinker, subjected my mother and grandmother to a life of verbal and physical abuse. Despite her mother's valiant efforts to shield them, they eventually escaped his clutches. However, the damage had already been inflicted. At the tender age of 15, my mother found herself pregnant with her first child, my brother Slick. The identity of his father remained uncertain. This heartbreaking reality compelled my mother to seek a fresh start, leaving behind the scars of her past.

As a teenager, pregnant with limited education, my mother arrived in Chicago, a city that offered her a glimmer of hope. With its towering buildings and unfamiliar rhythms, it presented a stark contrast to the country living, dirt roads, and cotton fields of her childhood. Within the walls of the Henry Horner housing projects, she found solace and support by reuniting with her grandmother, Melissa Redic, fondly referred to as "Mama Lissy." The aroma of freshly baked cakes and pies filled Mama Lissy's kitchen, replacing the harsh realities of her past with warmth and comfort.

Here, amidst the warmth of family, my mom began to mend the broken pieces of her life, laying the foundation for a future filled with the promise of overcoming adversity. Forced to start anew, she secured welfare and low-income benefits, leveraging her skills to find work as a housekeeper for a wealthy family in Evanston, Illinois, a suburb north of Chicago along the lake and home to Northwestern University. She established a foothold in her new life, settling into her own apartment in the Henry Horner projects at 140 North Wood Street.

A few years later, she met and married a man named Albert Butler. They had two children, my brother Buck, and my sister Tia. Unfortunately, the union was short-lived and took a tragic turn. Albert, a severe alcoholic, subjected my mother and siblings to relentless verbal and physical abuse. Stories of drunken tirades, hurled insults, and even physical violence against my mother and brother Buck left deep scars on the family. The constant fear became a daily reality, with Buck and Tia hiding for their safety. This trauma, we believed, contributed to Buck's seizures and learning difficulties.

My mother's mother and her siblings migrated barefoot on the bus from Tennessee to join her in Chicago. Witnessing the abuse, Madea confronted Albert, even resorting to threatening him with a gun to protect her daughter and grandchildren. This ultimately led to my mother's divorce, marking the beginning of her journey as a single parent, determined to provide a safe and stable environment for her children.

Coming from a rural background, my mother's family believed in self-reliance and self-defense, often resorting to carrying weapons. They also implemented strict disciplinary actions towards their children, including corporal punishment using belts, tree branches (known as switches), or even their bare hands. However, their volatile nature often resulted in frequent arguments and confrontations amongst each other.

Despite their harsh disciplinary methods, my mother's family cherished boisterous gatherings filled with laughter, card games, and trips back down south to Memphis. Their bond was undeniable, evident in their frequent visits and close proximity on Chicago's West Side.

# CHAPTER 2
# A MATCH MADE IN DIFFERENT WORLDVIEWS

*"It takes two to make a thing go right –
it takes two to make it out of sight.*
**Rob Base & DJ E-Z Rock (It Takes Two)**

My father, a United States Marine Corps Vietnam veteran with sharpshooter training, fell head over heels for my mother the moment their eyes met. He was a tall, light-skinned man with a good grade of hair, resembling the iconic actor Ron O'Neal, who was notoriously known for his role in the Blaxploitation movie 'Super Fly.' Determined to win her affection, he showered her with gifts and attention.

On the other hand, my father's family hailed from a world of affluence. With Creole and Native American descent, they had a light complexion and elegant mannerisms. He was raised in the affluent Hyde Park neighborhood; the same community where former President Barack Obama resided and began his roots in Chicagoland. Their lives stood in stark contrast to my mother's upbringing. Beautiful homes, lavish cars, and refined social gatherings were emblematic of a life vastly different from my mother's.

Upon learning of my mother's pregnancy with me, my father was determined to shield his child from the harsh realities of the projects. Swiftly, he whisked them away to a new home—a five-bedroom haven in West Englewood. It was a dream come true, characterized by lush greenery, a quiet neighborhood, and a stark departure from their previous life. While my father diligently worked, primarily as a butcher, my mother, at his insistence, became a homemaker, dedicating her time to her family. This familiar rhythm echoed her childhood, albeit this time caring for her own children.

My father's unwavering love for my mother was evident in his generosity. Diamonds, furs, and jewelry served as testaments to his affection, showering her with a life she never imagined. Although their backgrounds and experiences differed immensely, their love story began amidst the contrasting worlds they came from.

# CHAPTER 3
# LITTLE ANGIE BEGINNINGS

*"I was born by the river in a little tent- Oh, and just like the river, I've been running ever since."*
**Sam Cooke (A Change Is Gonna Come)**

My childhood was a kaleidoscope of vibrant memories, enveloped in love and surrounded by material comfort. My father ensured I was always impeccably dressed, while my mother meticulously cared for my well-being. Our home was a sanctuary of elegance, adorned with exquisite furniture, state-of-the-art electronics, and captivating fish tanks brimming with life. My parents delighted in providing a menagerie of pets, from a black miniature poodle named Gee-gee to hamsters, rabbits, and countless others.

Upstairs, a converted bedroom transformed into a bustling family room, resonating with music, laughter, and lively gatherings. Here, my parents, their friends, and extended family savored card games, gambling, and sumptuous meals. My father, a resourceful handyperson, showcased his craftsmanship by constructing a bar from scratch, while my mother, a skilled cook, infused her soul food with love, humming gospel hymns as she prepared feasts. Holidays, barbecues, and cookouts were cherished occasions, brimming with warmth and communal spirit.

Despite the abundance of joy in my childhood, one recurring disruption troubled my parents: unannounced visits from my mother's family. Initially welcomed, these visits became a source of frustration due to their frequency and lack of notice. Disregarding personal space and boundaries, they would enter the house, raid the refrigerator, and help themselves to food without permission. One particularly unsettling incident occurred while my parents were trying to relax in bed and watch a movie. Without warning, my mother's family arrived unannounced, outside honking that annoying horn call—beep, beep, beep-beep-beep—and they would walk into our house, loudly saying, 'Hey y'all, get up, we got some ribs and chicken to put on the grill.'

Another distressing incident from my childhood comes to mind, when I was around five or six years old. Our family was enjoying the company of my mother's relatives, including young children, while my cat had recently given birth to a litter of beautiful kittens. Amidst the jovial atmosphere, one of my male cousins entered the enclosed porch where the kittens were kept, wielding a pair of sharp scissors for an unsettling game of darts, using the defenseless animals as targets. Despite my pleas to stop, he persisted, leading to a horrifying turn of events. In a moment of shock and horror, he hurled the scissors once more, this time piercing one of the kittens' eyes. Witnessing the excruciating pain and hearing the helpless cries of the injured kitten left me utterly traumatized. I rushed into the house, screaming for help, devastated by the callous act committed by my cousin. The incident deeply affected me, and I cried inconsolably throughout the night, while my father, furious at the situation and its impact on me, expressed his anger and concern.

My parents grappled with this disruptive behavior for some time, which eventually led to numerous arguments and confusion between them. Despite my mother's inability to control her family's actions, she was adamant about not confronting them, further straining the relationship between my parents. Eventually, my mother took action to reduce their frequent unannounced visits, which gradually dwindled over time.

Concerned for my safety and well-being, my father made it a rule never to allow me to visit my mother's family alone. This decision created a sense of separation from my cousins and aunts, who enjoyed more freedom in their interactions. Despite my longing to spend time with them, my requests were consistently denied by my father, whose reasoning remained unclear to me. This restriction, however, was just one aspect of a complex family dynamic that occasionally caused tension.

Despite these limitations, I harbored immense love for my entire family, especially my cousins. I yearned to partake in their activities and experience the love and care showered upon them by my grandmother, Madea, who lived with my aunt Helen. However, the inability to fully connect with this part of my family remained a source of longing throughout my childhood.

Visits by my maternal grandmother were marked by a stark contrast. While I witnessed her showering my cousins with love and affection, I felt a distinct lack of attention and acceptance. Instead, I endured harsh words and hurtful remarks, leaving me feeling out of place and unwanted. On rare occasions when my grandmother took me out, the experiences were bittersweet. One such occasion was a trip to bingo when I was around three or four years old. I vividly recall her jubilant victory screaming "BINGO" at the top of her lungs, and everyone congratulated her. I believe she had won a huge coverall. The joy afterwards of me receiving treats from her, as we went to the concession stand together and she brought me some popcorn, a candy bar and soda pop. I was so happy. That was the first time she had ever bought me anything. I was ecstatic that she was treating me like I was her granddaughter for once. I felt special, like I was really a part of her life and that I meant something to her. I ate that popcorn as if it were the best thing I had ever had. I can still remember how good it was. I smiled that whole night, probably the whole week. My grandmother had finally done something with me, a rare display of affection that left a lasting impression on me.

However, another outing turned out to be a confusing and frightening experience. At around six or seven years old, we attended a church revival, where my grandmother urged me to join in; I agreed and said, "yes ma'am." Overwhelmed by fear and confusion amidst the chaotic atmosphere of fervent prayer and exuberant worship, I froze and failed to respond to her instructions. Disappointed and angry, my grandmother berated me harshly on the way home, condemning me for my perceived disobedience and likening me to my father by calling me a liar. This incident marked the last attempt at bonding between us during my childhood.

It is essential to understand that my father's Catholic upbringing and our family's quiet religious practices greatly contrasted with the intense and spirited environment of the sanctified church revival. The unfamiliarity and intensity of the experience left me paralyzed with fear, watching all those people running around the church, catching the Holy Ghost, speaking in tongues, falling out on the floor screaming, hollering, kicking, and shouting, it scared the hell out of me as a child. I didn't know what the heck was going on. I wasn't used to that type of behavior, making me unable to comply with my grandmother's wishes despite my desire to please her.

These contrasting experiences with my family members left a lasting impact on me, shaping my understanding of love, acceptance, religion, and familial bonds. Despite the challenges and traumas endured, I cherish the moments of love and connection shared with my family, as they have shaped me into the person I am today.

Regarding my father's side of the family, I never had the opportunity to meet my paternal grandfather. However, I am aware of a significant event involving my paternal grandmother. My grandfather made the difficult decision to commit my father's mother to a psychiatric ward due to complications stemming from a stroke related to her diabetes. Back then, options for caring for individuals with such conditions were limited, and my grandfather felt unsure about how to handle the situation. This unfortunate circumstance led to their separation and eventual divorce, with my grandfather relocating back to New Orleans and remarrying another woman.

I have a faint memory of my father bringing his mother, Bessie, to our house on one occasion. Despite her physical beauty, characterized by light skin and long, lustrous black and gray hair with a good texture, she used a wheelchair and had difficulty speaking due to the effects of her stroke. I was quite young at the time, around three or four years old, and felt hesitant and shy in her presence. I remember my father urging me to greet her, introducing her as my grandmother, but I couldn't bring myself to do so. There was a sense of unease and unfamiliarity surrounding her. I couldn't understand why she wasn't saying anything verbally to me. I remember her reaching her hand out for me, and I ran and hid bashfully behind my mother. It's unclear whether my apprehension stemmed from fear or if she was heavily medicated, but her appearance and demeanor struck me as different from any other Black woman I had encountered. This encounter remains my sole memory of meeting my paternal grandmother.

Among my paternal relatives, my aunt Helene shines brightly as a beacon of warmth and generosity. Her welcoming home, impeccable sense of style, and culinary skills left an impression on me. I fondly recall her attendance at my kindergarten graduation, where she bestowed upon me a generous envelope filled with money, a gesture that symbolized her love and support during my formative years.

Despite the limited connection with my extended family on my father's side, I found solace and enrichment in intellectual pursuits. My father played a pivotal role in fostering my intellectual curiosity by encouraging me to engage with educational television programs, laying the foundation for a lifelong love of learning.

Growing up, I found myself navigating between two distinct personas, a practice commonly known as code-switching. This duality was largely influenced by the contrasting expectations of my maternal and paternal families. When in the company of my mom's side, I felt compelled to adopt a persona that mirrored their country and ghetto demeanor. I had to project toughness and assertiveness, engaging in banter, and exchanging playful insults to fit in. Conversely, when with my dad's family, a distinct set of expectations prevailed. I was expected to embody elegance and refinement, maintaining a quiet demeanor while exuding intelligence and beauty. My father took great care to ensure I was impeccably dressed, and my behavior was always under scrutiny, requiring me to articulate myself with sophistication and propriety.

This ability to seamlessly transition between divergent social environments has proven invaluable throughout my life. I possess the adaptability to thrive in any setting, easily connecting with individuals from all walks of life. I can effortlessly navigate between hood culture and professionalism, seamlessly blending strength with sophistication. Whether commanding attention in the boardroom or engaging in a high energy spirited game of spades, I command respect and assert my presence with confidence. I take pride in my ability to communicate effectively, whether employing street vernacular or eloquent discourse, as it enables me to assert myself and navigate various social spheres with ease. This versatility allows me to uphold my identity while adapting to the expectations of different social contexts, showcasing the depth and breadth of my capabilities.

My dad was a heavy cigarette smoker and a jack of all trades, truly. Anything this man touched, he improved. If he found something interesting, he mastered it. He was a butcher, a chef, a photographer, and a funeral director. He played tennis and golf. He was a scuba diver, a fisher, and a hunter. He flew helicopters and drove boats. He taught martial arts. He skied and was even a professional pool player and swimmer. He was a limousine driver—a straight hustler. Oh, he was most definitely a hustler. My father was a con artist; he could con the best of them. He could lie quicker than a cat can cover up shit. He kept large sums of money coming in. I remember times when my dad would come in with big suitcases of money.

He would tell me to sit down and count this money out. I had to be around seven, eight, or nine years old. He would have me sitting there counting thousands and thousands of dollars. At one point, my father had a brand-new Cadillac, a brand-new Lincoln Town Car, two boats, and a camper home. He had our entire side of the street filled with just about all his cars, boats, camper homes, and trailers. He had all the neighbors complaining about the lack of parking spaces available. Unfortunately for them, my father was cool with everyone, even the entire police department. Most of the time, he would have the entire police department at our house kicking it, literally. They were supposed to be out patrolling the beat, and they had been chilling at our house hanging out. Eating, drinking, smoking weed, talking crap, taking pictures—you name it. And they were best friends with my dad. It was so cool.

My father was good friends with the famous singer Barry White and his wife, Mrs. White. She and my mom were good friends and would dress up to go out and get their nails and hair done when they were in town, and they would talk on the phone all the time. I remember Mrs. White having these really long fingernails. My mom would get her nails done in 14-karat gold. They really had great times together when they would sneak into town. I only saw them a few times growing up.

He was also great friends with some of the big names in Hollywood through his friendship with Hugh Hefner, whom my dad knew from hanging out at the Playboy Club in downtown Chicago. I remember Mr. Hefner offering my mother a great deal of money to pose in his Playboy magazine because of her voluminous breasts, and my father had a fit. LOL, quiet as kept; I think my mother was flattered by the suggestion. She would blush and be tickled pink while watching my father rant and rave about it.

My father was a very well-admired person. He had a way about him that was magnetic, and he was knowledgeable about a lot of things. He could hold the best conversations with people and knew what he was talking about. Plus, with his good looks and all that charm and charisma, he was a force to be reckoned with.

He was friends with all the locals—local politicians and funeral home directors. I remember him and his best friend James Jones, owner of one of the biggest funeral homes on the south side of Chicago, and his wife's name was Mary. Now, Ms. Mary and my mom were best friends, and when I tell you all these women did was dress, I mean, they were dressed too sharp when they would get up and go out. My father kept my mother on point and dressed in expensive furs, nice clothes, and fine jewelry, diamonds and pearls, the sharpest high heels, and stilettos. He would get her manicures with 14-karat gold nails added on. I would just look at them going out together, and I would be in awe of how beautiful my parents were and just watch the life that they lived together.

The way my mother looked; you could never imagine she was a welfare recipient. Now my mother kept her welfare benefits because she had three children before meeting my father, and she wanted to have something to help around the house. She mainly wanted to make sure she had her children covered. I would assume that her food stamps, welfare check, and medical card came in handy.

They really had a great life together. My mother was very, very much in love and happy with my dad. I watched her smile, and I watched him cater to her every want and heart's desire, even though my mother wasn't materialistic or hard to please. My dad would just shower her and pamper her with gifts; he would always surprise her. I remember this as a little girl, and it use to fill my heart and my life with so much joy and happiness.

My father had a gift of gab like none other. I mean, he really knew how to talk to people and get whatever he wanted or needed. He knew how to make friends and had friends in high places. Everyone who was anyone was friends with my dad. Everyone liked this man. He knew the mayor, the congressman, the alderman—you name it.

But what people didn't know was that my father was illiterate. He could not read at all. He only knew how to sign his name.

No one outside of our home knew this secret. It was a huge taboo. I could never tell anyone that my father could not read. Absolutely no one knew or even suspected that my father was illiterate. He had what I assume would be called a photographic memory; this is how he learned.

He would hear or see something, and he could remember everything about it; that is how he made it in life because of his memory. When I was a little girl, he used to call me on the phone and ask me questions like, "What is the name of this street?" and he would spell it out, saying "G-R-E-E-N," and I would say, "That's Green Street, Daddy." And he would respond, "Okay, thanks, Sugar; be good; I'll see y'all when I get off work." Then he'd hang up.

Around five or six years old, I became my father's unlikely confidante. Despite his outward confidence and numerous talents, he harbored a secret: illiteracy. Unable to read himself, he relied on me to decipher letters and navigate the written world. This responsibility, while challenging, fueled my own intellectual growth and inadvertently fostered a sense of isolation from peers my age.

My father's unconventional approach to education prioritized learning over traditional toys. While my classmates bragged about Christmas presents, I received typewriters and educational materials, shaping my path towards an intellectual pursuit. His ambitions for my future, however, came at a cost.

I became an unwilling observer of my father's manipulative behavior. He befriended an elderly woman, Ms. Love, gaining her trust and exploiting her kindness for financial gain. Despite my youthful age, I recognized the wrongness of his actions and felt a deep sense of unease.

Witnessing the consequences of my father's actions unfolded when his sister, Aunt Helene, discovered his betrayal of her best friend. Infuriated and heartbroken, Aunt Helene confronted him in a violent outburst, exposing the emotional toll his choices had on our family. He had befriended her best friend and gotten a lot of money from her. He conned her so badly—he made her fall in love with him and took her for all her money. He told her he was going to buy them a house, and she believed him. When my aunt Helene found out what my father had done to her best friend, she came to our house PISSED OFF! She came in screaming and yelling at my father for what he had done and started whooping his ass. She jumped up on his back and started swinging and scratching all over him uncontrollably. I remember she had her sons with her. There was so much commotion and hellraising. They were fighting like crazy. My mother was trying to break it up. My aunt told my father how low-down and dirty he was, and she told my mother how sorry she felt for her. She kissed me goodbye and never came to our home again after that.

# CHAPTER 4
# DYSFUNCTIONAL SIBLINGS LOVE

*"Some of The Most Poisoning People Come Disguised As Friends And Family"*
**(Unknown)**

Growing up alongside my sister, I felt a constant sense of separation. Unlike other siblings, she offered little companionship or guidance. This emotional distance left me yearning for a different kind of sisterly bond. I remember watching my sister as I was growing up. My sister always treated me like I was a pest; she was extremely selfish towards me. As a big sister, she never took the time to talk to me, play with me, or teach me anything. She never took me anywhere or did anything with me. I would see my sister eating some food or candy; I would literally have to beg her to share, and of course she never would. She refused to spend quality time with me as a little girl, cook for me, or even comb my hair, even though she was exceptionally good at French braiding, and later she attended hair school.

As she entered her teenage years, my sister's behavior shifted dramatically. She embraced rebellious tendencies, causing considerable strain within our family. Witnessing her struggles added another layer of complexity to my childhood experiences. Now, mind you, we are six years apart, so I was watching and learning a lot from my big sister, particularly. She started becoming fast-tail, hardheaded, and running the streets, and she gave my mom pure hell. She found a best friend next door named Thia. They had just moved into the neighborhood when my sister was in seventh grade. Thia used to put a ladder up our upstairs back window for my sister to sneak out of the house at night. They were around twelve or thirteen years old.

My sister's behavior took a troubling turn as she continuously engaged in risky activities such as sneaking out, experimenting with drugs and alcohol, and getting involved in inappropriate relationships. Despite my mother's efforts to discipline her, my sister began resisting and even fighting back. My mom used to walk up and down the streets through the neighborhood, searching for my sister, giving her whooping's, and making her return home. But nothing our mother said or done made my sister settle her wild behavior.

In a desperate attempt to address the situation, my mom summoned her siblings to intervene. They took matters into their own hands, delivering a stern whipping to her that left a lasting impression on me. I was made to wait outside as they collectively confronted and disciplined my sister, determined to instill some sense into her. They did a Soul Train line on whipping her ass. They tore her tail up something terrible.

She was screaming and hollering. This incident served as a turning point for me, as I silently vowed never to find myself in such a situation. They took my sister back to the Westside with them for the rest of that summer, hoping they could straighten her out.

Despite the disciplinary action, my sister's behavior escalated upon her going back to the Westside with them to reside with our aunt. She became entangled with an older man named LeRoy, who provided her with financial support in exchange for questionable favors. This risky behavior of interacting with older men eventually led to my sister asking for financial favors from my Aunt Helen's husband. Now my uncle Newt was a construction worker who made a lot of money. He was a great provider, but he always kept a bottle of Seagram's Gin in his back pocket and would get good and drunk every day when he got off work. Tia knew she could get money from him for her pills, drinks, and weed. But when my aunt found out, that's when all hell broke loose. This led to a confrontation with my Aunt Helen, resulting in my sister being expelled from her home and forced to return to our family.

Back on the Southside, my sister's rebellion continued, causing frequent clashes with our parents. One memorable incident involved a chaotic confrontation with a neighbor after my sister had an affair with the neighbor's husband. One evening as my mom and I were walking back home from the bus stop, as we approached our house, we saw so much commotion going on in front of it. The lady had found out about her husband's affair with my sister, and she came and busted out all our front windows. It was complete chaos outside. That lady was out of her mind and talking crazy to everybody. My mom tried to calm it down, but the situation escalated into a family brawl. Everybody got to fighting. My mom was fighting the lady for busting our windows, my sister and her friend Thia were fighting some other people the lady brought with her, and my father was chasing the man they were fighting over down the alley with our dog.

We had a huge Great Dane. As my father was chasing the man down the alley, the dog stopped and took a shit. That was the comedy of the year. Afterwards, we all laughed about it so much. Despite efforts to repair the damage of our windows, my sister remained a constant source of trouble. A particularly distressing incident occurred when she struggled with heartbreak, leading to a self-harming episode. I remember one day, my mom was in the kitchen cooking dinner, and my sister and I were lying in my mom's room, which was adjacent to the kitchen. My sister was constantly crying and super depressed over this guy on the block that she'd fallen in love with. She was slobbering and crying uncontrollably over the guy leaving her, hurting her feelings by not wanting to be with her anymore. As we were lying there, she just kept crying. I had to be at least seven years old.

I remember telling her it was going to be alright and to please stop crying; she just wouldn't stop.

When I looked down at what she was doing, she had a key in her hand and was cutting her wrist. She just kept cutting at it. I kept begging her to stop hurting herself, witnessing her distress, I got up and ran into the kitchen and told my mommy she was bleeding badly. My mom ran into the room, grabbed my sister, and immediately called 911.

When the ambulance arrived to take her, I remember them bandaging up her wrist where she was cutting herself and then strapping her down in this white jacket. They put her on the stretcher, and my parents followed behind the ambulance. I didn't realize it at the time, but they ended up taking my sister to the hospital for treatment, and she was later committed to the psych ward for evaluation. She eventually came back home after a few days. My mother was at her wits' end with my sister's misbehavior.

Following this incident, my sister attempted to turn her life around by enrolling in a high school on the north side, but her rebellious behavior persisted. She ended up going to live with another one of our aunts and then eventually with the older man LeRoy out west, further distancing herself from our family.

Switching gears to my brother, Buck, who was nine years my senior, he played a different role in my life. Although not as selfless as one might expect from a sibling, he demonstrated a more amiable demeanor. Being beaten so much as a child by the hand of his father caused Buck to suffer from a learning disability and dyslexia. Buck masked his struggles with humor, always eager to share laughter and joy. His coping mechanism involved reciting rhymes and jokes, creating a lively atmosphere whenever he was around. He was a very fun-loving guy, always singing, laughing, telling jokes, and slapping his knee while singing Hambone. "Hambone, hambone, have you heard?" He was notorious for reciting the rhymes by Dolomite, such as "Way down in the jungle deep, the badass lion stepped on the signifying monkeys' feet!"

There was so much fun when Buck was around because you knew you were going to get your laugh on.

In contrast to my sister's tumultuous journey, Buck's resilience and humor provided a welcome reprieve from the challenges our family faced. His ability to find joy amid personal struggles left a lasting impression, highlighting the power of laughter in navigating life's difficulties.

However, despite his vibrant personality, Buck faced his fair share of challenges. Dropping out of high school due to the overwhelming academic demands and the intimidation of gangs trying to recruit him in the neighborhood. He didn't contribute much around the house.

Frequently admonished by our mom for neglecting chores, he spent long hours lounging in front of the television, eating all day, and drinking soda pop, until he found a girlfriend. Buck eventually secured a job at Halo Lighting Company, working alongside our uncle and aunts after various stints at temporary agencies.

Reflecting on our childhood, it's essential to note the peculiar dynamics within my family. I, being the only child unable to visit my mother's side without parental escort, sensed an unspoken tension, akin to what I've come to recognize as a manifestation of the Willie Lynch theory. This tension, especially between my sister and me, stemmed from a range of factors, including the distinct treatment she received based on her physical appearance.

My sister, a strikingly beautiful young lady with dark skin, enjoyed privileges and material possessions that created a stark contrast with my own experiences. I was constantly subjected to derogatory names and exclusion by my siblings, which caused me to grapple with low self-esteem. This was further exacerbated by the pervasive belief that my lighter skin made me inferior. They would call me "Chinese" because I couldn't see without my glasses, and I would often squint my eyes. Every day, they would call me ugly and constantly make me feel unwanted.

My siblings would yell, "Get your little ugly yellow ass out of here!" They would always be together, my brother Buck and sister Tia, ignoring me or pushing me away. They were very stingy towards me and made me feel like they wouldn't accept me. This left me feeling unwanted and unaccepted within my own family. Growing up alongside siblings who relentlessly mocked my appearance, especially my brother Buck, took a toll on my self-worth. The hurtful remarks led me to believe that beauty was synonymous with being a dark-skinned woman, and my light complexion made me feel worthless. Nights were filled with tears as I yearned to fit in and be accepted like my sister.

Buck, who was once a major contributor to my emotional struggles, battled his own demons. At first, he used to smoke weed, drink, and pop a few pills. I remember one warm summer night when everyone on our block was out on their porches, relaxing and enjoying the breeze. Kids were jumping rope and riding their bikes up and down the block when suddenly we all heard this Tarzan-like scream. It was Buck's reckless behavior; he had jumped out of the second-floor window of our house and landed in the bushes. He was so high that he thought he could fly. I will never forget that day. The entire block was laughing, but it was truly no laughing matter. Buck had a serious mental problem, and his substance abuse only worsened the situation. We all stood outside, looking at him like, "Dude, you must be kidding right now."

Shifting to my oldest brother, Slick, who was thirteen years my senior, I loved, honored, and respected him almost as much as I loved my father. He was my father's right-hand man and would do all kinds of things with him. Out of everyone, he was the one who helped my mom and dad the most. Growing up, I always looked up to my older brother. He was the oldest among us. His father lived in Memphis, TN, and when we were growing up, he was never around. I loved my big brother unconditionally. He would always play games with me, talk to me, and let me watch television with him. He would buy me candy and chips; he was just a cool guy.

I'll never forget when I was about four or five years old. I was lying down in his room, and we were watching something on television. I fell into a deep sleep, but when I woke up, I felt his hands in my panties, rubbing on my vagina. I knew what I felt, but I was so petrified that I didn't dare open my eyes to see what was happening. My heart started pounding extremely fast, and I didn't know what to do. I looked up at him, and he quickly moved his hand away from between my legs. I was scared, so I jumped up and ran down the stairs as fast as possible. I got on the couch with my mom, bawling myself up and putting my shirt over my knees. I sat there in shock, not knowing what to do.

I was so afraid to tell my mom what my brother had just done to me. I sat there, my heart beating fast, feeling nervous, scared, confused, and in total disbelief. I was worried and unsure about what to do.

After a while, my brother came downstairs, acting as calm, cool, and collected as ever. He looked at me, looked at my mom, and casually asked, "Hey mom, are you alright?" My mom replied, "Yes," completely unaware of what he had just done to me.

I sat there, trembling, and filled with shame. I was terrified of telling my mom. I simply didn't have the courage, and I didn't want to hurt her or cause chaos in our family. Everyone loved my brother so much. I didn't want anyone to think I was lying, and strangely, I didn't want to see my brother leave, knowing how much my mom relied on his help. She didn't know how to drive, and my brother was always there, taking her to the grocery store and helping with everything my father couldn't do because he was working so hard to provide for us.

I never got over or forgot how disgusted I felt when I discovered my brother touching me inappropriately.

My brother, Slick, was quite something. He was cool and down to earth. He loved Earth, Wind & Fire, The Funkadelic's, and Michael Jackson. He always dressed neatly and had a carefree, long curl. He used to be by my father's side all the time. Whenever he got into trouble and got locked up, my dad would have his police friends help him get out of jail, arrange for bail, hire attorneys—whatever it took. Slick was always getting into trouble, but he always helped my mom and dad around the house.

My father favored Slick and rewarded him generously for his assistance. He bought him cars and nice clothes, kept money in his pockets, and took him places. I know they weren't far apart in age because my mom was born in 1943, and my dad was born in 1949, so there was a six-year age gap between them and about a ten-year difference between my father and my brother.

Unfortunately, Slick started going down the wrong path in life. He began pimping women of various backgrounds. I remember him bringing beautiful young Spanish, Caucasian, and Afro-American women to our house. They were really into Slick.

When he started bringing all these different women home, my mom would complain to my dad, saying, "He keeps bringing these whores into my house." They would sit and have conversations about my brother's new activities. As a kid, I observed and listened to everything.

Slick ended up stealing cars. He started driving all kinds of different cars around our house. But one day, he came over in this big white luxury car, a Lincoln Continental.

My father kept saying, "Mae, I don't care what you say; that car is stolen!" My mom said Slick told her he was working and that he was out there at Halo Lighting with my aunts and uncles. He claimed his white girlfriend was helping him buy those cars.

Then one day, my mom received a phone call saying Slick had been arrested.

My dad couldn't get him out of trouble this time. Slick had been in trouble so many times before, with an extensive arrest record. There was nothing my father could do because I think Slick committed this crime in Waukegan, IL.

On the day of the court hearing, the judge sentenced Slick to two years for grand theft auto. I saw the pain contorting my mother's face, a reflection of the heavy burden on her heart as she watched her son's future slip away.

Every other weekend, she would take the bus to the penitentiary to visit him. My parents always sent him money and paid for his calls home. During one visit, Slick persistently urged me to look under the table. Confused, I followed his gaze and saw a single peppermint candy in his hand. It was a silent gesture of affection, a reminder of his love amidst the harsh reality. Yet, a nagging doubt lingered in the back of my mind, an unspoken truth I couldn't confront. It haunted me, but I could never say anything to my parents. I knew they needed him, and he needed them.

Slick served a year and a half in Pontiac Penitentiary. His early release brought relief and joy to our family. He returned unchanged. He took care of household chores, did repairs around the house, and drove my mother around for her errands. He helped my mom a lot while my dad was working or hustling on the streets.

However, Buck's demons resurfaced. He fell deeply in love, but just like his father, his love turned destructive when fueled by alcohol. He mirrored his father's abusive behavior towards his girlfriend, leading him to eventually move out and went to the West Side to stay with my aunt Helen.

Meanwhile, my sister, Tia, embarked on a dangerous path. She entangled herself with an alcoholic named Lawrence, a volatile veteran, whose possessiveness manifested in brutal abuse. He used to beat the hell out of my sister, pulling and dragging her all up and down the streets, stomping her, and beating her to the point of fear. She would have bruises and black eyes. My mother, heartbroken and helpless, could only watch as Tia willingly entered this toxic relationship. Despite her pleas, Tia remained with Lawrence, enduring his controlling measures and physical violence. My sister went through hell with him. Even though he was fun to be around and real cool, always singing songs with his lovely vocals, and could cook something serious. He was extremely jealous. She couldn't go anywhere or talk to anyone—not even come visit our mother.

Amidst this family turmoil, a surprise emerged: my mother unexpectedly got pregnant and gave birth to a baby boy. Initially ecstatic, my father showered the child with gifts, briefly igniting a spark of jealousy within me, who had been his only child for a decade. However, I quickly embraced the idea of having a little brother and grew to love him dearly.

Unfortunately, the joy was short-lived. My mother received a devastating diagnosis of type II diabetes, and her health rapidly deteriorated. As her dizzy spells increased, managing her health became a top priority. The crack epidemic had a tight grip on Chicago, affecting the lives of countless individuals. Unfortunately, my older brother Slick fell victim to its allure and became deeply involved in the drug trade, establishing himself as a prominent figure in the neighborhood alongside a guy name King. Together, they operated a drug house in our vicinity. Slick's newfound wealth manifested itself in extravagant displays of cars, clothing, jewelry, and lavish parties. Unbeknownst to me, a ten-year-old unaware of the gravity of the situation, Slick confided in me about his hidden stash of money.

As my father struggled to make ends meet through Lawful means, the stark contrast between his legitimate earnings and Slick's drug money fueled frustration. This tension escalated into frequent arguments between my parents, with my mother fiercely defending Slick while imploring him not to bring drugs into our home.

Rumors circulated that my father, who still had connections to the local police, had tipped them off about the drug operation, ultimately leading to a raid on the neighboring drug house where Slick conducted his business. While the source of the information remained unconfirmed, Slick suspected my father's involvement.

One day, Slick approached me and asked for a favor. He called me by my nickname, "Teet-leet," and offered me money for candy. Excitedly, I agreed, unaware of the true nature of his request. He instructed me to take a book bag and deliver it to King's house, emphasizing that I should not stop, open the bag, or look inside it. Upon reaching King's house, I handed over the book bag, and King instructed me to wait on the living room couch for a few minutes. He assured me that he had something for me to take back to him. During this time, he would disappear into the basement before reemerging, placing the book bag back on me, and giving me candy and money. He would playfully tease me, asking if I was still engrossed in my books and reminding me that I should continue being a good girl, or else he wouldn't buy me any more candy. Unbeknownst to me, I was unwittingly serving as a drug mule, transporting illicit items without understanding the gravity of my actions. The conflicting emotions I experienced during these encounters were a mix of excitement over receiving candy and a nagging sense that something was amiss. Slick would often caution me not to reveal that he had bought me candy, as he knew it would upset others. He emphasized that I should never give him the book bag in front of anyone, not even our parents. I dutifully carried out these tasks, shuttling back and forth multiple times a day, unaware of how long this arrangement would last. It wasn't until much later in life that I came to understand that I had been used as a pawn in the drug trade.

Slick would store shoeboxes filled with money in the attic of our house, specifically in a small crawlspace located in my room. Accessing it required squeezing through a tiny space. He entrusted me with the task of hiding his money there, resulting in stacks upon stacks of cash.

I recall one night, around 3 a.m., when Slick began knocking on my locked door, quietly calling my name. Startled, I inquired about his purpose, and he whispered, "I need you." Feeling a sense of unease, I asked what was wrong, and he responded, "I need to lie down next to you." The situation sent chills down my spine, and I replied firmly, stating, "You can lie on the edge of the bed." He then asked, "Can I hold you?" I adamantly declined, asserting, "No, I'm good." I promptly got up and went downstairs, overwhelmed by the same fear, and panic I had experienced when he had touched me inappropriately during my childhood. I couldn't believe he had attempted to engage in a sexual manner with me once again. All I could do was sit downstairs and cry, grappling with the emotions that flooded my mind.

During this time, our family's circumstances rapidly deteriorated. My mother's health deteriorated due to her diabetes, resulting in strokes and frequent hospitalizations. My father turned to heavy drinking, and the once joyful atmosphere of our home crumbled. The tension grew intense, and the stress overwhelming. I vividly remember our last Christmas together as a family.

Despite the challenging circumstances, my father managed to gather all of us—him, my mother, my siblings—for a grand Christmas celebration. We ate, laughed, watched movies, and sang songs. The older members of the family indulged in drinks, and it felt like the best time we had shared as a family. The Temptations' Christmas song played softly in the background, and my parents joined in singing along. We received wonderful gifts, and there was an unmistakable and poignant sense of something different about that particular Christmas.

Somehow, Slick got involved with a woman named Jerry who lived in the drug house where they sold drugs. I'll never forget that it was Jerry and her daughter who resided there. Jerry was also involved in drug usage. My brother became heavily involved with her, and before we knew it, he started using crack cocaine. Let me tell you, he began stealing anything that wasn't bolted down, and I witnessed it all. King stopped associating with him and treated him like any other drug addict in the neighborhood.

Now, keep in mind, my dad had over $100,000 worth of darkroom equipment for his photography. Slick stole all of it, along with jewelry, furs, electronics, and everything valuable from our home.

I recall a specific incident when I was around 12 years old. I was sitting upstairs, gazing out the window when Slick burst into the room with extreme excitement and said, "Hey, Teetleet, what's up?" I replied, "Nothing," and he began talking to me about life. I shared my dreams of becoming a nurse or achieving fame when I grew up. He started speaking strangely, saying,

"Yeah, life's a bitch, and as you grow older, you'll go through a lot of shit," as he pulled out his crack pipe.

He proceeded to smoke crack rock; it was my first time witnessing him do crack. I stared at him, thinking, "Is this really happening?" He was feening for it so bad that he couldn't wait for me to leave the room. Then, he looked me straight in the eyes and offered, "Here, do you want to try it?" as he passed me the pipe. I stepped back and firmly replied, "Hell nawl, I'm good." I looked at him as if he was crazy.

Not long after, he stole drugs from King. That night, Slick was incredibly paranoid, pacing back and forth and constantly looking out the windows. I remember King putting a hit out on him for it. I believe that Slick's knowledge of King's drug operation led to him robbing them. King ended up posting an obituary with my brother's picture and sticking it on our front door. He rang the doorbell and left. My mother answered the door, saw it, and just broke down crying. My parents agreed that they had to get him out of there. Somehow, my dad managed to safely remove Slick from the house in the back of a hearse he'd borrowed from his friend's funeral home, and he was sent down south.

Now that Slick was gone, Buck was back around the house to help take my mom back and forth to the hospital and the grocery stores. Tia was still in and out of these tumultuous relationships. She ended up getting involved with a guy named Miguel who lived across the street from us. He was a complete asshole; he just played entirely too much, even though he was known for being physically strong. He was the only one who was brave enough to stand up to Lawrence, the guy who was abusing my sister. He said something to him in the sense of "She's my girl now, and if you even look at her again, I'll kill you." And my sister never had any more issues with Lawrence. She ended up marrying Miguel, but she didn't visit us across the street too often. My dad wasn't at home much anymore during those days, so it was just me, my mom, and my little brother.

# CHAPTER 5
# FROM SUGAR TO SHIT

*"When A Family Breaks Apart, The Pain Reverberates Through Each Member, Leaving Scars That May Never Fully Heal"*
**(Unknown)**

At this point, I was about 12 years old, witnessing my life transition dramatically. I shifted from being a spoiled little girl to finding myself in a situation where I felt helpless, constantly questioning, "What do I do? What can I do? What should I do?" Yet, there was nothing within my control. My mother began experiencing dizzy spells, desperately trying to maintain balance by clutching onto walls. In public spaces, anxiety attacks overwhelmed her, and I became her source of stability, holding her hand through the tremors. Her health rapidly declined, and she struggled to care for my brother and me. Cooking and cleaning diminished, and I vividly recall her sitting on the edge of the bed, utterly drained. I assumed more responsibilities, tending to my little brother and assisting with household chores upon her more frequent requests.

My father, overwhelmed by the chaos surrounding my mother's children engaging in harmful behaviors, became frustrated and tired. The tension led him to withdraw from home, spending nights away and growing distant. His escalating alcohol consumption and neglect of household repairs exacerbated our living conditions—the porch breaking down, the roof leaking; there was a big hole in the roof you could look straight up and see outside—and financial strain tightening its grip. Sometimes he would come in late and drink Nyquil to try to sleep. My dad was not paying the bills, and the gas and other utilities were constantly being shut off, putting us under financial strain. Our decline was swift.

After the initial dizzy spells, my mother suffered a full-blown stroke in 1984, spending days in the hospital. Her speech slurred, the left side of her face slightly twisted, yet I managed to understand her. Occasionally, my brother Buck drove her to speech therapy. Christmas of that year proved particularly challenging. My parents had nothing for me that year, and I think my mom was hoping that her family would have something for us. Visiting my mom's family house, expectations of a joyful celebration were shattered. While the other grandkids received gifts, my brother and I were left empty-handed. I was thinking, "Dang, we did not get anything." I was hurt, but I was trying to be a big girl in front of my mom and dad, so even though I was crushed and really hurt because it was a dry Christmas, I couldn't cry or be a baby about it. I didn't want to worry my parents; I knew something was wrong. I remember my cousins asking what I got for Christmas, and I tried to play it off by telling them we had been running around all day and hadn't opened my gifts yet. I was too embarrassed to tell them I did not have anything for Christmas. The silent ride home was heavy with disappointment, signaling the beginning of tougher times to come.

As the year progressed, our situation deteriorated. My father's absence increased and his financial support for our family and home ceased, leaving me, a 12-year-old, burdened with caring for my ailing mother and younger brother. Older siblings showed little concern, rarely checking in on us. I vividly recall the chilling winter when the gas supply to our home was abruptly cut off. The freezing temperatures made our bedrooms uninhabitable, prompting my resourceful father to transform the dining room into a makeshift living space. He covered the dining room windows and doors with plastic and blankets, providing some insulation from the bitter cold. In this improvised living quarter, my mom shared one couch with my little brother, while

I occupied the other. To combat the cold, my dad introduced a kerosene heater and a small camper stove connected to a propane tank, serving as our source of warmth. Despite the challenging circumstances, we clung to a sense of normalcy by gathering in that room, where my dad's state-of-the-art projection television became a focal point.

Our struggle intensified when the freezing temperatures caused our water pipes to burst. The lack of running water meant we couldn't bathe, shower, use the toilet, wash clothes, or engage in basic daily activities. To cope, my mom utilized her few food stamps, sending me on daily trips to the corner store for sustenance. My limited culinary skills at that age led to a menu dominated by lunch meat, hot dogs, Parker House Polish sausages, and ramen noodles. As my mom's health deteriorated, my dad's presence dwindled. He rarely visited and would only come over when he knew my mom received her food stamps and welfare check. He would take her money and most of her food stamps, claiming he had to pay the mortgage, and then leave, neglecting essential tasks like changing the propane tank or bringing kerosene regularly. Instead, he prioritized a new relationship with a woman named Dawn, diverting his attention and resources away from our already struggling family. Dawn, with her bright blonde afro and fair complexion, had a mentally ill son residing in a handicapped facility. My father had taken me to meet her once or twice, saying she was going to be my stepmother and how much he loved her.

The neglect reached a heartbreaking climax during a shopping trip for Easter. My father came to pick me up, and then we went to get his girlfriend Dawn. I was eager for the prospect of new and desperately needed clothes. At this time, I was growing into maturity; my breasts were forming, and I was growing out of the few pieces of clothing I had. I excitedly selected items for both me and my little brother. However, my joy was short-lived as my dad insisted that I put back everything I had chosen. When we got to the register, he pulled out a handful of cash, all twenties and hundred-dollar bills. He then only bought me and my brother one outfit with some underwear, while a shopping cart full of clothes went to Dawn's son. The stark contrast between their abundance and our meager possessions left me crushed and deeply disappointed.

At this point, my father's neglect was all-encompassing. My limited wardrobe went unwashed, and the difficulties I faced at home remained hidden from those around me as I navigated the challenges of seventh and eighth grade. It was beginning to be so damn hard on me. I was not able to wash up properly or take a bath. Basic necessities became luxuries; I wore the same bra and panties for an extended period, lacked essential items like deodorant, pads, tampons, perfume, and hair supplies. Improvised solutions with old socks, shirts, and towels served as makeshift sanitary napkins, highlighting the stark contrast between my reality and the carefree lives of my peers. My hair, a simple part down the middle with two French braids, reflected the limited options available to me during these challenging times.

I will never forget Cindy, my friend down the street. During the harsh winter when our pipes froze and burst, she provided a lifeline by allowing me to bring buckets into her backyard for rinsing and refilling with fresh water, as our home's toilet became unusable. On my way through the alley to her yard, I discreetly disposed of the waste in garbage cans. Once there, I would clean the large waste bucket and fetch fresh water in a smaller bucket so we could brush our teeth and wash our faces. Cindy's kindness extended to letting me come into her house and use her bathroom to wash under my arms, between my legs, and even rinse the only bra and panties I owned, which happened to be stolen from my sister because I had no other way to get any. My sister would not willingly let me have any of her clothes or underwear no matter how desperately I begged. This support from Cindy was crucial in maintaining a sense of decency as I faced the challenges of going to school every day without the means for proper personal hygiene.

My first job became a turning point. Recognizing that something was amiss, my teachers assisted me in obtaining a work permit at thirteen, and they helped me get a job at Central

Community Hospital, conveniently located near our house, bringing a newfound sense of empowerment. I thought to myself, "Oh my God, I can finally do something for myself, my mother, and my little brother." I toiled in the kitchen, finding solace in the routine, away from the tumultuous home environment. I eagerly embraced the opportunity to work two to three hours each day after school and eight hours on weekends. The bi-weekly paycheck of $200, though modest by adult standards, brought immense joy to a 13-year-old facing financial hardships.

However, this newfound independence was abruptly curtailed when my father intercepted me on payday. He took me to cash my check at the currency exchange and shockingly confiscated the entire amount, leaving me with only $5. I had planned to buy underwear, clothes, deodorant, and other necessities that I desperately needed. It was like my entire paycheck vanished. I was deeply disappointed and frustrated. Despite his apologies and explanations of dire financial circumstances, I couldn't shake off the devastation I felt. He kept promising to get the utilities restored, but those promises were never fulfilled. I continued working for a little over a month or two, enduring the recurring cycle of my father taking my paycheck on payday. Unable to bear the emotional toll of providing for my family while being deprived of my hard-earned wages, I reluctantly quit my job.

This decision left me in a state of profound depression, feeling trapped in a life where I couldn't participate in typical activities enjoyed by my peers. While other kids in the neighborhood went on outings to places like skating rinks, bowling alleys, and amusement parks, I couldn't attend any of these events because my responsibilities to care for my ailing mother and younger brother consumed all of my time and energy. The stark contrast between their teenage experiences and my isolated reality served as a constant reminder of the sacrifices I made in the name of familial duty. One vivid memory encapsulates the challenges I faced: One day, while I was outside jumping double dutch, I glanced down our gangway and saw my mother lying unconscious on the ground in the alley. She had fallen and hit her head on an iron garbage can while attempting to take out the trash. Summoning inner strength, I rushed to her aid, lifted her onto my shoulder, and carried her back into the house. I laid her on the couch and noticed that her eye was swollen shut. This moment represents the daily struggles and sacrifices that shaped my teenage years.

I was strictly instructed by my father never to call the police or an ambulance in case of emergencies. Instead, I had to contact him first. I vividly remember dialing his girlfriend Dawn's house and urgently asking, "Can I speak to my dad? It's an emergency." In a dry, authoritative tone, she inquired, "What is the emergency?" Frantically, I replied, "Please, can I speak to my father? It's urgent." She responded, "You have to tell me first, and then I'll get your father if it's important enough." I explained, "My mom is unresponsive; I just found her in the alley by the garbage can." Finally, she handed the phone to my dad, and he instructed me to wait for 15 minutes before calling the ambulance. Panicking, I followed his instructions.

My mother appeared gravely ill, but I was powerless to call the police or an ambulance due to the fear instilled by my father. He had made it clear that if authorities discovered we were alone and our mother couldn't care for us, they would intervene and separate us. Despite the situation, I remained committed to caring for my mother and younger brother. Those 15 minutes of waiting were agonizing, filled with worry for my mom.

When the time came, I called 911, and both my father and emergency services arrived almost simultaneously. My father took charge of the situation upon his arrival. My mother was rushed to the hospital, where it was determined that she had suffered another stroke, leading to an extended hospital stay. Meanwhile, I stayed home, looking after my younger sibling. My father expressed gratitude for following instructions and emphasized the need to keep our family struggles confidential.

Upon my parents' return from the hospital, my father took exceptional care of my mother, especially since during this same time her mother had passed away from complications related to diabetes and strokes. He made sure she was impeccably dressed for her mother's funeral, providing her with a beautiful cream-colored dress, an exquisite hat adorned with feathers and a netted veil, and elegant hair, makeup, and nails. The limousine he arranged for the funeral services reflected his desire to give her a dignified farewell to her mother. However, at my grandmother's services, I was really worried about how my mother was going to handle it. She took it very well until we got to the burial. During the burial, as they began lowering her casket, my mother let out a short, piercing, and painful scream that I will never forget. It hurt me deeply to witness my mother having to endure such an ordeal in her already fragile condition.

Despite the hope that this ordeal might bring about positive changes, my father's behavior worsened in the aftermath. I persisted in my efforts to attend school, attempting to balance my academic responsibilities despite frequent absences. My father somehow managed to evade truancy officers, instructing me to come home directly from school to care for my mom and refrain from leaving the house. These challenges persisted, creating a delicate balance between my academic pursuits and my familial obligations.

During my eighth-grade year, I found myself in a distressing situation. Growing up in a close-knit neighborhood where everyone knew each other like family, I never expected to experience such a traumatic event.

There was an older guy named Jab, two years my senior and a high school sophomore, who lived down the street on my block. One day, as I was walking home from school, Jab began playing pranks on me. He snatched my jacket and started running, goading me to chase him. Eventually, we ended up on his front porch, both laughing. In a playful manner, I jokingly but seriously mentioned that I was hungry and asked if they had anything to eat. Jab responded, "I don't know; go in there and look."

With that, I walked towards the back of the house, intending to reach the kitchen. I opened the refrigerator, searching for food, and mentioned that I wanted a sandwich. Jab agreed, and as I started making the sandwich and began eating, he called me over to talk. Standing in the back bedroom, I approached the door and asked, "What's up?" Naively, I had no idea what he had in mind. He requested, "Come sit down right here on the bed; I want to talk to you."

At that moment, a sense of unease crept over me, reminiscent of the discomfort I had experienced before with my brother Slick. Sensing something was wrong, I replied, "I'm good. I have to get home now." Jab insisted, "You ain't going nowhere until you kiss me." Feeling trapped, I reluctantly gave him a quick kiss. I then tried to leave through the front door, only to find it locked. I asked him to open it, but instead, he grabbed me and repeatedly said, "Just come here for a minute; let me talk to you." I struggled to free myself, but he lifted me up, carried me back to the bedroom, and forcefully threw me onto the bed.

He proceeded to yank my pants down and rape me against my will, taking away my virginity. I was in shock, questioning whether this horrifying experience was real. Ignorant about sex and its implications, I couldn't comprehend the white creamy substance that was left on my body. Confused and repulsed, I asked, "What is this? It's nasty." Jab handed me a towel, and as I wiped myself off, I put my pants back on and went home. I felt violated, disgusted, and utterly confused. I couldn't fully grasp the gravity of what had just happened to me, as I lacked knowledge about sex and its consequences. Mentally, I couldn't process the encounter.

When I arrived home, I couldn't bring myself to tell my mom. I knew that revealing this incident would devastate her, especially considering her ongoing illness and the struggles our family was already facing. I couldn't confide in my dad or anyone else either. I felt utterly alone, with no one to turn to for protection or support. Consequently, I chose to keep it all to myself, carrying the burden in silence.

Not even two weeks later, I began experiencing severe nausea, which ultimately led to uncontrollable vomiting. My mother noticed that something was wrong and, summoning her strength despite her own health issues, she accompanied me to the hospital, which was about six blocks away. Initially, she assumed I had caught the flu.

As I sat alone with the doctor, he delivered shocking news: I was pregnant. Overwhelmed with fear, I pleaded with my mother, begging her not to tell my father, repeatedly crying and saying, "Please don't tell Daddy." I was at a loss, uncertain of what to do. Walking home slowly with my mother, tears streamed down my face. I cried uncontrollably, while my mom remained silent. Once we arrived home, my mother, inevitably, informed my father of the situation.

Later that evening, my father arrived at our house, consumed by a fit of rage and anger. Without asking any questions, he immediately lashed out at me, swinging at me, hurling insults, and derogatory terms, and physically assaulting me. He completely lost control. Eventually, he demanded to know who the father of the baby was. When I told him it was Jab, he spiraled even further without seeking any explanation. I was devastated and so hurt that I ran into the kitchen, grabbed a knife, locked myself in the bathroom, and threatened to take my own life. It was an overwhelming moment, and I couldn't fathom the reality of what had happened to me.

With a knife in my hands, I contemplated self-harm by attempting to cut my own stomach. However, my brother Buck broke down the bathroom door and pulled me out before any harm could come to me. My father tried to calm down, and that's when I mustered the courage to explain to him that I had been raped by Jab and that I had never engaged in any sexual activity with a boy before.

I poured my heart out to him, recounting everything that had transpired, why I was afraid to tell Momma, why I felt too ashamed to confide in anyone else, and how terrified I was. I didn't fully grasp the magnitude of what had happened to me, and the pain was shared by my father and my mother. It was incredibly difficult to recount the events to my parents and explain the ordeal I had endured. My father and mother were devastated, and I felt utterly broken. Sharing my experience with them was one of the hardest things I have ever done. My father was sickened by what had happened. He told my mother, "Mae, get you, Angie, and Jr. ready; I'll be back to pick y'all up later," and he left. Later that evening, he called to check on us and instructed my mother not to give me anything to eat.

The following day, he came to pick us up and took us to his girlfriend's apartment on the east side. The pain etched across my mother's face was unbearable to witness. They proceeded to starve me for two or three days, denying me any sustenance, not even a cracker. My mother sat there watching, and as I pleaded, "Mom, I'm hungry. I'm hungry," she tried to comfort me, but it was of no avail. On the second or third day, my father's girlfriend declared, "It's time." I will never forget the sight of my father handing me a gallon of vodka and saying, "Here, drink this." I protested, saying, "No," but he insisted, "Just drink it straight." They placed a straw in the bottle and instructed me to consume the entire contents.

They made me drink the entire bottle of vodka, whether it was a fifth or a gallon, I'm not sure. I was intoxicated to the point of being completely drunk, and it was a terrible feeling. After that, my father's girlfriend gave me some pills. I remember reading the label, and they were called Quinines. I will never forget that name. Then they turned up the volume of the music they were playing, some kind of rock or heavy metal. I exclaimed, "What the hell?" and she told me to lie down on the floor. Despite being heavily intoxicated, I was fully aware of what was happening.

They forced me to lie on the floor, and they proceeded to spread my legs. The music grew louder and louder. Confused and frightened, I asked, "What are you doing?" They instructed me to remain quiet and still. My mother watched intently, sitting in a chair, and rocking back and forth, clutching my little brother tightly. I began experiencing excruciating pain and started screaming, "Ma, Ma, Maaa!" Before I knew it, my father was holding my legs and pinning my arms down. His girlfriend attempted to insert a bent wire hanger into my vagina, and I screamed, cried, and begged them to stop. The pain was unbearable, and I pleaded with them to cease their actions.

My father asked her if the procedure was done yet, but she replied, "No, turn the music up." I was screaming, pleading for them to stop, while she continued to dig deeper inside me. I looked at my mother, desperately begging for her help to make them stop.

His girlfriend pressed down forcefully on my stomach, pushing the hanger deeper inside me in an attempt to abort the pregnancy. It's important to note that I was a virgin before the rape, so my vaginal opening was not stretched or accustomed to such traumatic experiences. I had never encountered such extreme measures or surreal situations. I was being attacked, but she wouldn't stop. I screamed, yelled, and begged them to stop, growing louder and louder. However, she kept turning up the volume of the music drowning out my cries and screams.

It was a chaotic scene. I cried uncontrollably, screaming at the top of my lungs. I squirmed and fought, doing everything in my power to make her get off me. I pleaded with my mom to intervene and make them stop. My mom cried, my little brother stared in disbelief, and I continued to cry out for help. Eventually, my father told her to stop. I just endured it. My mom cried, and my father, with remorse in his voice, said, "Come on, I'm going to take y'all home." My mom continued to cry, while I sobbed, trying to catch my breath. It was an unbearable experience. I cried and, in my intoxicated state, I vaguely remember getting into the car. I passed out completely and only woke up when my brother Buck carried me into the house. I'll never forget how he started joking and laughing, saying, "Damn, you're fucked up." He didn't know what had happened. He laid me down on the couch, and I slept for two days straight.

A couple of days later, my parents took me to an abortion clinic downtown. My father couldn't afford or didn't want to pay for the procedure, which is why he initially attempted to do it at his girlfriend's place. However, when we entered the room, they positioned my legs in the stirrups and prepared to use the medical equipment on me. Nervously, I asked, "What is this? What are you doing? No, STOP!" I screamed in panic. The nurse went out and informed my dad, "We cannot proceed without anesthesia." My father paid for them to put me to sleep, and they performed the abortion. My parents took me home, and I felt completely drained. It was heartbreaking to see my mother witness everything I went through. I felt helpless. This all happened during my eighth-grade school year, and it was an incredibly challenging time.

I was deeply embarrassed, as if the entire world knew what had just happened to me. I was hurt beyond words, unsure of how to cope with it all. A few days later, I returned to school, but it was incredibly difficult. They threatened to fail me in eighth grade, despite being one of the smartest students in the school. There was only one other person, Tijuan, who was just as intelligent as me; we were neck and neck. The only advantage he had was that he was able to physically attend school every day.

I barely made it through eighth grade, and during that time, my father grew increasingly distant and neglectful towards us. My mom would receive a small monthly welfare check, but my father would come and take all the cash, claiming it was for the mortgage. He would also take all the food stamps, saying he needed to sell them to help pay the bills. This left us with only a $65 book of food stamps to get us through the entire month.

There was an Arabian man named Joe who owned the corner store, and he took pity on us. He extended credit to my mom, and I would write letters on her behalf to get essential items that we couldn't afford because she had nothing. Joe allowed us to get bread, milk, cereal, lunchmeat, and occasionally some potato chips and candy. Most of the time, I would get us ramen noodles and Parker House sausages.

I will never forget that Thanksgiving. We were incredibly hungry, and we had to wait for my father to bring us some food. We waited and waited, and finally, around 11:30 p.m., he arrived with a box of leftover food from him and his girlfriend's family. My mom, little brother, and I devoured that food as if it were the best meal we had ever eaten. We were overjoyed to have turkey, dressing, greens, spaghetti, and a pineapple coconut cake. We didn't care where the food came from; we were just grateful to have something to eat. The entire cake was gone that night. I can't fully explain how I felt in those moments, knowing the circumstances we were in, but as a 13-year-old, I felt powerless to change anything. But I found strength in being there by my mother's side. I was all she had, as well as she was all we had.

There is one particular morning that will forever be etched in my memory. It must have been around 4 or 5 a.m., and I was sleeping on the couch. My brother Buck was getting ready for work, and suddenly, I felt a large rat running up and down my body on top of the blanket. I woke up frozen in fear, knowing I had to do something. I swiftly flung the blanket off, and all I heard was the rat hitting the wall and squealing loudly. Buck jumped and exclaimed, "What the fuck?" before bursting into laughter, saying "Damn that was a big ass rat!" I was utterly disgusted.

Around this time, I pleaded with my mother to leave that house because it had become unbearable to live there. We were taunted and teased, with people referring to our house as the "igloo," unaware of the suffering we endured inside. It was truly a terrible situation. I suggested that once I graduated from eighth grade, we could find an apartment somewhere, and I would work to take care of us.

We desperately needed to escape that house, find safety, and better living conditions. However, my mother said no, stating that I couldn't take care of us. I could see the pain on her face. The worst incident occurred during the winter. I was playing with my little brother, who was around two or three years old, in the only room of the house that was warmed by a kerosene heater. As we were laughing and having fun, he tripped and fell into the heater, severely burning the bottom part of his stomach. He screamed and cried in excruciating pain, shaking me to my core. I was devastated. In a panic, I grabbed him and looked at my mom, unsure of what to do. I poured some water over the burn using a bottle I had and applied petroleum jelly to it. I was terrified and cried uncontrollably. My baby brother's skin was blistered, and he was in agony; it was a severe burn. I was afraid my dad was going to kill me, and I couldn't tell anyone because I thought for sure they would take us away from our mother. Every day, I did my best to clean the burn and ensure he was okay. I felt an overwhelming sense of guilt and sorrow.

I remember the time leading up to my luncheon and graduation. It was a challenging period for me, as I didn't have anything suitable to wear. I had to go to my sister's house across the street and ask her for something to wear. Initially, she said she didn't have anything for me, but I kept pleading with her because I really needed an outfit. Eventually, she reluctantly let me borrow a more mature outfit—a silky gray skirt and matching top that resembled something you'd wear to a nightclub. It wasn't exactly what I had in mind, but it was better than nothing.

On the day of my graduation, my father arrived to drive my mother, my little brother, and me to the ceremony. I was disappointed that my sister or any of my family didn't show up or get me a gift. At the end of the graduation, my father attempted to show off, acting like a big shot. He gave me a diamond ring as if it were my graduation gift. He was out there taking numerous pictures, boasting, and exaggerating about his daughter and his own achievements, trying to impress everyone and maintain his image as a loving father.

I was ecstatic that he gave me a diamond ring. I thought, "Wow, my daddy gave me a diamond ring!" However, as soon as we got home, he promptly took the ring off my finger. I was taken aback and thought, "Are you serious?"

He explained that he would get me something later, but he couldn't let me wear such an expensive ring around. He told me to stay on the porch while he went to work, saying that we would celebrate my graduation soon. He drove off in his fancy Lincoln, leaving me feeling incredibly dejected on the porch. At that moment, I started to despise my life.

While all the other graduates were headed downtown, attending graduation parties, and enjoying themselves, I couldn't go anywhere. I had to stay home to take care of my mom and brother. I didn't mind taking care of them, but I wished this one day could be different, something special just for me. Unfortunately, I was stuck sitting on the porch, feeling utterly downcast, watching everyone else go out and celebrate their graduations.

Then, my mom came to the door and called me by name. She looked at me with a profound sense of care and said, "Here." She stretched out her words, conveying how proud she was of me. In her hand, she held a single $1 food stamp. She said, "This is all that I have," and instructed me to go buy some candy. The gesture touched me deeply, more than I can adequately express. All I could do was look at her and say, "Thank you, momma. I love you, and I promise I will take care of us and make you proud one day!"

I walked down to the corner store, bought some penny candy, and returned to the porch. My little brother and I sat there, savoring the Now and Later candy, wine candy, chips, and penny cookies. In those days, chips cost around 10 to 15 cents, and I had a dill pickle and a peppermint stick. It was a simple but meaningful moment, cherishing the treats with my brother and feeling grateful for my mother's love and support.

I will never forget that summer. There was a boy named Davis who was 16 years old. I was feeling extremely hungry when he walked past me, eating a gyro and fries. Without thinking, I asked him if it was for me. Surprisingly, he offered me the whole sandwich. I didn't waste a moment; I grabbed it from him and rushed into the house where my mother, little brother, and I devoured it within seconds. It was such a satisfying meal after being so hungry. After finishing the sandwich, I went back out to the porch to thank Davis. We sat there, talking, and laughing, and it felt great to have someone to connect with. Davis offered to bring me another gyro the following day, and I eagerly anticipated his return.

True to his word, the next day Davis came down the street with another, this time a large gyro plate. He mentioned seeing my little brother enjoying my sandwich the previous day, so he wanted to bring me a bigger one. He continued this kind gesture on the third day as well. I expressed my gratitude and thanked him profusely. From my window, I could see my mom watching us on the porch, laughing and smiling—a rare sight in our difficult circumstances. Davis and I spent the entire summer sitting on the porch, having conversations about diverse topics, including our neighborhood, schools, families, and friends.

Although he visited every day, I never felt comfortable inviting him into our house. I couldn't bear to let him see the extent of our living conditions and how challenging life was for us. As winter approached and the weather turned colder, we relied on kerosene heaters to keep warm inside the house. Davis started noticing that I wore the same bra and the same clothes every day. To help, he began buying me things like Levi's jeans, T-shirts, and shoes. He would bring me gifts daily, such as socks, underwear, and personal care items. Despite his generosity, he remained unaware of the true extent of our circumstances. However, it's important to remember that even with these gifts, I was still unable to go anywhere. I was confined to home, spending my days sitting on the porch or inside the house as the cold and rainy days set in.

As the temperature dropped and winter settled in, I wondered what I should do next. My mom, brother, and I found ourselves back in that one room we had taped off to keep it warm. We had set up our sleeping arrangements in the dining room, where we also had the TV. We were still dealing with the issue of the busted pipes, which meant we couldn't use the bathroom or bathe. It was during this time that Davis started noticing the situation and asked me what was going on.

We had a heart-to-heart conversation. One night, while we were on the phone, we ran out of kerosene. I desperately tried calling my dad, but he wouldn't answer. I could see my mother and brother starting to freeze, and I knew I had to take action. I told Davis about our dire situation, explaining that we were extremely cold. It was around 2-3 a.m., but without hesitation,

Davis came over to my house. He brought a can of kerosene and walked all the way to the gas station on 55th and Ashland to get us more. Not only did he bring us kerosene, but he also brought us food.

That's when he began to realize that I was dealing with a serious problem on my own. He started cooking breakfast, lunch, and dinner for us, bringing us food every day. When his parents went to work and nobody was at his house, he would help me walk my mother and my little brother to his house so we could all take baths. We hadn't had a proper bath in such a long time. My mother sat in the tub, finally able to wash herself, and we were able to clean our hair. He not only cooked us food but also washed and neatly folded our clothes and underwear.

Once a week, he would help me walk my mother to his house so we could sneak in and take baths. During one of those visits, he expressed his concern about our living situation. He said, "What are you going to do? You can't keep living like this. This is terrible, and no child should have to suffer like this, nor should you have to bear so much responsibility on your own." I told him, "I don't know what to do, but I cannot leave my mother or risk her going into a care home."

By that time, my father had realized that I was seeing this boy because I wasn't calling him as often, and we had kerosene, food, and clean clothes. He started asking questions about where we were getting these things from. I told him I had a friend and that we were just friends. At this point, we were indeed just friends, but he was doing so much for us. My father expressed a desire to meet Davis, so I arranged for him to come over one evening. It was an awkward and tense meeting, as my father was suspicious of his intentions. However, as they talked and got to know each other, my father's attitude softened. He realized that Davis genuinely cared about our well-being and was simply helping us out of kindness. My father told him that we couldn't be in a romantic relationship because I needed to focus on school. However, he said it was okay for him to visit sometime. Davis and I continued talking on the phone every day, and he started coming over more frequently, providing us with much-needed help.

One day, that spring, while Davis and I were talking in the living room, my father came home and told me to pack my things because he was taking me to live with him and his girlfriend, Dawn. I refused to leave my mother and brother behind to live with someone I barely knew. I asked him about my mom, and he assured me that he had taken care of things. I panicked and argued with him, refusing to go anywhere with him. Davis stepped in and told my father, "You are not taking her anywhere." An intense argument ensued between Davis and my father. My mother was deeply shaken, and I could see the stress on her face.

My little brother cried uncontrollably due to the overwhelming chaos and confusion. So, in that moment, I made a decision. I ran. I ran as fast as I could, escaping from the tense situation. I hid under the porch in the backyard of Davis's house. Davis was looking for me for about an hour or two. I later knocked on his door. I had to make sure the coast was clear, and I wanted to get to him before his parents came back from work. I told him, "I can't; I can't go back there. I'm tired of the neglect, the abuse, and the inhumane ways of living there." I told him I was tired of the mental abuse and the starvation; I had to find a better way of life, and I had to find a way to help save my mother and little brother. I kept crying to him, saying that I could not go back to that house. I was just so worn out and tired from all of the neglect, pressure, responsibility, and abuse I was living under. I simply refused to go live with my father at his girlfriend's house. I just had to do something to save us.

Davis said, "Okay." He went into his house, packed a bag, and said, "Let's go." We walked up to the bus stop on 63rd and Ashland. I was so afraid. My heart was pounding so fast and hard. I thought my father was going to catch us. We went to his sister's house, who lived on the west side. I called my mom immediately to tell her not to worry. I figured my father was gone and had left her and my little brother in the house alone. She somehow stuttered that I could come back home. I told her I was okay and not to worry; I was going to get us help and fix it. I told her I loved her and my brother and not to worry. I was crying, and she was crying as well. I told her I was going to fix it and I was going to take care of us.

# PART
# TWO

# CHAPTER 6
# HERE COMES THE CALVARY

*"If you are silent about your pain, they'll kill you, and say you enjoyed it."*
**(Zoro Neale Hurston)**

After getting off the phone with her, I was in complete worry mode. There was no way I was going to leave my mother and little brother in that house by themselves. I simply could not rest, so I felt the only thing I could do was call someone. The only person I could think of was my mother's youngest sister. I called my aunt and told her what was going on in the house, and how bad it really was. I explained what happened between me and my father and that I had run away. I went on to say that I was calling them because I couldn't leave my mother and my little brother in the house by themselves.

I told them absolutely everything that my father was doing to us—how bad it was and how badly we were struggling. I shared all the details. My aunt said, "Don't worry, we'll go get them." She asked if I was okay and said, "You can come over here." She told me they had to hurry up and go. She thanked me for calling and being truthful about what was really happening because they didn't have a clue it was that bad over there. They had just felt like they weren't wanted around, and everything was okay because they hadn't heard from us in so long. They said they didn't even know my mother was having all those strokes and that we were starving and stuff.

I pleaded, "Please, just go get my mom and little brother; I'll be okay. I'll be okay." And they went that night to get my mom. At first, my mother wouldn't answer the door. So, they just kicked the door open. Surprisingly, my father was there with them. They started telling my mom they knew what was going on, and they were taking her out of there. She kept resisting and telling them, "No, it's okay; everything is okay." They looked around the house and saw everything I had described to them.

They observed the gas being turned off, an empty fridge, piles of dirty clothes, and the fact that we were all cramped in one room, relying on a kerosene heater for cooking. They witnessed the collapsed roof, which exposed the sky above, as well as the porch in disrepair and plastic covering the windows. It was evident to them that everything I had described was true. They inquired about my whereabouts, and my mother informed them that I would return soon. They informed my mother that they were aware of the situation and presented her with two options: either she could willingly leave with them, or they would forcibly remove her from there. Overwhelmed with emotions, my mother began to cry. My father, on the other hand, demanded that they leave, which led to an argument between them.

Among the family members present were my uncle Bubba, my brother-in-Law Miguel, my sister Tia, my aunts Helen and Tee-Tee, and their partners. They repeatedly threatened my father, ordering him to remain silent. He tried to argue back, defending his home, and insisting that they wouldn't take his wife and son away. In response, my aunt Tee-Tee declared, "Fuck this, let's go, Odie Mae." She lifted my mom from the couch and proceeded to guide her out of the house towards the car. She asked my mom if there was anything she wanted to take from the house because she would never return. My mom pleaded, "No, no, please stop," but her pleas were ignored. Meanwhile, my little brother cried in fear. In a desperate attempt, my father commanded the dog to attack them. My uncle then began to physically assault my father, while my aunt Helen joined in the altercation. As I was told, everyone in the house was involved, beating the shit out of my father. They took my mother, grabbing whatever belongings they could, and exited the house. The neighbors applauded and cheered as my mother's family rescued her and my little brother from the situation.

Everything happened so quickly. I recall hearing that my aunt Helen struck my father in the head with an air pump, causing him to lose consciousness. They inflicted severe physical harm upon my father, and to be honest, he deserved it for the way he neglected, abandoned, and abused us.

Later that night, around 2-3 a.m., I called my aunt to inquire if they had successfully gotten my mother and brother out of that house. They confirmed that they had, assuring me that they were safe. They acknowledged that everything I had relayed to them was accurate. The only discrepancy was that since I had left earlier that day, my father had returned to watch over them that night.

Immediately after, I secured a job at McDonald's and diligently went to work every day. I felt a strong determination to return to school and complete my education.

I made it a point to call and check on my mom and brother daily because, in my mind, I still had the responsibility to look after them. My aunt reassured me not to worry and urged me to come and live with them, as they were willing to assist us. At this point, I was around 14 years old, in my freshman year of high school. I knew deep down that I wasn't quite ready for such a move, but I was willing to do whatever it took to take care of my mother and brother. My mother requested that I come and stay with them to provide support. I agreed, and my aunt said, "Come on, Angie, you're intelligent, and it's time for you to experience a more normal life." I complied, informing Davis that I would be with my mother and brother at my aunt's house, where she would help me reenroll in school and assist us. He understood and promised to visit me every other day, ensuring I had everything needed as usual. With that settled, I packed my belongings and headed to my Aunt Tee-Tee's house to be with my mother and little brother.

Aunt Tee-Tee had always been known as the family gossiper. She regularly called relatives, both near and far, to share details about other family members' lives and personal business. I remember her behavior being quite extreme. One moment, she would be deeply involved in church, waving the Bible everywhere talking about the goodness of the Lord, participating in the choir, and attending church events five days a week, and twice on Sundays. She even experienced spiritual manifestations. Then, seemingly out of nowhere, she would immerse herself in the nightlife, going to clubs, partying every night, indulging in alcohol and drugs, and spending weekends at card games with her friends.

Aunt Tee-Tee had a volatile personality. One minute, she would shower you with love and treat you like her favorite person in the world, and the next minute, she would develop an attitude and refuse to talk to you. She had a knack for keeping family members mad at each other.

When I arrived at Aunt Tee-Tee's house, she immediately enrolled me at Orr High School out west and provided me with everything I needed to start school. It's worth noting that she lived in a small two-bedroom apartment on the Westside. The apartment consisted of a living room, one bathroom, and a small kitchen. Aunt Tee-Tee was the youngest of my mother's siblings, and she was down to earth. She had four little girls of her own and was in a long-term relationship with my uncle Lamar, although they never married. Three of her children were fathered by him. In Aunt Tee-Tee's apartment, my mother and brother slept in her daughter's room on one of the twin beds, while two of her daughters slept in the living room on a pallet on the floor or on the couch. Spending the night at each other's houses was a customary practice on my mother's side of the family.

So, when my Uncle Bubba visited, he and his sons would also sleep in the living room on a pallet on the floor. That's just how they did things over there. Aunt Tee-Tee, and my uncles, all worked at Halo Lighting, so they had to wake up around 4 a.m. to get to work on time.

Initially, everything was going well. I was attending school and finally feeling like a normal teenager. Davis and I continued to talk on the phone every day. My mother would spend her days in the living room with my brother, watching television. I would come in to do my chores, homework, and comb my little cousin's hair. Everything seemed okay for a while.

Then one day, my uncle said, "I'm taking all the kids to the movies." I was thrilled and told Davis about it. He wanted to come along; I told him I would ask for permission. Of course, he offered to pay for both of us. Now, my cousin Lydia, who was Uncle Bubba's daughter, warned me against it. She said, "No, Angie, that's not a good idea." I asked why, explaining that it had been so long since I saw Davis and that I missed him. I also wanted him to come over to make sure I was okay and see my mom and brother.

So, I approached my uncle and asked if Davis could join us for the movie. He completely lost his temper and demanded to know who Davis was. I explained that Davis had been my boyfriend for over two years and had been there for me, my mom, and my little brother. I expressed how much I cared about him. My uncle forbade me from seeing him and threatened that he was going to beat the hell out of me if I ever saw him again. Initially, I told Davis, "I can't see you anymore. My uncle said "no!" But the next thing I knew, Davis showed up at my school the next day, and when classes ended, he walked me home. I told him that he couldn't come to the house because of my uncle.

This continued for a while, but eventually, Davis said, "This isn't working. I want to sit down and talk to your uncle, get to know him, and let him get to know me." I told him I couldn't do that, but he urged me to try. I approached Aunt Tee-Tee about the situation, and she told me that my uncle was old-fashioned and that it was okay for me to see Davis and hang out with him occasionally. She even said he could come over sometimes. I asked about Uncle Bubba, and she responded, "This is my house. That boy can come over. I'll deal with Bubba." I also mentioned the situation to my cousin Lydia, who once again warned me, saying, "Angie, you don't want to do that. I'm telling you, my dad does too much."

"He doesn't mind whooping anybody; my mother had to intervene before when he caught me talking to a boy. Now, please note that I was living in very harsh conditions and was completely neglected. However, I had never experienced physical abuse or beatings from my parents, so the idea of getting a whooping was unimaginable to me. I told my uncle that it was Valentine's Day and that Davis wanted to bring me a gift. I asked him to just drop it off, but my uncle threatened me once again, saying that if Davis came to the house, he was going to beat the hell out of me.

Davis came to my aunt's house that day. Just to drop off my gifts—a big teddy bear, flowers, and candy—and we shared a quick kiss, and I made him leave immediately so I wouldn't get in trouble. Unfortunately, one of my cousins informed Uncle Bubba about Davis's visit, and he confronted me about the gifts. I explained that Davis had brought them, and that Aunt Tee-Tee had given her approval.

He said, "But what did I tell you? Since you want to be hardheaded and act grown, get your ass in that room and get that leather belt." All my little cousins looked at me with horror on their faces. He instructed me to go get the belt, go into my aunt's room, and pull my clothes off. In utter and total disbelief, I asked him, "What?" He replied, "You heard me!" I couldn't believe how extreme his reaction was and thought he must be joking. Loud and angrily, he announced it again for everyone in the house to hear him, "Angie, you better have your clothes off and your head under that mattress by the time I get in that room." My cousins were looking at me, shocked. My mother seemed as though she had a heart attack and couldn't breathe. I tried to stay strong and brave, not knowing what was about to happen.

I went into the room, trying to gather my courage. Shortly after, he entered the room, furious, and asked, "Why haven't you taken your clothes off and put your head under that mattress?" Refusing to comply, I stood my ground and told him that I wouldn't undress or put my head under the mattress. He violently struck me in the eye, and a struggle ensued. He mercilessly beat me; using an extension cord, he whipped me and inflicted pain all over my body. By the time he was done, I was covered in bruises and welts, unable to sit or stand without feeling intense pain. My body was literally raw from the beating. I was swollen and discolored, with a swollen shut eye, and my entire body was tender to the touch.

I couldn't sit down or stand up; I was in terrible shape. When I walked out of the room, my mother was sitting at the end of the couch, looking helpless with a pained expression, for there was nothing she could do to save or help me.

Later that night, I managed to call Davis and tell him about the horrifying incident. Fueled by anger, he insisted on coming to rescue me immediately. However, I knew we needed a different plan to avoid escalating the situation further. Davis suggested that I pack my things and wait for a taxi the next morning when everyone would be leaving for work. We arranged for a cab to pick me up at six in the morning; so, throughout the night, I quietly packed my belongings, making sure none of my cousins noticed. While doing so, I constantly glanced at my mother, torn between wanting to protect and support her and the urgent need to escape this toxic environment.

Examining my battered face and body in the bathroom mirror, I couldn't believe the pain I was enduring. I felt like a victim of slavery, subjected to the cruel punishment of a whipping from a heartless overseer. Finally, I came to understand what my father had been trying to protect me from and why he wouldn't allow me to be around this slave mentality and toxic Post Traumatic Slavery Syndrome mindset. I was in complete disbelief and shock that my uncle would beat me to such an extent.

I realized that I had to leave, no matter how much I wanted to stay and help my mother and brother. My own safety had to be the priority. When morning came and everyone had left for work, I quickly carried my bags downstairs and got into the waiting taxi that Davis had arranged. We went to his sister's house, where we were given a room. Davis found work with his brother at a construction site to support us financially, while I got a job at McDonald's. Despite being only 14 years old, I had already adopted a mature mindset, focusing on survival rather than enjoying my teenage years. To cash my paychecks, I obtained a fake ID stating that I was 18, highlighting the level of responsibility I had taken on at such a young age.

# CHAPTER 7
# A TWISTED FAMILY

*"She was powerful not because she was scared but because she went on. so strongly despite the fear"*
**(Atticus)**

As we worked and saved money, our relationship eventually took a turn. Davis became possessive and controlling, and then started picking fights over trivial matters. His behavior changed, and I began to question the person he had shown himself to be. His possessiveness even extended to his sister, whom he accused of being too promiscuous. One night, she invited me to go to a club with her and suggested that I shouldn't be confined to the room while Davis was out having fun. I usually stayed at home, so being in the house reading books during my time off didn't bother me. Reluctantly, I agreed to go out, as I rarely had the opportunity and wanted to experience something different. However, this decision only fueled Davis's jealousy and anger.
During this period of my life, my focus was on work and saving money to secure our own place and eventually return to school. Despite facing challenges and uncertainties, I was determined to break free from the abuse I had endured and create a better future for myself.

When we entered the house after a night of dancing and drinking at the club, Davis immediately confronted me. Our fights became a regular occurrence, happening almost every day. I distinctly remember one incident when our argument spilled out into the alley. Now, it's important to understand that

I was only 14 years old and, on the run, so I had to be extremely cautious. As we were fighting in the alley, a police car drove by and noticed the commotion. I quickly ran upstairs to hide while the police questioned Davis about my identity and whereabouts. As expected, he refused to provide them with any information. I'm not sure how the situation was resolved, but somehow, I managed to remain concealed under the bed, terrified of being caught.

Eventually, Davis began having an affair with Kay, who happened to be his sister's best friend. Kay was considerably older, around 25 to 30 years old. She had a petite figure, and some might consider her to be unattractive, with a missing front left tooth.

I never could have anticipated that Davis would become involved with someone like her. Kay was a regular marijuana smoker and consumed alcohol daily, which were activities that Davis also enjoyed. I later learned that Davis was smoking Sherm sticks, a combination of marijuana dipped in PCP or embalming fluid. He once engaged in a high-speed chase with the police while under the influence of that substance and refused to pull over after a hit and run. This incident prevented him from obtaining a driver's license,

Although I never smoked marijuana or drank alcohol, Davis did manage to get me into smoking cigarettes, specifically Newport 100's—an unhealthy habit that I now regret developing.

Now, here's the thing. I was working tirelessly at McDonald's, so I wasn't paying much attention to what was happening at home. I failed to notice Kay's increasing presence and the changes in her behavior when she was around Davis. I never even considered her to be any form of competition because I believed I had a strong and loving relationship with Davis. After all, he had witnessed the hardships I had endured and had been there for me since the day we met. I genuinely thought he loved me.

But looking back, I realize how young, naive, and ignorant I was. I didn't fully grasp the situation I had gotten myself into. All

I wanted was a normal life after everything I had been through. However, I eventually discovered that Kay had taken over the domestic responsibilities in the house. She cooked meals for her and Davis, prepared their lunches for school and work, and even took care of their dinner and snacks. I was so oblivious and clueless at the time that I didn't notice any of this happening right under my nose.

It's important to note that I had to wake up at 4:00 a.m. every day to make it to my shift at McDonald's by 5:30 a.m. I worked as a cashier for breakfast and lunch, and the restaurant opened at 6:00 a.m. My days were consumed by work, and I often worked overtime to make ends meet. Consequently, I wasn't available to cook breakfast or lunch for Davis, nor could I clean, wash, or iron for him. I couldn't even join him for dinner because I was at McDonald's from morning till night, sometimes closing the restaurant. Additionally, I relied on the bus for my daily commute to and from work.

By the time I returned home, all I wanted to do was take a shower and go to sleep. I wasn't paying attention to what was happening around me, and I didn't feel the need to. I simply didn't know any better. However, Davis's sister eventually informed me about what was going on, and I began to notice how Davis and Kay acted towards each other—the physical affection and terms of endearment. Suddenly, it all became clear to me. There was a major confrontation between Davis and me, and I called him into the bedroom to confront him about the affair.

He admitted that they were together. He told me how happy she made him feel and how they had so much in common. He began criticizing me, saying that I wasn't woman enough for him, that Kay took better care of him and his needs. She cooked for him, and she was fun because she loved to drink alcohol and smoked weed and knew how to have an enjoyable time, far more sociable than I was. He said he felt I was boring because all I did was stay home, read books, and work all the time. I was deeply hurt and devastated. I sat there crying, asking him what I was supposed to do. He reassured me that he still loved me and that he wouldn't abandon me.

We ended up leaving from there and moving south to his brother and girlfriend's apartment on 79th and Damen. She was Puerto Rican and had two children with his brother. His brother had a few women around town, but this one was named Pat. She was really cool and around 20 years old, maybe a little older. Nevertheless, she had a cute 2-bedroom basement apartment, and the rent was really cheap. She and her children slept in the front bedroom, and she rented the back room to Davis and me for about $100 a month. We also had to help with groceries and utilities.

I ended up changing jobs at McDonald's and transferred to the Southside location right around the corner on 79th Street. I found a second job working at Toys R Us. At this point, I was just trying to learn how to be more attentive, give Davis what he wanted and needed from me as his woman, and be able to save so I could get my own place. I was in survival mode. I felt like I was going down from all the stress I was under and working so hard. I was getting increasingly tired every day. I was so drained and tired that I was sleeping all day long and eating everything I could get my hands on. I was always hungry.

Every time I opened my eyes, I was eating. Lo and behold, it turned out that I was pregnant! Davis questioned, "We're going to keep the baby, right?" I told him yes because I loved him, and after the psychological trauma I had experienced from the abortion my father and his girlfriend tried to perform on me, I was so messed up that I simply couldn't imagine ever having another abortion.

So, there I was, 15 years old and pregnant. My mother and father were not in my life at this point. I only had Davis, and I wasn't attending school. When Davis's mother found out I was pregnant, she felt bad and started trying to help us out. However, Davis was still running back and forth to the Westside, still messing around with Kay. We started arguing and fighting more about it every day. Eventually, he left me for her while I was pregnant because she kept telling him to go and be with his family that he created since I was pregnant with his child. Out of nowhere, he up and married her. I was overly emotional about the whole situation. I felt as if my life was falling apart all over again. That's when I first started listening to the song by the Spinners, "Love Don't Love Nobody."

My relationship with Pat had started to deteriorate. She would become angry because Davis's brother wouldn't come to see her, and she would take out her anger and frustration on me, cursing me out over every little thing. One day, while I was sleeping, she started banging on my door and suddenly burst into my room with a nasty attitude, berating me about the dishes. Exhausted and half-asleep, I told her I would take care of them. However, she began pulling and pushing me, forcefully dragging me into the kitchen, shouting and demanding that I do them immediately. I couldn't tolerate her behavior, and I snapped back at her, which initiated a fight between us. She grabbed a dough roller from the counter and attempted to hit me with it. In response, I started swinging at her, and we ended up wrestling and struggling on the floor. Throughout the altercation, her children were screaming and crying. In the heat of the moment, I grabbed her head and forcefully banged it against the wall and radiator while continuing to punch her in the face. The fight was intense and violent. I looked at her children, still screaming and crying, and I felt a sense of guilt and remorse for subjecting them to such a disturbing scene. At that point, I made the decision to stop the fight and walked away.

During that time, while my mom was still living with my aunt Tee-Tee, my aunt was granted a Section 8 housing choice voucher and relocated to the Southside. Despite being pregnant, I made it a priority to secure employment so that I wouldn't have to rely on my mom financially. I didn't want to burden her further, as she was already struggling to make ends meet with only public aid supporting her and my little brother. Therefore, I took responsibility for myself and managed to support my own needs while also attempting to help my mom and offer assistance if they needed it.

However, even with a job, I couldn't afford the high cost of medical insurance for myself. Considering my pregnancy, it was crucial for me to attend prenatal visits and access necessary medications.

Although I was eligible for a medical card and welfare assistance due to my pregnancy, I deliberately refrained from applying. I knew that I was already covered under my mother's medical card, and she was receiving benefits such as cash, food stamps, and a medical card on my behalf. I wanted her to keep those resources to support herself and my little brother. Additionally, it helped me avoid unwanted attention and inquiries. It's important to remember that I was only 15 years old at the time and was lying about my age to secure employment. Very few people were aware of my homeless and unstable situation.

Consequently, I would take the bus to my aunt's house to retrieve the medical card from my mom whenever I needed it. It was an opportunity for me to spend some personal time with my mom while checking on her and my little brother. Since my aunt and uncle were at work and my brother was in kindergarten, I would often visit early in the mornings when my mom was alone. I would bring her small snacks, cookies, candy, and gifts—things I knew she enjoyed. I missed her immensely, but I was doing my best to navigate the challenges of being alone on the streets, finding a place to stay, and establishing stability so that I could eventually rescue her and my brother.

Whenever I arrived at my aunt's house, my mom's face would light up with happiness, and she would embrace me tightly. Unfortunately, I didn't have much time to sit and talk as I would have liked because I was always in a rush. I needed to catch the bus on time for my doctor's appointments and work. However, during the brief moments we had together at the door, I would update her on how I was doing (although not always entirely truthful), as I couldn't bear the thought of her worrying about me struggling on the streets. I wanted to provide her with some comfort, believing that Davis and I were doing okay. I would always express my love for her and how much I missed her.

My aunt Tee-Tee's oldest daughter, Tay-Tay, was around 12-13 years old at that time. One day, my sister went to my aunt's house to check on our mom. My mother managed to tell my sister, "Tay-Tay slapped my face and took my money." She gasped for air and continued, "She hit me in the head with the broom and stole my money. She threatened me and told me to keep quiet. She slapped my face and told me to shut up!" As soon as my sister heard this, she packed clothes for our mother and brother and immediately left that house. She rushed to the school to pick up my little brother, and then she called me and told me to come to her house urgently.

After finishing work, I went straight to my sister's house, where my sister and mother explained to me what had happened. I was deeply hurt and in disbelief. I couldn't believe that my cousin would do such a thing.

Eventually, Tee-Tee arrived at my sister's house with Tay-Tay. My sister said, "Tee-Tee, we need to talk," and she explained to her that Tay-Tay had been abusing our mom and stealing her money. She shared everything that our mother had told us about the situation. It's important to note that our mother had difficulty speaking clearly due to her speech impediment and stuttering from the damaging effects of her strokes. Her words were often confusing, but she managed to convey what was happening to her.

This wasn't the first time Tay-Tay had been accused of stealing. A few years earlier, she was accused of stealing money from my aunt Tee-Tee. My aunt had severely beaten her with an extension cord, causing her ear to be partially detached. However, it later turned out that the boy who lived downstairs in my aunt's apartment building had actually broken into her apartment and stolen the money while they were at work.

My aunt felt guilty and remorseful for beating her daughter so severely for something she didn't do. She tried everything to make it up to Tay-Tay. So, when my mom finally told us that Tay-Tay was abusing her and taking her money, my aunt Tee-Tee didn't want to believe it. She tried to blame me because I would visit when no one else was around. I insisted, "I have no reason to ever steal from my mom. I would never hit, abuse, or steal from her!" Tee-Tee became furious and screamed at my mother, desperately trying to make her say that anyone else but Tay-Tay was responsible. But my mother used hand gestures to point at her face and head and kept repeating, "No, it was Tay-Tay. She slapped my face, took my money, and hit me with a broom." In the end, my aunt Tee-Tee screamed at her daughter, threatened her, and pinned her against the wall by her throat with her forearm, shouting, "If I find out that you did this to my sister, I'm going to fuck you up, Tay-Tay!" Tay-Tay continued to deny everything, but we all knew she was lying, and our mom had no reason to lie about her doing these vicious acts to her.

My sister told Aunt Tee-Tee that she would keep our mother and little brother at her house from then on. Strangely and ironically, around 18 years later, my cousin passed away at an early age due to medical complications from lupus. She died on my mother's birthday.

After leaving Pat's house following our fight, Davis's mother arranged for me to live with his sister Lena. At that point, I was four months pregnant, and Davis's mother had helped me get back into school. I had been expressing my strong desire to finish high school, and despite working two jobs, she insisted that I stop working so much due to my pregnancy and school commitments. She enrolled me in a maternity school called Simpson Alternative High School, which catered to teenage pregnancy students.

During my pregnancy, I experienced a lot of fatigue, which made it challenging for me to perform daily tasks like cooking and cleaning. I would often feel exhausted and spend most of my time sleeping. When I was awake, I would watch educational television programs, keep up with the news, and read books. I was also still dealing with the heartbreak and depression of Davis leaving me and abruptly marrying Kay. I was utterly miserable, spending my days lying around, feeling tired all the time, attending school, doing homework, and just staying at home.

His sister worked night shifts while I attended school during the day, so we often missed each other around the house, except on her days off.

Despite presenting herself as saved and sanctified, she was involved with the pastor of her church. I remember vividly that we lived just a block away from Davis's and her parents' house. It's worth noting that Davis's father would periodically check on me. I genuinely believed that he cared about me, especially considering I was carrying his son's child. He was aware of my situation and consistently inquired about my well-being, offering assistance and support without hesitation. I expressed my gratitude, saying, "Okay, thank you!"

One day, as he drove past, he noticed me sitting on the front porch. Rolling down the window, he asked if I was alright. Taking the opportunity, I requested, "Could you please bring me some Pepe's tacos?" I had been intensely craving them, as they were one of my father's all-time favorite foods. Without hesitation, he replied, "Sure, I'll get you some." Approximately thirty minutes later, he returned, rang the bell, and handed me a 10-pack of tacos! I expressed my gratitude, and he entered the house as usual. We sat down at the kitchen table, and I savored the delightful meal. His father's care for me made me immensely happy.

As we sat in the kitchen, talking about Davis and how he had treated me unfairly, I became overwhelmed with emotion. His father spoke about the need for me to mature and become a strong woman, considering I was about to become a mother.

Then, something unexpected happened. He started making advances towards me. He gently grabbed my hand, started rubbing it, and embraced it, telling me how much more he could offer and do for me. I pushed him away and guided him towards the front door. I couldn't believe he had tried his luck like that. I was appalled. He followed behind me, and all I could say was, "It's time to leave." I was trying to get him out of the house. He pleaded with me not to tell his wife, claiming he meant no harm. But as I approached the door, he grabbed my arm and turned me around. He began wrestling with me, eventually pinning me to the floor, and he raped me!

He threatened that if I were to tell anyone, he would accuse me of luring him in and forcing myself on him, saying all sorts of craziness. I couldn't believe that my baby's grandfather had just raped me while I was pregnant! I had genuinely thought he cared. He knew I had nowhere else to go. This man came in and violated me.

So, I found myself sitting at his sister's house crying, and asking myself, "What am I going to do now?" I bathed and douched, desperately trying to rid myself of his stench. It was absolutely disgusting. I felt sick to my stomach! All I could think about was how to tell Davis that his father had raped me. Here I was pregnant, alone, abandoned by Davis, who had run off and married another woman, and I still held on to the hope that he would come back to me once I had our baby. I was still deeply in love with him. I was willing to stay with him, no matter what he had done, because I was pregnant with his child. But now, I realized I couldn't tell him. He would never return to me. I had to be strong.

Years later, I discovered that his father had also raped his stepdaughters, including the sister I had been living with when she was younger, and he had a son with another sister. These were the children Davis's mother had prior to marrying his father. She had three children from a previous relationship and three children with him.

I never told anyone, not even Davis, about his father raping me. I kept it to myself. I believed it was the best course of action. I didn't want to be judged, and I had nowhere else to go. At that time, I was still attending school, trying to find a way out of that situation. I was pregnant and dealing with so much. It was a terrible experience.

Then, one day not long after, Davis's brother, Homicide, came over to his sister's apartment and rang the bell. I told him Lena wasn't home, and he said, "No, she wanted me to come over and do some repairs." I simply replied, "Okay," and opened the door to let him in. He walked around, inspecting the house. I asked him if there was something specific, she wanted him to do, and he said, "Nah. I actually came to see you. I heard about what you've been going through, and you and my brother aren't together anymore, I told him, "No, we aren't," and reassured him that I was fine and there was no need to worry about me.

Homicide was known in the neighborhood as an intimidating figure, someone not to be crossed. However, he had always been respectful towards me whenever we saw each other at their family gatherings. As I stood up and thanked him for stopping by, I guided him towards the front door. Unexpectedly, he started expressing his desire to be with me and made explicit comments about wanting to engage in sexual activities, saying how he could fuck me way better than his brother ever could. I felt panic rising within me, and fear consumed me. I ran towards the front door in an attempt to escape but ended up falling and hitting my head on the living room table.

After I fell, he began assaulting me, strangling, hitting, and punching me relentlessly. I felt my life was in danger. I had no doubt that he would kill me based on the sudden outburst of violence. He struck my ear with such force that I could only hear a loud pitched ringing sound and saw a blackness with speckled stars. I desperately tried to fight back, but I was no match for him. I screamed, and he responded by choking me harder, threatening to kill me if I didn't shut the fuck up and stop fighting. In the end, I gave up and closed my eyes, silently praying for my life. He forcefully removed my panties, as I was wearing a duster gown, and proceeded to rape me on the living room floor, just weeks after his father had done the same in almost the exact same spot.

Once he left, I was in a state of profound shock. I couldn't comprehend that I had experienced such horror again. My mind was in turmoil. Shaking and crying, I held my belly protectively, as if shielding my unborn baby, while rocking back and forth on the couch. I immediately gathered what belongings I could carry and took a bath. I had to leave; I couldn't endure it any longer.

The men in Davis's family were dangerous. I was pregnant, and two of them had raped me within a month of each other.

With my bag in hand, I started walking down the street. Being familiar with the neighborhood, I knew some people there. I decided to go to the White's family house, which was about four blocks away. Lawrence, the person my sister had once been involved with, was part of that family.

# CHAPTER 8
# CHILD SEXUAL EXPLOITATION

*"Family Is Supposed to Be Our Safe Place. Very Often, It's The Place Where We Find The Deepest Heartache"*
**(Iyanla Vanzant)**

The White's Family house was known as the neighborhood's social hub, where people gathered for parties, cookouts, and drinks. Growing up in the area, I knew the family and their friendly nature. When I arrived on their porch, they recognized me as Tia's big ole little sister and welcomed me warmly. I ended up spending time with them, particularly Lawrence sister Theresa, who had daughters around my age and a son named Rob.

Later that night, I asked Theresa if I could stay over, and she kindly allowed me to sleep at the foot of her bed. Throughout the night, worries about my next steps and where I would go plagued my mind. Unfortunately, Rob, Theresa's son, made unwelcome advances towards me, which bothered me. I didn't particularly like him; he had a peculiar appearance; we didn't share any common ground. However, I felt compelled to find a reason to stay and justify my presence there. In order to have a place to stay and spend my nights, I pretended to be interested in Rob, even though I truly wasn't. It was a situation where I had to make compromises.

Given my pregnancy and lack of family support or transportation, continuing my education became impossible. I had to shift into straight survival mode and managed to secure a job downtown at the First Business School of Chicago. With my income, I approached Rob's mother about staying at their place, and she agreed, mainly because she needed the rent money as she was unemployed. Initially, things seemed fine, but then the house was raided, and I lost my entire paycheck and savings. During the raid, the police forced everyone to the floor and confiscated all the cash from my purse.

I had been diligently saving up, intending to get an apartment, but losing all my money in the raid was a devastating setback. I was left with absolutely nothing to secure a place to stay. It was incredibly disheartening. Staying in that house was no longer an option for me, especially since Rob's sister's boyfriend was constantly selling drugs from there, which was how Rob's mother managed to pay the rent. I had nowhere else to turn and no one to rely on. In my mind, I was determined to get back on my feet. I continued going to work every day, doing my best to rebuild my life and gain some stability.

I began my search for a new place, nonetheless. I received my next paycheck that Friday, and I found a lady who was willing to rent me a nice two-bedroom apartment on 53rd and Honore for $400 a month. She agreed to let me pay the security deposit along with my monthly rent for a year. I wasn't concerned about furniture because I knew I could find discarded items from affluent neighborhoods. Davis and I used to do that when we lived together at his sister's place out west. One person's trash is another person's treasure, as the saying goes. Alternatively, I considered renting furniture from a rental center or purchasing items from Goodwill. My main priority was finding a safe place for myself and my unborn baby. Finally having a safe and secure roof over my head brought immense happiness. The apartment was cozy and perfect for me and my soon-to-arrive baby.

Now, it's important to note that after Theresa's apartment got raided, her landlord told her they had to leave. Meanwhile, I had just secured my own place. She couldn't believe that I had found such a nice apartment.

I appeared to be doing well, while all Theresa had was a social security check and food stamps. She had some decent furniture, and she asked if she could move in with me because she needed a place. It was impossible for me to refuse her request, especially considering the help she had provided me.

However, it turned out to be the worst mistake ever. Firstly, she didn't like the fact that I wouldn't allow her other children and their boyfriends to move in with us. She also didn't appreciate me having any say over her behavior in my own apartment. To give an example, she became upset when I refused to let her daughter and her drug-dealing boyfriend come over every day. I didn't want drugs entering my home. One day, while I was at work, she went and told my landlord that I was a minor and a runaway, claiming that she had no business renting the apartment to me.

When I returned home that evening, the landlord asked for my identification. I presented the fake ID I had been using, but when she requested my birth certificate, I couldn't provide one showing that I was 18. Just like that, Theresa managed to get me kicked out of my own apartment, and she ended up taking it for herself. I was devastated.

Rob and I had to move to his aunt's house, and soon after, I went into labor and gave birth to my baby boy, Dell. I returned to Rob's aunt's house, but I wanted my mother to meet my baby. So, I went to visit my sister, and she offered for me and the baby to stay with her. She mentioned hearing about the things happening with me in the streets. I responded by saying, "Okay, I'm trying to get myself together to find another place." In truth, I didn't want to be with Rob. I never really liked him, and he was becoming clingy and extremely irritating. He engaged in dishonest and criminal activities, and he kept getting in trouble with the law. I desperately wanted to distance myself from him, but I didn't have anywhere else to go.

At this point, my baby was about two to three weeks old, and I was sharing a room with my mother and younger brother. We were all sleeping together in my mother's bed. Then, in the middle of the night, around three o'clock, my sister's husband, who was intoxicated, entered the room, and touched me inappropriately while I was sleeping in bed. In a state of panic, I yelled, "Miguel, what's going on?" I immediately jumped up and firmly told him, "Don't you touch me. Don't you dare touch me." I quickly left the room and went to my sister's bedroom, urgently knocking on the door and begging her to wake up.

I said, "Tia, please wake up." Eventually, she responded, and I pleaded with her, "Could you please come and get your husband?" She asked, "What is he doing?" I replied, "He's in there trying to touch me." She began shouting, "Miguel!" and called him into the room. She told me to go back to bed and said, "We'll discuss this in the morning." It was difficult for me to sleep that night. The next morning, she got up and started cooking breakfast. She called me into the kitchen and instructed me to sit down at the table and eat. Then she said, "I don't know what happened between you and my husband, but you must have done something, to make him want to come into the room and try to get into bed with you."

Afterward, she continued, "I need you to gather your belongings and your baby's things. I have a place for you to go. I won't leave you out on the streets. I'll do my best to help you." Even my mom tried to explain to her that Miguel had attempted to get into bed with me. She struggled to get the words out to my sister, saying, "Miguel tried to get into bed with her., Miguel touched her!" My mom did her best to convey to my sister that her husband had made advances towards me, but my sister refused to listen to anything that either I or my mother were trying to tell her.

She made me gather my baby and my bags and get into the car with her. I had no idea where she was taking me or what she had planned. I was terrified, but I had no choice but to follow her instructions because I had nothing and nowhere to go with my baby.

My sister drove me out west to Chicago Avenue and Homan in Chicago. She took me to the older man named LeRoy apartment, whom she used to have sex with for money. She said, "Angie, just do whatever he wants you to do. He is going to take good care of you. He will make sure you and your baby get everything you need. You will have a roof over your head, and he will provide you with some money." She was instructing me to comply with his desires, assuring me that it would be over quickly and that it wouldn't hurt. She told me to act like I enjoyed it. She said, "I promise it won't hurt because he can't even get an erection."

She went on to explain, "Just lie down and take it. It won't bother you at all, but you have to do what you have to do until you can get yourself together, because I can't have you at my house around my husband, and I don't know where else to take you. But you will be alright here with him." At that time, the old man was about 65 or 70 years old, and I was 15 years old with a newborn baby trying to navigate life. I felt completely helpless and didn't know what to do.

To my horror, it seemed like my sister wasted no time before leaving the apartment, leaving me alone with this man. He immediately made me lie down on the bed, beginning his abusive behavior. Despite my reservations, I felt compelled to comply with the demands of this older man, even though deep down I knew it was wrong. The moment he climbed on top of me, I felt an overwhelming sense of disgust and violation. My soul literally shattered. It was as if I was reliving the trauma of being raped all over again. I felt dirty and repulsive, unable to comprehend how my own sister would subject me to this in order to survive.

As he engaged in these acts, I kept telling myself that it wouldn't last forever and that I needed to endure it until I could find a way out of this dreadful situation. Adding to the distress, I was still recovering from giving birth and was experiencing physical discomfort, including bleeding. Dealing with this older man on top of me, demanding me to perform sickening acts, made me feel even more nauseous. He repeatedly uttered disturbing phrases like, "Yeah, Daddy is going to take good care of you. You're safe now. I will make sure you're okay. You're mine now, and you don't ever have to worry about anything. Just be a good little girl and take care of Daddy." Once he finished, he asked if I wanted something to eat and bought us some Church's chicken and drinks.

He sat up and began sharing details about his life, as if I had any interest in hearing it. All I could think about was how to escape from this situation. Despite my exhaustion, I told him, "Okay, I'm really tired. I want to go to sleep now." But to my dismay, he climbed into bed with me and resumed touching me all over again. I felt a wave of nausea as he got on top of me, breathing heavily and making unpleasant sounds. It was unimaginable that I found myself in this situation, with a newborn baby who was not even three weeks old, and this older man on top of me. I felt sick to my core and had an overwhelming urge to vomit. I questioned God, wondering what I had done to deserve such an ordeal.

My sole focus was finding a way out of this predicament. I desperately tried to come up with a plan to escape. I stared at the ceiling, attempting to block out his presence, while my mind raced, considering any place I could go to get away from this repulsive, perverted sexual predator. I wondered if there was anyone, I could seek solace with, anywhere I could find refuge. "Where can I go? I have to get out of this situation," echoed in my thoughts.

Eventually, I started spending more time at my cousin Lydia's house in the projects on the west side. I didn't want to go back to the older man's house because every time I went there, he would make advances towards me.

I was constantly subjected to his unwelcome touches and perverse, lewd comments. I felt deeply disturbed in his presence, fully aware that I was being exploited as a child. I had nowhere else to turn, and I felt utterly lost. I didn't know what else to do for myself; all I knew was that I had to survive this moment. I continued to pray, desperately seeking a way to extricate myself from this harrowing situation.

One day, while I was at my cousin Lydia's house, I met her brother's uncle, named Mike. That night, he and I started spending time together. It was rather serendipitous how it happened. He had recently become a father, and my cousin Lydia wanted to visit the baby's mother. Unfamiliar with who Mike was, I accompanied her around the corner. As we admired the adorable baby, Mike walked in, and as soon as his eyes gazed at mine, he couldn't help but smile and stare at me. I immediately understood his intentions. I must admit, he was an attractive individual with his charming demeanor and rich dark skin tone.

My cousin Lydia introduced us, and upon seeing me, Mike exclaimed, "Wow." I blushed and shyly laughed off the comment. We returned to Lydia's house without giving it much thought since I was accustomed to men being attracted to me and flirting. I suppose you could say they were drawn to my beauty. Shortly after, Mike showed up at my cousin's house with a big smile on his face, reintroducing himself. He mentioned that he was no longer with his baby's mother. I wasn't bothered by it since I wasn't in a relationship with my baby's father either. As he continued talking, he mentioned that he had a car and invited me to hang out with him for a while. At that moment, my baby was asleep, and my cousin encouraged me to go. However, I declined, as I wasn't much of an outdoorsy person. I preferred staying at home, and I was preoccupied with figuring out how to handle my situation.

Instead, we ended up lying on my cousin's bed with the lights off, illuminated only by the moonlight streaming through the window. We engaged in conversation about various topics, laughing and enjoying each other's company. He had a cocktail, and I had a Pepsi. We genuinely had an enjoyable time together. I learned that he was 35 years old, while I had recently turned 16. Nevertheless, I wasn't concerned about the age difference because I wasn't actively seeking a romantic relationship. My primary focus was finding a safe place and stability for myself and my baby.

While we were talking, his baby's mother ran up the stairs, approached the room, and an intense argument ensued between them. Mike quickly got up to address the situation. I fell asleep after they left, unaffected by their dispute as I had no involvement in it. Mike returned and informed me that he had given her a black eye in response to her having given him a busted lip. He asked me to spend more time with him. It was around 2 a.m., and my cousin Lydia advised me to go, as she believed his baby's mother would only return to cause more trouble.

We continued talking for an hour or more, and he suggested, "I can drop you off at home." I agreed because I had to tend to some business early in the morning. Before I knew it, we started spending a lot of time together and frequently visited his sister's house. His sister resided in Lathrop Homes, a public housing project on the north side of Chicago. She soon became my best friend. Her name was Brenda. From the moment we met, she exuded a vibrant and lively personality. We laughed, talked about several topics, sang, and danced around the house. We enjoyed drinks and engaged in silly games and singing competitions with Mike and her partner, Donnie, who was the father of her two children. When I met Brenda, her sons were 2 and 4 years old. Despite Brenda being 10 years older than me, we connected well. I always found myself vibing with older individuals as I didn't quite fit in with people my age. I had experienced a lot at an early age, and my intellectual curiosity couldn't be satisfied by teenagers.

I made a conscious effort to avoid spending time at the old man's house. Instead, I would spend as much time as possible with Mike throughout the day. However, I would have him drop me off at the old man's house after 10 p.m., as that was the only time when he was away working as an overnight security guard at the local grocery store. It was during those hours that I could finally find some respite from his constant unwanted advances and have a moment of rest. I vividly remember dreading the moments when he would climb on top of me. To cope with the situation psychologically, I would stare up at the ceiling and imagine a different life. On one occasion, the situation felt so absurd and repulsive that I found myself laughing. It was a defense mechanism, a way for me to process the disturbing reality I was trapped in. Being confined to that apartment with him was an absolute nightmare, and I despised every moment of it.

Mike remained oblivious to the situation, and he had no issue dropping me off at night because he was living with the mother of his other children in the Henry Horner Housing projects. So, after spending the entire day together, he would go home to her, and I would be left at the old man's house. It worked out conveniently for him because he didn't have to be tied down with me all night, allowing him to have the best of both worlds.

To reduce my time at the old man's house, I started seeking refuge with my friend Brenda. She welcomed me into her life more frequently, and I began opening up to her, revealing the harsh reality of my situation. Brenda did her best to help me in any way she could, offering support and assistance.

I will always remember the time when my sister had a grand birthday party. She invited me to join in the celebration, so I made my way to her house. As I stepped off the bus, I saw Mud-bone, an old friend from our childhood on the block. Mud-bone was like a big brother to me, and I greeted him with a warm hug and said, "Hey, Mud-bone." I asked if I could borrow a few dollars to buy diapers for my baby. He seemed surprised and asked if I didn't have any diapers at all. I sadly admitted that I didn't.

Without hesitation, Mud-bone told me to get into his car with my baby. He drove us to Toys R Us, a place where I used to work. There, he generously purchased a case of diapers, baby clothes, socks, and bottles for my little one. We left the store with the car packed full of supplies. To top it off, he even gave me $100 for myself and took me to McDonald's because I was hungry. I felt an overwhelming sense of joy and gratitude when he bought me a Big Mac meal. Throughout our encounter, Mud-bone kept encouraging me, emphasizing that I was intelligent and beautiful. He urged me to turn my life around and wished me nothing but the best. He assured me that if I ever needed him, I could reach out without hesitation.

Upon returning from our shopping trip, I saw my auntie Tee-Tee standing in the doorway of my sister's apartment. Her facial expression was filled with anger and hostility, as if she believed Mud-bone and I were involved in something inappropriate. As I exited the car with my bags and food, I greeted her, but she remained silent, glaring at me with intense rage and hatred. The very next day, the Department of Children and Family Services (DCFS) showed up at the old man's house looking for me. Fortunately, I wasn't there at the time. When I returned, the old man informed me that DCFS had been looking for me. They explained to him that I was being investigated as a runaway, and they wanted to speak with me. The news struck me with disbelief, and panic immediately set in. The thought of them potentially taking my baby away was the last thing I wanted to imagine.

# PART
# THREE

# CHAPTER 9
# TRYING TO FIND MY WAY

*"Either I Will Find My Way or I Will Make One."*
**(Philip Sydney)**

Eventually, one morning, as I was getting ready to leave the house before he came home from work, DCFS caught me. I was at the old man's house, and they began interrogating and questioning me about my baby and myself. They inquired about who I was living with, mentioning that they had received a call suggesting that I was engaging in a romantic relationship with this old man in exchange for a place to stay. I explained to them that he was family and had allowed me to stay there until I could get my life together. Despite being aware of the old man's actions of molesting and exploiting me, I felt a strange compulsion to protect him and remained silent. Perhaps it was because he provided for me and my baby. I couldn't fully comprehend it, but I refused to disclose that he was forcing me into sexual relations. Instead, I continued to lie, claiming that I saw him as a grandfather figure and that he had never touched me, fully aware that I was being dishonest. However, I felt trapped and didn't know what else to say. Numerous thoughts raced through my mind at that time. I feared that my sister would never forgive me if I had him arrested, and my family would criticize me since he was the step-grandfather of my aunt Tee-Tee's children. I simply couldn't do it. I couldn't bring myself to confess, even though he deserved to face severe consequences for the sick acts he subjected upon me sexually.

They threatened me, stating that if I didn't leave the apartment and go to the shelter, they had arranged for me, they would take my baby away. I genuinely didn't want to go to a shelter, but in a way, I felt a sense of relief knowing that I would be escaping from this repulsive old man. I was conflicted and unsure of what to do.

Upon entering the shelter, I was confronted with a horrifying reality. I couldn't help but think, "Oh my God, what is this?" I was unaccustomed to being surrounded by individuals plagued by such severe drug addiction and alcoholism. Some of the people in the shelter appeared repulsive and left me with a feeling of disgust. While there were regular individuals present, others warned me, saying, "Watch your back, watch your baby, and never trust anyone around you or your child. Don't leave any valuables unattended and be cautious not to sleep too deeply."

Sleep became elusive as people would approach my bunk in the middle of the night, staring at me. This terrified me to no end. They would reach out, attempting to touch my face and hair, complimenting my appearance, and sharing their sexual desires and intentions. They even tried to touch my baby. Throughout the night, they would roam the floors, coughing, singing, begging for cigarettes, craving crack, and drugs, and attempting to steal my belongings, including my clothes and shoes. I feared for the safety of myself and my child. Some of these individuals had volatile temperaments and were always ready to engage in fights and arguments. It felt as though I was trapped in a chaotic zoo. While not everyone behaved in this manner, there were enough individuals exhibiting erratic behavior that I desperately wanted to escape from that environment.

Once again, I found myself repeatedly questioning both myself and God, pondering how I could extricate myself from this dire situation. I turned to Brenda and poured out my heart, disclosing every detail. She responded, "Angie, I would let you move in with me, but I can't. I live in low-income housing, and they closely monitor us in this building. However, we'll find a way to help you. You're only 16 years old, with a baby. Isn't there anyone you can reach out to?" I kept replying, "No, I don't have anyone." She began suggesting various family members, and I proceeded to explain the circumstances surrounding each one, emphasizing my lack of support.

Brenda proposed, "Let's try to locate your father." I confessed, "I don't know where he is." She asked for his name and searched for it in the phone book. To our surprise, we found him. She dialed the number listed and, astonishingly, he answered. She verified if it was him, and he confirmed. She inquired, "Do you have a daughter named Angela?" He replied, "Yes." He bombarded her with questions, concerned if something had happened to me. Brenda reassured him, explaining, "No, she's fine. She's safe here with me." She conveyed to him that I found myself in a dreadful situation and needed his help. My heart raced as I stood there in shock, tears streaming down my face. I was petrified of his potential rejection or how he might react to me. It's important to note that I hadn't seen him since I was 14, and I had run away from home.

Brenda said, "I'm going to let you talk to her now." With trembling hands, I took the phone and nervously uttered, "Daddy, I have nowhere to go. Can you please come and get me and my baby?" He responded, "Yes." Surprised, he asked, "You have a baby?" I replied, "Yes, I have a newborn baby boy." He began sobbing even harder. He inquired, "Where are you?" I answered, "I'm living in a shelter, and I have nowhere to go." His tears intensified. Both of us were overwhelmed with emotions. He assured me, "I'll be there in about an hour." I explained that I needed time to gather my belongings. True to his word, he arrived at the shelter to pick me up. We ended up going back to his house, and to my surprise, he had remarried. He was residing in an apartment on 64th and Campbell in Chicago with his wife, Roxanne. She had three teenage children — a daughter and two sons — living with them.

The situation mirrored what had occurred with my mother, her two boys, and her daughter when my father met her. Her daughter was slightly older than me, and she had a son younger than me and another son around my age. I arrived at their home with my baby, Dell, who was just a few months old. Now, bear in mind that my father had married Roxanne some time before my arrival. However, the twist was that she had no knowledge of his two children.

He hadn't disclosed anything about his previous life with my mother or our existence. Neither me nor my younger brother — nothing! Roxanne was utterly devastated to discover that not only did he have two children, but he also had a grandchild. When we arrived, Dell was still an infant. We engaged in conversation, and I explained my situation and the circumstances that led me to the shelter. My father, although taken aback by the revelation, expressed concern and empathy for my situation. Roxanne, on the other hand, was furious and felt deceived by my father's omission. She confronted him, demanding an explanation for his secrecy and the fact that he had never mentioned his previous family.

Amidst the tension, I sat there, holding my baby, feeling a mix of relief and anxiety. I had escaped the shelter, but now I found myself in a new and complicated situation. Roxanne's anger was palpable, and it created an uncomfortable atmosphere. My father tried to mediate, explaining that he had made mistakes in the past and was trying to make amends. He assured Roxanne that he loved her and that his intentions were to help me and my child.

Now, she was on Section 8 housing voucher and had a four-bedroom apartment with two bathrooms. She and my dad had a bedroom, her daughter had a bedroom, and both her sons had a bedroom to themselves. They told me I had to sleep on the couch in the living room with my baby. I didn't care; I just wanted to be out of that shelter and off the streets. They asked me what I had to bring to the table. I told them I didn't have anything but the clothes on our backs and the few clothes we had in our bags, and I had some food stamps at the shelter; they were making me save because meals were free. My father said, "We'll go get them tomorrow." I told them I was looking for a job, but all I had was my little welfare check coming in once a month—it was $250 a month—and I was getting WIC for my baby milk. They said I had to give them all the food stamps for groceries and half of my check. I could keep the other $125 for diapers, clothes, etc.

Roxanne immediately explained that they were not going to make her boys bunk in the same room so that I would have a room. But they said, "Well, you can stay here until you can get yourself together." I explained that I was expecting my income tax check to come in; I just needed to file it. Remember, while I was pregnant with Dell, I worked till the day I went into labor with him. I informed them, "Well, as soon as my income tax check comes, I'll be able to get a place." Now, this was back in the old days when you used to have to file a paper tax return, and it took months for it to come back.

I had filed my taxes, and I was just waiting for them to come back so I could try to find a place. I slept on the couch in the living room with my baby, but I felt extremely uncomfortable and out of place at my father's house. My stepsister had recently graduated from high school and was on her way to college. She was dark-skinned, soft-spoken, and had a snobbish demeanor. To my father and stepmother, she was the epitome of perfection. My father worshiped the ground she walked on. They were sure to always praise her and rave about her accomplishments. How smart she was, and her being a good and respectable young lady, almost in a teasing fashion. It made me feel like a complete disgrace and embarrassment, as if I had completely messed up my life. Having a baby at such a youthful age and having been in a shelter seemed to be a source of shame for them.

My father's wife had two sons who were both involved in sports. Henny, the oldest, was in high school, and the younger one was in the eighth grade. I will never forget how they used to come to the living room early in the morning before going to school. They would disturb my sleep, and I was already exhausted from taking care of my baby all night, preparing bottles, changing diapers, and so on. It got to the point where they started pouring water on me, waking me up, and laughing and teasing me. I tried not to cry or complain, but it became unbearable.

Moving in with my dad actually helped resolve the situation with DCFS (Department of Children and Family Services) because the shelter had informed them that I had left. They were given the address of my father's house so that I could receive the food stamps I had saved up. Consequently, the caseworker and the police came to my father's building, knocking on all the doors and intensely searching for me and my baby throughout the building. My dad opened the door and explained that I was staying with him, that we were safe, and that he would help me get my life together. Finally, I was relieved of that stress.

After staying there for a little over a month, I approached my father one day and asked if I could have a room to sleep in. I explained that I was constantly being bothered during my sleep, and as a young lady with a baby, I didn't feel comfortable sleeping out in the open. I just needed my own little space. He nodded as if he were listening, but at that point, he and his wife were dealing with their own problems—being evicted. The Chicago Housing Authority had discovered that my stepmother hadn't reported her marriage to my dad nor his disability and pension income from the VA. As a result, her Section 8 voucher was terminated. They started telling me that I needed to figure out what I was going to do because they wouldn't be there for long, and they couldn't take me with them. I responded, "Okay, I'm trying to find a place." I was just praying for my tax refund to arrive soon because I didn't know where else to turn.

I tried to reach out to anyone I could—family, friends—anyone who would let me stay with them until I could get back to work, receive my tax refund, find a place, and stabilize my life. Dell's father never offered any support; he had moved on with his wife. I attempted to visit his mother's house in the old neighborhood so she could meet her grandson. She and two of Davis's sisters were on the porch. Now, it's important to note that nobody in his family knew that I had been raped twice, which was the reason I had packed my bags and left. They simply thought I was being ungrateful. As I approached, their expressions turned sour, and they asked, "Why are you coming around here?

Our mother won't help you anymore, and she won't take care of you or your baby." Their mother looked at my baby, seemingly glad to see him, but she didn't want to get involved now that Davis and I weren't together anymore, and he had married someone else. I quickly took my baby and left the porch without looking back. That was the last time I saw his mother or any of his family members. I vowed never to go back to them. After everything I had been through, it didn't feel right to seek help from him or his family. Being around them didn't feel right at all.

My dad reached out to his sister, my aunt Helene, and asked if I could stay with her. Her response was, "No, that whore can't come to my house with a baby. I'm not trying to raise a promiscuous girl who has been out on the streets with a baby. I have too much going on in my own life. I just adopted these two little boys, and I simply can't take in Angie. I'm sure you guys will figure something out. It's unfortunate what she's going through, but Mae's family should step up and help her. They were the ones who brought them into this situation. I don't have the time or patience for those ghetto ass people."

I was still going out with Mike, now as a means of escaping from my father and his wife, since I wasn't employed or attending school and didn't feel welcome or comfortable living with them. I continued to go out and tried to spend time with my sister, the only family member I felt close to no matter what. During that period, she frequented nightclubs often. One particular place she hung out at was called the Van Club, where older, intoxicated men were a common sight. To become a member, you needed to own a van. Since the club was located near my father's house, I would meet up with my sister there, hoping to find solace. I did anything I could to escape my father's wife, who treated me poorly and made me feel insignificant, worthless, and unwelcome in their home.

I would visit the Van Club on weekends. My sister was involved with a guy named Smurf, who was tall and dark-skinned. Personally, I had no interest in him as he wasn't my type. However, when he saw me, he became infatuated. Unaware of his feelings, I was dancing with another guy on the crowded dance floor when Smurf approached from behind, dancing provocatively with me. I tried to distance myself, but he persisted.

Feeling trapped on the crowded dance floor, I continued dancing without engaging in any intimate or inappropriate behavior. I was simply dancing with the person I had initially been dancing with. After the song ended, I went to sit at the bar. To my shock, my sister came up from behind and struck me on the back of my head with a beer bottle. I turned around, holding the back of my head, only to find my hand covered in blood. She stood there, screaming, accusing me of trying to engage with her man and saying, "Stay the fuck away from my man, you bitch!" Without thinking, I instinctively hit her in the face, leading to a scuffle and fight inside the club. I tried to explain that I hadn't been involved with the man she accused me of pursuing, that I didn't even like him. However, she continued to fight back, screaming, and accusing me of wanting her man.

When the fight was broken up, we ended up outside, still arguing. Earlier, my sister had driven us to the club in her car, and now it was around 2 a.m. with no means of transportation for me to return home. Refusing to get back in the car with her, I started walking toward her house. Smurf, in a stern voice, insisted, "Come on, I'll take you home. I'm not going to let you walk alone." He kept repeating, "Your sister is crazy." Realizing I needed to retrieve my baby from her house, I told Smurf, "I need to go get my baby." My sister begged me not to get in the car with him, but I responded, "I'm not getting back in the car with you. You just hit me in the head with a beer bottle for no reason."

At that moment, she began chasing Smurf around his car after he had opened the door for me. He repeatedly told her she was mistaken and that I hadn't done anything wrong. Eventually, he got into the car, and we drove off. He took me to my sister's house to collect my baby, who was in the room with my mother. I informed my mother about the situation and that I was leaving. As my mother helped gather my baby's belongings, my sister stumbled into the house, heavily intoxicated, attempting to fight me once again. Her best friend, Thia, encouraged her throughout the night to fight me and accused me of being involved with Smurf. I told my sister that I hadn't done anything to provoke her, but if that's how she wanted to treat me, so be it.

I tried to brush her off and focus on retrieving my baby and his belongings. She pleaded with me not to get back in the car with Smurf, but I told her she had lost her mind, and I was done with her because of how unfairly she had treated me. Thia said, "Forget her; let her go, Tia. You don't need her; I'm your sister!" Those words hurt deeply because my sister had already developed a closer bond with Thia and would do anything for her. Despite my bleeding head, my mother attempted to intervene and separate us. Seeing her distress, I realized that any further altercation could trigger another stroke. I didn't want to cause my mother any additional stress, so I kissed her and made the decision to get back in the car with Smurf. We drove away.

It's important to note that I genuinely had no romantic interest in Smurf. He dropped me off at my father's house, and we sat in front of the house, laughing and talking throughout the night. Suddenly, the phone rang. They had contacted me, informing me that I needed to rush to the hospital because my mother had suffered another stroke. So, Smurf and I hurried to the hospital. Upon arriving, my sister emerged from the room with my mom, engaging in an intense argument with both me and Smurf. She criticized him for bringing me there, and tensions escalated. I entered the room, kissed my mom, and reassured her that everything would be alright and that I loved her. This stroke was the most severe I had ever witnessed. Her mouth was twisted, tears filled her eyes, and she couldn't speak coherently. However, I could tell she was aware. Paralysis had overtaken the left side of her body, rendering her immobile, and her face was etched with stress and worry. The reason I avoided arguing with my sister in my mother's presence was that Tia was unaware of how stress and worry could trigger another stroke, as she had never been present during my mother's previous episodes.

Subsequently, I left the hospital where my mother's entire family had gathered. I preferred not to be around them, particularly my aunt Tee-Tee, who harbored jealousy and ill will towards me. I learned that she had reported me to DCFS, falsely portraying me as promiscuous and in the wrong in my dealings with my sister, which had fueled our intense arguments that night. Moreover, my family looked at me with suspicion, as my sister was their favorite. I refused to sit among them, enduring their judgment without knowing the full story. It had turned into a chaotic scene, with everyone exhibiting callousness, pointing fingers, and engaging in gossip. Even my abusive uncle, Bubba, was present, intensifying my feelings of resentment and animosity towards him. I shook my head in disappointment and declared, "Nope. I can't handle this," and promptly left.

As Smurf and I drove back from the hospital, I was overwhelmed by a mixture of emotions. The hurt and anger stemming from my mother's stroke, the shattered relationship with my family, and my sister's continuous accusations of my involvement with Smurf consumed me. I felt that our relationship had reached its end, and if that was the case, I wanted there to be a reason behind it. Consequently, I made the regrettable choice of having sexual intercourse with him intentionally and purposefully in the driver's seat of his car.

I engaged in a passionate activity, driven by my emotional turmoil. It was one of the worst decisions I have ever made in my life! It provided no relief whatsoever because I did not have genuine feelings for him, nor did I desire him. He held no appeal or attractiveness in my eyes. After he dropped me off, he persistently attempted to pursue me, but I evaded him and ignored his calls. He even made multiple visits to my father's house in search of me, but I refused any further involvement with him. Truthfully, I never desired him, and I felt foolish for engaging in a sexual encounter, believing it would alleviate my pain. Or give me a sense of revenge against my sister for her actions towards me.

So anyway, after that, I distanced myself from my family for a significant period. I focused on getting my life together and continued my search for employment. Despite my powerful desire and need to do so, I didn't have the luxury of time to consider returning to school. Instead, I had to figure out how to provide for myself and my baby and secure shelter. It remained a challenging ordeal. Due to the fallout with my sister over the Smurf situation, I found myself alone. I started spending more time at my father's house. When Dell reached around eight months old, I began searching for Dell's father. I wanted him to be involved in our son's life.

I desperately needed his help and support in raising the baby. My only wish was for him to embrace his role as a father. I had heard that he and his wife had separated, so I deliberately frequented places where I knew he would be and visited mutual acquaintances. The few times I encountered him, he was always under the influence of drugs or alcohol, showing no interest in being a father. It seemed like he was not in the right state of mind. I was simply trying to get him to be a part of our son's life, but he vehemently rejected us.

Subsequently, I began spending time with Roxanne's eldest son, Henny, and his girlfriend, Nay-Nay. Now, Nay-Nay and I were roughly the same age; she was 15, and I was still 16. Together with her mother, Diane, we started going to nightclubs. I would often accompany them because Nay-Nay and her mom enjoyed drinking, dancing, and partying. Nay-Nay's mother always kept herself well-groomed and adorned with stylish jewelry and clothing.

We spent so much time together that Nay-Nay and her mom eventually suggested, "Why don't you and Henny just come and move in with us?" This proposal arose as the time came for my father and his wife to relocate. They had sent Roxanne's daughter off to college, and my father, his wife, and her youngest son went to stay at Roxanne's sister's house. Consequently, Henny and I moved in with Diane and Nay-Nay.

She said, "I can't just allow you and your baby to be out on the street. You come stay with me to get yourself together," and I told her that I'd be gone as soon as I could get my income tax check. I would have enough to get a place of my own. I ended up moving in with them. I found a job way up north at a call center by O'Hare airport and was going to work every day. I gave Diane rent and money for babysitting while I went to work. She loved keeping my baby for me. She said it gave her something to do around the house every day.

Diane had a mom named Rev. Rosie Lee Wilson. This woman was so deep into the Bible. Every time she'd see me, she'd say, "Hey there, girl." She always called me Angel and would say I was such a sweet little angel. She would also say to me, "You keep being blessed; God is going to take care of you! You are truly an angel, and God is going to bless you." She loved to talk to me about God and tell me about the Bible. It was just so pleasant around her; she was such a sweet old lady and had such a warm spirit.

So, when I called to check on my mom, I was told that my sister put her in a nursing home not too far from Diane's house. I finally got a day off, went to the nursing home to see my mother, and took my baby. I went to tell my mom I was stable, working, and trying to find a place. I told her about the family I had met and that I was learning about the Bible, Jesus, and the Word of God. She looked at me and smiled. I told her that as soon as I was able to get an apartment, I was coming to get her out of that nursing home, and she was coming to live with me. I told her not to worry; I was going to get myself, her, and my little brother back together again. I wasn't going to allow her to stay in that nursing home. I fed her what she could eat and told her I needed her to be strong and not worry. I combed her hair and told her how much I loved her.

I just wanted her to know that I was okay out there on those streets, and I promised her I was going to make it for us. By this point, the strokes had really taken a toll on her. She was bedridden and couldn't speak much at all; she mainly just looked at me, and I remember the tears rolling down her eyes. I told her, "Don't worry, momma, I got us. I promise we are going to be together again real soon, and I am going to get you out of here."

Although she couldn't talk anymore, somehow, she was able to mutter quietly in my ear that she loved me and to be good. She also told me to stay with God, pray, and take care of my baby. I promised her I would! I told her I would be back on my next day off to spend the day with her and bring her favorite food. She smiled and silently cried as I walked out the door.

One day, soon after, not even a week later, the phone rang early that morning; it was my neighbor Cyndi. I got on the phone and said hello. She said, "Hey, how are you doing, honey? Are you sitting down?" I nervously responded, "Yes." She said, "I got something to tell you, and before I do this, I just want you to know that I love you. And I'm always here."

I just came out and asked, "Did my mom pass away?" She said, "Yes, Angie, your mom passed away." I just felt hurt and sorrowful. I felt so lost, empty, confused, and alone. I felt like my life was over. That was so hard on me. I was screaming and crying uncontrollably. Nobody could get me to calm down. I felt like I was going insane. Nothing could soothe me. I was crying out loud for my momma... I wanted to hold her, see her, save her, and kiss her. I just wanted her to tell me she loved me just one more time.

# CHAPTER 10
# CAUGHT IN THE CLOSET

*"Some People Aren't Loyal to You. They Are loyal To Their Needs. Once Their Need Change, So Does Their Loyalty"*
**(Anonymous)**

Diane ended up calling her mother, Rev. Wilson, to help calm me down. She got on the phone and started praying instantly. Then, in an authoritative tone, she said, "Hey, Angel, why are you screaming and hollering like that? Do you trust God? Do you really trust God? Did you do right by your mother while she was here? Did you do the best you could for her?" I said yes, and she said, "So why are you acting like a fool? Only people who didn't do right by their parents' cry and act like that. Your mother is in a better place now, get up and thank God for her. Thank God for giving her rest and relief from all her suffering on this earth. You need to calm down and take care of yourself and your baby."

Her words hit me hard, but they also brought some sense of clarity. I realized that I needed to be strong and carry on, not just for myself but also for my baby. I was listening and calming down. But all I could think about was that my mother was so young—only 47 years old—and gone. I kept thinking about my little brother. It was sad. I didn't know what to do. But I knew I had to snap out of it. I had to pull myself together. I had made a promise to my mom that I would take care of her and my little brother, and even though she was no longer with us, I knew I had to honor that promise.

My dad and Roxanne came over to see me at Diane's house. Everyone was there, including Mike and Brenda, friends I grew up with. None of my mother's family, none of my siblings—no one reached out to me. I didn't know if I could go to my sister's house because of what happened regarding Smurf. There was still bad blood between us. My aunt Tee-Tee was still mad as hell and jealous, thinking I had messed around with Mud-bone. It was a mess. No one came to see me. They didn't even call to let me know my mom had died. Even though I was technically still a kid, I was only 16 years old with a newborn baby, and I was my mom's baby girl.

I was so grateful that Diane allowed my friends to come to support me, but I literally felt numb. Now the very next day, my income tax check had finally come to my dad's house. I guess they were going over there to get the mail from the house we got put out of, or they were holding it at the post office. But they called and stated, "Hey, we got your check. You can come pick it up." I happily responded, "Oh my God, this came in right on time. I can get something to wear to the funeral for me and my baby. And I can finally get us a place to stay." I was so happy. I asked Diane if she could take me to get my check and to get something to wear for the funeral.

I had to meet my father and Roxanne at White Castle on 69th and Western in Chicago. So, when we got to White Castle, I went in to get the check, and my father said, "Angie, you know we do not have a place to stay right now. We've been staying with Roxanne's sister, and we wanted to tell you that we're getting a place. You can stay with us. We'll make sure that you have a bedroom to sleep in and can keep $200 a month out of your aid check, but you have to give us this income tax check so we can get us all a place to stay."

I must've looked at them like they were crazy. I angrily responded, "I can't give y'all my check, my mom just died. Me nor my baby have anything to wear. And I want to get my own place. I need my own space and my own privacy. I'm just not comfortable living with y'all. Roxanne, your sons bother me in my sleep, you all degrade me and make me feel stupid and worthless. It's just hard, living with other people, especially another woman who's not my mother. I just prefer to be on my own and try to get my own life together, dad."

They looked at each other and said, "Well, you can't get this check. Either you give us this check so we can get us all a place to stay, or no one is getting a place to stay! Because we are not going to give you this check to go blow it. We all need a place to stay, and you need to help us." I got up and walked out of White Castle, crying. I got in the car. Diane looked at me and said, "You got your check?" I said nah, and she said, "Why not?" I sadly said, "Just forget about it. They just told me that if I didn't give it to them, I couldn't have it because they need it to move."

Diane said, "What the hell do you mean they need it to move? Aw hell nawl, you need your check! This check is yours!!! It's for you and your baby. You and your baby are out here, homeless. You do not have any place to go, and your mother just died, are they crazy? They're grown, and they have each other! You don't have anyone! Aw, hell nawl, fuck that! They better give you your check, or I'm going to go in there and beat their ass!!!" I fearfully responded, "No, no, no, don't try to defend me; I'll be okay somehow. Maybe they can mail me a new check to your house." She said, "What you're going to do is, you're going to go and call the police on them right now. Go to the phone booth. Call the police and tell them what's going on!"

I nervously did as instructed by Diane. Roxanne and my dad were still sitting in White Castle drinking coffee. The police pulled up; they went in with me. I pointed at them and said, "This is my dad and his wife." I explained, "They have my income tax check, I'm homeless, and I am broke. I got a ride here to meet them with somebody. I need to get me a place to stay, my mother died yesterday. I have a baby, and they won't give me my check." I started crying badly because it hurt me that I had to go to this extreme to get what I had worked so hard and waited so long for.

I desperately needed to find a safe place for myself and my child to stay. I simply did not want to live with them anymore;

his wife had treated me so badly when I was with them. They went on to question my father and asked him about the check. The police officer told them either they surrender the check, or they were going to search them for it, and if they had it on them, they were going to lock them up. Roxanne reached down into her bra and pulled out my check, handing it over to the officer. I politely took my check and walked straight out the door.

Diane took me straight to cash my check at the local currency exchange. She refused to accept any kind of money from me that I offered for her help. I went to get myself and my baby an outfit to wear to my mom's funeral. I put my security deposit down on an apartment. I had found a cute little one-bedroom apartment right on 59th in Fairfield. It had a big living room, an eat-in kitchen, a stove, and a refrigerator. It was perfect for me and my baby. I think my rent was $300 a month. Catholic Charities helped me get some furniture. Diane gave me a few sheets, blankets, and some pots and pans. I was just receiving so many little blessings there and stood there in awe, thinking, "Okay, it's just me and my baby."

Leading up to the day of my mom's funeral, neither my siblings nor my family ever called or tried to reach out to me. They did not come to get me for anything. They didn't offer to let me ride in the family car or help make any plans or arrangements for my mother's funeral. They didn't try to see if I was alright or if I needed anything—absolutely nothing! I had to get to my mother's funeral the best way I could. Diane, her husband, and her family went with me. They supported me and helped me through it all. The funeral services were so hard on me. I literally do not even believe I was there mentally. I numbed myself during the entire ceremonial service. I don't remember anything other than when they were rolling her casket down the aisle and out the door. I felt like I had died. I just fell to the floor with so much hurt and grief. I was so broken. I just felt numb; I didn't want to go any further. I had nothing left in me, and I knew life wasn't going to get any better for me. I had lost everything. My dad wasn't there for us. I looked at my little brother; he just looked lost and confused. It was so sad.

After my mother's funeral that night, they wouldn't allow me to congregate with the family for the repast. They kept pretending as if the family wasn't going to do anything, which was a lie. They just did not want me there. The entire family treated me terribly.

The following day was my mom's burial. However, I couldn't find anyone to take me there. Diane wasn't feeling well, and her husband had work obligations. In hindsight, I believe they didn't want to be around my mother's family due to their ignorant behavior towards me. But I couldn't bear to let my mother go without being there with her. I had to go that last mile of the way with her. I was determined to go, no matter what or who I had to face. I would have walked, if necessary, just to be by my mother's side.

I called my sister's house early that morning, begging and pleading with anyone who would listen to come and pick me up. Finally, my brother Buck agreed to come. At the burial, I was overcome with so much emotion and cried uncontrollably. I felt lost, empty, broken, just shattered. I had already endured so much pain and suffering in life, and at the time of my mother's passing, I was sick to my stomach, lost, and confused. I didn't know how I was going to move forward. I didn't care about getting back home; I was simply devastated. My aunt Tee-Tee had finally told me to get into the family car with them and ride back to her house.

Once we arrived at my aunt's house, the funeral home called and informed my sister that someone had already picked up the death certificates for my mother. My sister immediately assumed that my father and I had a life insurance policy for my mom. Cornering me in the hallway near the bathroom, my sister and her best friend Thia confronted me, yelling and accusing my dad and me of having a secret policy. They were saying negative things about my father and me, calling us all kinds of names, threatening to jump on me and beat me up. My cousin Lydia intervened, her anger evident in her voice, and said, "No, you're not going to treat her like that. I won't allow it! If you try to jump on her, I'll defend her." Lydia managed to defuse the situation and protect me from their aggression. Then the entire family loaded up in cars and went to the funeral home to review the video camera footage, only to discover that my mother's brother, Jack, was the one who picked up the death certificates and had a secret policy on my mom.

My sister apologized to me; Thia and Lydia were still arguing. Lydia kept telling Thia to stay in her lane and that she didn't have anything to do with our family's business. We all went back to my aunt's house, and that's when the big fight broke out over who was going to take custody of my little brother. My sister ended up calling the police, and the police told them that the siblings had the right to get my little brother, so my sister got my little brother, and they left.

Now, it's important to note that when my mother and little brother were taken out of our house on Winchester, my parents still had nice furniture and belongings. My sister had rented a U-Haul and retrieved their belongings from my parents' house. However, my sister had given my mother's new living room furniture, decorations, and other items to her best friend, Thia. When I asked my sister if I could have something of my moms, she told me that she had given everything she wasn't using to Thia. She mentioned that she had just recently bought my mom the bed that we were sleeping on at her place, as well as a 13-inch black-and-white TV. She insisted that I had to pay her for these items because they were still new. She made me give her $250 for my mother's bed, dresser, and the TV. I complied because those items belonged to my mom, and I didn't have these things for my apartment.

To make matters worse, a few months before my mother passed away, she had instructed Tia to add me to her life insurance policy. However, Tia never added me to the policy and didn't give me any of the money. Instead, she and my older brothers divided the remaining money from the life insurance policy among themselves, leaving me with nothing. During this time, the most hurtful thing my sister ever said to me was, "I hate you because you look like that motherfucker!" Referring to my father. Somehow, that never left my heart, my mind, my soul, or my spirit. Knowing that my one and only big sister, whom I loved, adorned, and looked up to so much for acceptance, help, and guidance, despised me simply because I looked like my father.

After burying my mom, I began to rebuild my life. Rev. Wilson continued to share her wisdom and faith with me, reminding me to trust in God and find strength in Him. While the pain of losing my mother never fully went away, I knew I had to keep moving forward. I found solace in my faith and the love of my baby. I made a promise to myself to be the best mother I could be and to provide a loving and stable environment for my child. Over time, Diane and her mother became like family to me. They were always there to offer guidance, support, and a listening ear. Rev. Wilson continued to share her deep knowledge of the Bible, and I found comfort in our conversations about faith and spirituality. I learned to rely on my faith, trust in God's plan, and take things one day at a time. Living with Diane and having her mother's spiritual guidance had a profound impact on my life. They helped me heal from the loss of my mother and provided me with a sense of stability and love that I desperately needed. I will forever be grateful for their presence in my life during that difficult time.

Now that I had my small apartment and was trying to figure out how to improve my situation, it was incredibly challenging without my mom. I had already gone through a lot with my dad, and now I was doing my best to make it on my own. It was tough. My rent was $350 a month, and I was receiving $250 from public aid and food stamps, approximately $300. I would sell half of my food stamps and use the other half to buy groceries, do laundry for myself and Dell, purchase a carton of cigarettes, diapers, and some personal hygiene products every month. I lived on a very tight budget and was actively searching for another job because I had lost my previous one.

Most of the time, I was alone, but Brenda would come over and visit me on weekends. I also became friends with Kat, who lived next door and was around my age. We would spend time together, laughing, talking, taking care of our kids, cooking, and helping each other with babysitting. I didn't go out much except for job hunting, attending interviews, grocery shopping, and running errands. Kat had a tendency to associate with drug dealers, but I personally avoided any involvement with them. I had a strong aversion to drug dealers due to what happened to my brother Slick. No amount of money could convince me to associate with them. Additionally, I was always afraid of getting caught up in legal trouble or having drugs brought into my house. I had experienced being caught in a raid before, and I wanted no part of that lifestyle. I refused to ever get involved with drug dealers.

Now, Mike still used to drive to my place to come see me, but I wasn't into him anymore, either. Because he had these two women, he kept having all these kids back-to-back with them. It seemed as if they competed to see who could have the most children with him. The sad part is that both women were way older than me; both were living in housing projects. Not to mention, they were both receiving social security benefits for themselves and their children, making them pretend they were slow, couldn't read, communicate well, or understand anything. Making them act like they were crazy, telling them to tell the social security administration they see dead people and would talk with them, things like that.

Then, when they would get their monthly checks, they bought Mike everything he could ask for, keeping him in nice cars, clothes, and jewelry, buying him drinks, and giving him money to have in his pocket. I said to myself, "Oh hell nawl, not me. He can miss me with that." I was not trying to take care of a grown-ass man!

I was barely able to take care of myself and my own baby. I was so glad God spared me, and I didn't fall into the trap that these two women had fallen into. All the fighting and arguing amongst each other over a man who wasn't doing anything for them was just not for me. I simply could not see a future with him. I was pretty much this young, cute little fun girl he had because his kids' mothers were between 10-15 years older than me; they both drank and were not doing anything with their lives. Work was the furthest thing from their minds. Mike, even though I cared a lot about him, and he was a lot of fun to be around. In all reality he was just a way of survival and a means of transportation for me. He truly did not want much more out of life than what he had set himself up for with these women. That was the reality of that relationship, so it soon faded away.

I was really to myself. I was just trying to figure out how to get my life together with this baby. One day, I went to the meat market called Moo & Oink right off 74th and Racine in Chicago. I was walking around grocery shopping, minding my own business, and this guy named Hook was in the butcher department. He just kept staring at me, while over there cutting some fish and kept looking at me with these really pretty brown eyes.

He walked over to me and asked, "Can I get your number?" With a shy voice, I answered, "Yeah." We started talking that night. I kind of felt good having someone around my age to laugh with and talk to. We ended up setting up a date where he and one of his homeboys were going to come over to my place so we could hang out. I responded, "Cool, I will call one of my girls." So, I called Cindy; she came over, and the guys came shortly after. Now, Hook and I were really into each other; he was very cool, we laughed and joked a lot, he DJ'd, and he could dance something fierce and loved house music.

We all stayed up late, laughing and kicking it. I had cooked us some fish and spaghetti, hush puppies, and coleslaw with some homemade garlic bread. We played cards, drank, danced, listened to music, and had a wonderful time together. He was very talkative and put it on me thick and heavy in our conversation. I was checking him out and really getting to know him. He was getting to know me. He was telling me what he could do to help me. Now, mind you, I had this apartment that I could barely afford. I didn't have a car, I hadn't found a job, and things were really tight for me. Even though I was in my own apartment, I was holding on by the grace of God, because I had no one to help me survive. At this point, I was about 17 years old. As I was struggling to survive, Hook kept coming over, always talking about how he could help me. He said I wouldn't have to worry about groceries anymore; he would give me half the rent and bills. Constantly telling me, I could use my money and start doing more for me and my baby.

He was living at home with his parents then; he had never been out on his own. He was 20-21 years old and had a daughter who also lived with his mother. Because her mother was young and unstable with housing, she would often be out running the streets. Since he was over at my place almost every night, eventually after struggling so hard, and wanting and needing some help, I simply gave in and said, "Okay, come on, we can work this out. You can move in." His parents, sister, and nieces came to help him move in with me. I remember his mother and father telling him he had a beautiful girlfriend and that he better not mess this up.

Sure enough, he immediately started helping me with everything when he got there. He was able to get groceries at a discounted price because he worked at Moo & Oink. My house was overflowing with food; we had groceries for days, meats, fresh produce, and vegetables. I didn't have to spend my food stamps on anything other than canned goods and seasonings, and he would bring groceries home every night. By giving me half of the rent and bills, I finally felt a sense of relief. I was able to take my limited funds and buy decorations for the house, as well as toiletries, household supplies, and personal hygiene products. I could also purchase things for my baby, such as diapers, wipes, cute outfits, and shoes. I really started to enjoy having help around the house. He would go to work, and I would spend my days looking for a job while ensuring that I took care of cooking, cleaning, and looking after my baby.

Soon, Hook began going out and spending a lot of time with his friends. Initially, I thought, "Okay, maybe I'm overthinking this." I was more of a homebody and didn't go outside much, but he was a social person. He would often attend house parties and spend time with his friends from the neighborhood. They would hang out on the block, drinking, smoking weed, having a good time, and engaging in casual conversations—nothing too alarming for me. Since he would come home every night and help me with the bills, I didn't see any reason to be concerned. I was just grateful to have some assistance.

Before Hook moved in with me, my neighbor Kat and I went to file my income taxes at H&R Block, which was located inside Sears on 63rd and Western. As we were sitting there talking, she said, "Girl, I'll be right back. I'm going to go see if I can find a few things." I said OKAY because I knew it was going to be a while before they got done with me because they were really crowded. While I was sitting there, she kept coming over and showing me all these pretty bras and panty sets she had in the bag. I kept saying, "Oh, that's cute. I can't wait to get my income tax check; I'm going to buy myself some really nice stuff, too." There wasn't anything suspicious about her buying all these bra and panty sets because she messed around heavily in relationships with dope boys. She always had a drug dealer in her apartment with her laid up and relaxing. She kept money; the drug dealers she was messing with would give her extra cash because she stored and bagged up their drugs for them.

As I was sitting there waiting my turn, she kept coming over to show me all the stuff in this bag she brought. As we were walking out of the store, tell me why security stopped us as we got to the door, saying, "We're going to need you to come with us." I hesitantly responded, "Who?" They said, "Both of you." I confusingly questioned, "For what?" They said, "Ma'am, we saw you stealing; we need you to follow us." I said, "No, the hell you didn't see me stealing nothing." They questioned me and asked, "Are you two together?" Not having a clue as to what's going on, I nervously responded, "Yes, we're together." They said, "Y'all got to come with us."

Now Kat was just standing there, quiet as a mouse. I was seriously panicking because I didn't know what the hell was going on. They put me in handcuffs and walked me to the back with

Kat. I kept telling them I hadn't stolen anything; I was just there in H&R Block filing my taxes. I only walked through their store to get to the tax place; I didn't even shop for anything because I didn't have any money.

They called me an accessory to the crime. They said that I knew exactly what she was doing. I explained, "I had no clue she was stealing those bras and panty sets. I don't know what you are talking about. Y'all are tripping. I haven't stolen or touched anything." They kept saying, "We have you on camera looking at the stolen merchandise she kept bringing over to show you, and you were nodding your head with a yes signal." I told them I was saying, "Yes, those are cute, and I am going to buy me some when I get my check. I was not stealing, and I did not know she was there stealing."

Because I kept arguing with them and going back and forth, simply because I knew I hadn't stolen anything and I wouldn't admit to the crime, they called the police and had me locked up. I was able to get out on an I-Bond. They gave me a court date. Now, this goes to show you how young and naïve I was. I felt as if I didn't have to go to court because I didn't do anything. In my mind, I'm thinking, I haven't committed any crime, nor did I steal anything; that was on her; she was the one that stole the stuff. I'm not going to go to court for this foolishness because I haven't done anything wrong. Not thinking twice about it, I just went on with my life as usual.

Now, let's return to the situation with Hook. We were living our lives, paying our bills, and I believed we were happy and compatible. However, one early morning, I went next door to Kat's place. Her kids let me in, as it was per the normal that we frequently visited each other's apartments throughout the day. When I entered her room, I noticed that the door was partially closed. Kat was sitting on her bed, covered up, pretending to have been sleeping and just waking up without any clothes underneath. This didn't bother me much, as we were accustomed to barging in on each other. So, I sat on her bed and began complaining about Hook not coming home the previous night. While

I was talking, I noticed movement in her closet. I assumed it was one of her kids eavesdropping on our conversation, so I got up, pulled the covers off, and to my surprise, it was Hook!

Angry and shocked, I exclaimed, "What the fuck? Are you serious?" Now that I had caught him looking guilty as hell in her closet, I started screaming and yelling, venting my anger at both of them. Hook pleaded, "No, no, no, please calm down, Angie. I came over to talk to her, and you caught us off guard. I didn't want you to think something inappropriate was happening, which is why I hid in the closet." We argued back and forth. I told Kat that I was done with her. I couldn't believe that she had my man in her house, hiding in the damn closet. I knew they were involved with each other, regardless of what they claimed. Hook followed me back to our apartment, attempting to talk to me and convince me that nothing was going on. We had a discussion, and deep down, I knew he had been involved with her.

However, I also needed his support, and he was a cool guy whom I genuinely liked. I wasn't in love with him, but I wanted to work things out. We were compatible when it came to survival, and he had a strong work ethic, willingly bringing home his paycheck to contribute to the bills. I believed that because he came from a stable family and his parents had been married for a long time, he understood the importance of settling down and resolving conflicts.

So, one day, he was lying in the bedroom, and I was feeling extremely aroused. I decided to climb on top of him and engage in sexual activity. However, as we proceeded, he suddenly started yelling and telling me to get off of him! Confused and alarmed, I shouted, "What the hell is wrong with you?" He rushed to the bathroom, and I noticed that his penis was bleeding. I questioned him through the bathroom door, asking if he was okay. He responded, "Yes, I need to go to the doctor." He washed up, got dressed, and left, but he didn't return that day or the following day. Three days later, I started experiencing fluctuations in body temperature, feeling sick and unwell. I had no idea what was happening to me.

Concerned, I decided to go to the emergency room, suspecting that I had the flu or some other illness. The doctor informed me, "Well, congratulations, you're pregnant! But not only that, we need to provide you with treatment for gonorrhea." Shocked, I exclaimed, "Gonorrhea?" The doctor confirmed, "Yes, we will administer a shot in your buttocks and prescribe pills for you to take over the next seven days. You should start feeling better soon. Make sure to schedule a follow-up appointment with your OBGYN." I sat there, overwhelmed with emotion, and couldn't help but cry. I had never experienced an STD in my life. I was in disbelief. I was pregnant, and now I have an STD. I kept repeating to myself, "I can't believe this." I felt sick to my stomach, completely stunned.

# CHAPTER 11
# THE FRUIT OF MY WOMB

*"Resilience Is knowing That You Are the Only One Who Has the Power and The Responsibility to Pick Yourself Up"*
**(Mary Holloway)**

All I could manage to say was, "Wow, I'm pregnant again." I called his mother while crying uncontrollably and asked, "Can you please come and pick me up? I don't have any money to get home, and I'm feeling unwell." His father came to the hospital to get me, displaying deep concern as I couldn't stop crying. When I informed his parents about the pregnancy and the fact that Hook had given me a STD, they were in utter disbelief. I sat at their house, sobbing at the kitchen table, feeling lost and uncertain about what to do. His mother prepared dinner for me, and we had a conversation where I expressed my intention to kick him out. She sympathized with me, understanding the gravity of the situation. Upon returning home, I packed his belongings, threw them out the window, and changed the locks. I firmly believed that he had to leave.

Now, it's important to note that I did not want to undergo an abortion. Based on my previous experience with abortion, I didn't want to go through that again. I was determined to keep my child, love it, and care for it the way a mother supposed to. I simply couldn't bring myself to go to the clinic and terminate the pregnancy, despite his insistence. He provided the money for the abortion, but emotionally, I couldn't go through with it.

One day, while I was at home, I happened to glance out the window towards the back of my building and noticed a detective coming up the stairs. We made eye contact, and there was an odd and unsettling feeling that washed over me, but I didn't pay much attention to it.

Shortly after, there was a knock on my door. I opened it to find an officer standing there. It's worth mentioning that my sister, Tia, had come over earlier that morning to take me grocery shopping, and she was resting on the couch before heading back to work. The officer asked, "Are you Angela?" I nervously replied, "Um, no, why?" The officer demanded, "Can I see your ID?" Confused, I asked, "Why?" In a stern tone, he stated, "I have a warrant for your arrest." I questioned, "Why? I haven't stolen anything, so why should I have had to go to court?" He replied firmly, "It doesn't matter. You were supposed to appear in court, and since you failed to do so, there's a warrant for your arrest. I have to take you in."

I turned to my sister and asked if she could look after my baby. She responded, "How long will you be gone? I have to go back to work soon. I was just on my break, and I need to get back to the school bus." The detective assured her, "She'll be back soon. I just have to take her in, and once she's processed and appears before the judge, she'll be released."

It's important to note that I had never been involved in any legal matters before, so I was completely clueless about what was happening. The officer placed me in the police vehicle and took me to the police headquarters on 51st and Wentworth. I sat there, waiting for the processing to be completed. This happened on a Friday afternoon, and I didn't get an immediate court hearing. They kept me in lock-up on 51st street for approximately 24 hours before transporting us, chained, and linked by hand and ankle cuffs, on a bus resembling a penitentiary transport vehicle, along with several other women, to Cook County Jail. I tried to inquire with the guards, asking, "Why am I being taken to the county jail? What's going on?" We were placed in a large holding area. I sat there, scared, listening to various jail stories shared by the other women. They acted like experts when it came to the Law, predicting what would happen based on the charges we disclosed. Naively, I shared everything, as if seeking advice from a Lawyer. They presented me with worst-case scenarios, intensifying my fear and panic. I kept reminding myself not to show any fear, recalling scenes from movies depicting people in jail.

One of the guards noticed the distress on my face and pulled me out of the holding area. She showed me kindness by sharing her sandwich, recognizing my pregnant state and the fact that I appeared famished since I hadn't eaten since my arrest. She said, "Girl, you don't belong here." She asked what was troubling me and proceeded to explain why I was in the county jail and the legal situation I was facing. She could tell that I was completely unaware and had never been incarcerated before.

She informed me that my initial I-bond had been revoked due to my failure to appear in court. The next judge I encountered might grant me another one, but it would ultimately depend on the judge's decision. It was possible that the judge would require me to pay a cash bond. She inquired if I had any money or family members who could post bond and secure my release. Overwhelmed, I burst into tears and replied, "No, I don't have anyone. It's just me, and I'm doing my best to make it on my own." I went on to explain that I had a son at home and was pregnant with my second child. She genuinely tried to console me as I wept, consumed by feelings of regret, fear, and sorrow. I couldn't believe I had found myself in this situation, surrounded by hardened criminals. Some of the women there were incarcerated for prostitution, drug dealing, and violent crimes.

I swear, I didn't want to be in this bullpen with them, but the officer had to put me back there after a while.

She said she knew I didn't fit in, but she had to do a head count and complete her paperwork. Being behind those bars felt as if my oxygen had been shut off. I couldn't breathe. I felt claustrophobic, nervous, anxious, irritable, angry, scared, and cold. Being locked up and losing your freedom is truly a terrible experience for someone who isn't suited for that life. While we were sitting in the bullpen, they began processing the inmates by conducting exams, blood work, and providing orange jumpsuits. The only way to avoid this processing and entering the system completely was to be granted a bond before being processed. As they called the women back one by one, I vividly remember praying and asking God to help me out of this situation. One of the ladies emerged after having her blood drawn, and her arm was bleeding profusely. She told me they had performed a pap smear on her and taken her blood. She described it as a rough and uncomfortable experience, almost as if they had stabbed her and taken her blood. Her words terrified me.

"Oh my God, they're calling my name," I thought to myself. I was incredibly scared. When I approached the processing desk, where I was supposed to be processed, they informed me that the judge had granted me an X-bond, if I recall correctly. I'm not entirely sure, but it was a different type of bail bond, not an I-bond. They released me at approximately 2 a.m. They asked if I had bus fare to get home, and I replied that I did not. They provided me with two tokens to use for transportation. Now, I had to get from 26th and California to 59th and Fairfield. Unsure if the buses were running late, I decided to walk home. It was 2 a.m., and I found myself walking alone because I didn't have money or a means to call anyone for a ride at such a late hour.

Throughout the entire journey, I prayed, expressing gratitude to God for getting me out of that situation and seeking His help for what was to come. Above all, I thanked Him for my freedom. I arrived home around 4 a.m. When I reached my apartment, my brother Buck was there with my baby because I had been locked up all weekend. My sister Tia had instructed him to stay at my house and take care of Dell until I was released. She mentioned that I had plenty of food at home, and he willingly accepted the offer. The conditions for my release were that I had to be back in court the following day at 9 a.m. They warned me that if I missed this court date, I would be incarcerated again without the possibility of a bond, and I would have to fight my entire case from inside the county jail. Keep in mind, I didn't have a car, but in order to secure my release from jail, I agreed to comply with whatever terms they imposed.

Thankfully, my brother Buck was available. His friend Mud-bone stopped by early the next morning to check on Buck, and when he honked his horn outside my window, I jolted awake. It was 8:15 a.m., and I began screaming, "Oh my God, I'm going to miss the court date!" I pleaded with Mud-bone, "Can you please take me? I don't want to get locked up again. Please, I can't be late; I can't miss this court date." Mud-bone agreed to take me, and we barely made it in time.

I had to attend a few more court dates, but Sears never showed up against me, so they eventually dismissed the case, and I finally escaped that situation. It was one of the most challenging experiences I had ever faced, but I learned from it that jail simply wasn't for me, and I had to be cautious about the company I kept. From that day forward, I was very mindful in my life. I knew that jail wasn't the lifestyle I wanted. I cherished my freedom and everything it entailed, so I proceeded with caution.

Now that I was 18, I had a baby and was expecting my second child. I was still alone and ended up moving because I found a more affordable apartment. I discovered a 2-bedroom basement apartment with a spacious living room, an eat-in kitchen, and a laundry room at the back. I told myself, "Okay, I can afford this rent." It was only $200 per month, including heating. I thought, "I'm going to get my life together now. I can handle this on my own." Despite being pregnant with my daughter, I persevered and applied for jobs every day.

I ended up finding a job at a call center in Skokie, IL. I was trying to work, but it was challenging. I had to wake up at 5 a.m., take Dell to daycare on the bus, and then commute all the way up north to work by 8 a.m. every day. The same routine applied in the evening. I would finish work around 4:30 p.m. and arrive at the daycare around 6:00 p.m. Sometimes, I would be late, and although the lady tried to work with me, I didn't have enough money to cover the entire bill along with the late fees.

Consequently, I constantly felt defeated as I struggled to get my life in order.

One day, I was feeling depressed because I couldn't afford Dell's childcare payments. My sister came over and suggested, "Come to work with me. I want you to meet this guy. He's really cool, has money, and he's always driving extra routes and working a second job." She spoke highly of him, believing he could be a significant help to me. I was bored at home by myself and expressed my hesitation about getting involved in another relationship. However, she insisted that I should just get to know him and emphasized how he could assist me. Despite my wariness about my sister setting me up with someone again, I trusted her because she was my older sister. So, I went to work with her, and she introduced me to him.

When he laid eyes on me, his face lit up. I could tell that I wasn't what he was expecting. He was tall, dark, and quite handsome. He had an athletic build, was about two years older than me, and carried himself like a gentleman. His name was LAW. The first thing he asked me was, "Are you pregnant?" I replied affirmatively, and he started laughing. He said, "Where's the father?" I explained that we were no longer together and that I was alone. He responded, "Don't worry; I have a baby on the way too, and the mother and I aren't together either." He went on to share that he lived on the west side with some Mexican friends and was focused on working and taking care of himself.

While we were conversing, my sister mentioned, "I'm having a fish fry tonight. You guys can come over and hang out at my house." She, Michael, and LAW all worked at the school bus company. We ended up meeting at her house and had a fantastic evening. We laughed, talked, drank, and played cards.

As it got late, LAW said, "I'll drop you off at home," and he ended up taking me back to my apartment. We shared a kiss, and he asked, "Can I come see you again sometime?" I responded, "Yes." Surprisingly, the very next day, he showed up unannounced with flowers and candy. He had listened when I mentioned that I loved Butterfingers, so he brought me a giant-sized one. He continued to visit me, and a few weeks later, I planned a lovely candlelight dinner for us. He came over and was surprised at how well I could cook. We had an enjoyable conversation, which eventually led to us making love. Now, I had never experienced a man leaving money on the dresser before, but as he was getting ready to leave for work, he left me $200. I looked at him curiously and asked, "What is this for?" He replied, "You might want to buy yourself something. I'm sure there's something you want. If not, just keep it in your pocket." It felt strange to me. I knew I wasn't a prostitute, but it almost felt like it.

He returned that evening after finishing work. He told me that he had been through some challenging times in life. He had recently been released from the penitentiary after serving a year or two for selling weed. He explained that he was trying to get his life together and increase his income. He was working a lot of overtime at both jobs, driving on special bus trips, and working at a downtown gas station at night.

He came over every day to assist me with bills and household tasks. Our sexual chemistry was intense. We spent most of our time indoors, making love without pause. Our routine consisted of him going to work, returning home, having dinner, making love, showering, and heading out to his night job. This continued for a while. Eventually, I became heavily pregnant and unable to work. LAW provided financial support every pay period. I was reluctant to enter another relationship like this, but I desperately needed help with the bills, especially with the impending arrival of my baby and my small son. We decided it was best for him to move in, considering our passionate and sexual connection. Our desire for each other was constant throughout the day. We couldn't resist each other and made love anywhere and at any time.

I expressed to him that we couldn't just have a causal relationship; we needed to discuss commitment to each other. We obtained our marriage license but decided to delay the actual marriage until after our deliveries. He was expecting his first child, and I was having my second. However, having the license made me feel that our relationship was official, and marriage was on the horizon.

His daughter was born in mid-August 1991, followed by the birth of my daughter, Makeba (Makeba), two weeks later. LAW accompanied me to the hospital and was present during the delivery. I also called my daughter's father, Hook, who arrived at the hospital later. LAW respected our privacy and stepped away to allow Hook and me to discuss matters concerning our daughter.

Hook was thrilled to be at the hospital and expressed his desire to name our daughter. He wanted to name her Makeba, as those names were popular in the 90s. I agreed to the name Makeba, although I wasn't particularly fond of it. However, I insisted on choosing a more suitable middle name. I suggested Makeba, which he accepted, and he jokingly referred to her as "Makeba-Makeba." Hook's best friend and Makeba's godfather, Eric, was also present at the hospital. Eric was the person who accompanied Hook to my apartment when we first met. We all spent time together, laughing and enjoying each other's company. Hook held Makeba and remarked on her beauty. He asked about Law and me, to which I replied that we were a couple. Hook inquired if we could reconcile and raise our daughter together. I firmly declined, expressing my continued frustration with his past actions. He apologized and understood my decision. He kissed me on the forehead and acknowledged my worth, while Eric teased Hook about losing a good thing he didn't appreciate.

I returned home with the baby, and LAW continued to assist with rent and bills. It seemed like we were going to make it as a family. We made plans to marry soon. Despite LAW having a recent child with someone else, I was willing to accept it since my relationships with my children's fathers hadn't worked out either.

LAW showed dedication to me and the children. We shared responsibilities in raising our children, and I stayed home to take care of them. LAW remained employed, and I focused on managing the household by cooking, cleaning, washing, and ironing. It was like having twins, considering our daughters were born two weeks apart. As our relationship stabilized, some of the pressure I felt began to ease. I started to contemplate how I could improve my life. I became more independent and pursued better job opportunities. I didn't want to spend my entire life working at minimum wage or telemarketing jobs.

I knew I was much smarter and capable of obtaining my high school diploma. At the age of 18, I witnessed my peers graduating from high school, and it deeply bothered me that I couldn't participate in prom or walk the stage with my diploma, despite knowing that I was intellectually superior to them. This realization sparked a motivation within me, and I made up my mind to take the GED test. I decided that I didn't need to take lengthy GED classes; I would simply take the test.

The following day, I contacted Olive Harvey Community College and scheduled my GED test. A few weeks later, filled with supreme confidence, I took the bus to Olive Harvey. The GED exam was an 8-hour session, and I positioned myself at the front, ready to begin testing. The test comprised several timed sections, and I finished each part early, taking breaks outside to enjoy a snack while others were still testing. Once the 8 hours were over, I returned home, and two weeks later, the test results arrived. I achieved high scores in every category, and I felt an immense sense of accomplishment.

After obtaining my GED, I aspired to attend college, but I knew that I couldn't afford it financially. My financial situation was already precarious. I witnessed many individuals burdened with financial debt from student loans, their credit scores suffering, and their income tax returns compromised due to the loan repayments. What saddened me the most was that the majority of these individuals hadn't even completed their intended degrees. This fear and discouragement about going to college weighed heavily on me. Additionally, I had no knowledge about the application process, scholarships, or applying for financial aid through FAFSA. I was completely clueless about college, and I had no one to turn to for guidance. Neither side of my family had ever pursued higher education, nor I didn't have any friends who had attended college. Moreover, I had the responsibility of taking care of my children, and LAW's work schedule left me without much assistance. With my GED in hand, I began searching for better job opportunities, believing that I had the chance to earn a higher income and secure a better position.

Eventually, I discovered that he was cheating on me with his ex and the mother of his child. I would think he was at work, but instead, he would be spending time at her family's house. Despite being ten years older than me, she was unable to support herself and still lived with her mother and extended family. They all resided together, with numerous siblings and their children. One of the reasons he had initially told me he had left her was because she lacked independence and showed no desire to leave her mother's house and establish a life of her own. That was precisely what he appreciated about me. She had a 10-year-old son, and she and LAW had recently welcomed a new baby together.

She possessed a rather ignorant demeanor and was a heavy marijuana user. This shared affinity for marijuana was a connection between her and LAW. However, I had no interest in smoking weed. He persuaded me to try it once, and I ended up hallucinating. I ran through the house, screaming and convinced that he was the devil. I genuinely believed he was the devil. I don't know how he managed to calm me down from that intense high, but I was greatly affected. That experience deterred me from ever trying marijuana again. I had tried it once before, during my initial apartment days with only Dell. My cousin had come over, and we were all hanging out when she passed me a pre-rolled joint. I ended up passing out and sleeping for what felt like three days. I had no awareness of my surroundings or what was happening. Those two dreadful encounters solidified my decision never to smoke weed again. I knew it simply wasn't for me.

I remember one day; I was continuously paging LAW. I needed him to come home early from work so that I could ensure he would be there on time with the children, allowing me to go for a job interview the next morning. However, he wasn't responding to my paging messages. It was around midnight when I decided to call his baby momma's house. To my surprise, she answered the phone. I asked her if she knew where LAW was, and she confirmed that he was there with her. I requested that she give him the phone, emphasizing the importance of the call. She replied, "He saw your pages. I'm sure he will get back to you; he's busy right now." I questioned, "Busy?" She started moaning and said, "Yeah, he's busy." I was taken aback by her response, and before I could react, she abruptly hung up the phone.

I was furious beyond words. I couldn't believe that LAW was at her house, engaging in sexual activities with her. I was overcome with anger and called my girlfriend over for support. Together, we gathered all of his belongings, stuffed them into a plastic garbage bag, poured bleach over them, and drove to her house. We dumped everything on her porch and set it on fire. At that time, I was young and blinded by my strong sexual attraction to him, mistaking it for love. However, his infidelity had reached an intolerable level, and I was seething with anger.

Despite everything, I couldn't help but feel foolishly infatuated with him. He returned and apologized, claiming that he was only there to see his baby and that she had blown the situation out of proportion. Naively, I fell for his excuses and took him back. We immediately resumed our physical relationship. He knew precisely how to satisfy me, and I was completely under his control. As time went on, he continued to cheat on me relentlessly. One night, he stayed out all night, and it became clear to me that he wasn't with his daughter's mother. I started questioning his whereabouts, wondering why he would leave me with the car, riding off on his bike, disappearing for extended periods. A voice inside me urged me to follow him, and so I did, trailing him to an apartment building a few blocks away from our place.

I patiently waited outside the apartment he entered, and to my dismay, he emerged with another woman and her children. She had five boys. They walked together towards her car, exchanging kisses, and engaged in conversation. Deciding not to reveal my presence, I drove home before he noticed me. When I arrived home, I packed his belongings while he entered the house, pretending he had been at work. We started arguing and fighting.

In the heat of the moment, I grabbed his clippers and swung them around, attempting to hit him in the head. The altercation continued, and I rushed into the kitchen, grabbing a hatchet. He hurriedly fled down the back stairs. In my anger, I threw the hatchet, aiming for his back. He let out a scream, "Aaaah," but stumbled over a shoe or boot, tripping in his attempt to escape. Unbeknownst to me, I was pregnant again during this chaotic event. After I kicked him out, he went around the corner to live with the other woman. I would often see him driving her new car in the neighborhood. It was summertime, and I spent time with my friends, not yet showing my pregnancy.

One of my friends had male acquaintances, and one of them owned a brand-new white sports car. On a particular day, I purposely presented myself in an attractive manner, wanting LAW to see me. I wore a cute outfit, had my hair done, and went outside.

When LAW spotted me lying across the hood of the guy's car, looking exceptionally stylish, he must have been taken aback. He swiftly got out of his car and approached me, saying, "Get in." I replied, "I'm not getting in your woman's car, you're crazy." In response, he discreetly pulled out a gun, showing it only to me. He demanded, "Get your ass in this car." Fearful of what he might do or if an altercation would ensue with the car's owner, I reluctantly got into the car. I was flattered, thinking that his jealousy was a demonstration of his love for me, not wanting to see me with anyone else.

We eventually reconciled, but the pattern of him leaving and returning persisted. Meanwhile, I was pregnant with my third child when a neighbor living above me, who had several children of her own, approached me. She understood the hardships I had faced in life and introduced me to a program called Section 8. She explained how it could be a perfect fit for me, as it had been a blessing in her own life. With Section 8, I wouldn't have to constantly struggle and worry about rent payments. It seemed like a wonderful opportunity, particularly with my responsibilities as a young mother.

She provided me with the necessary instructions, saying, 'To apply for the program, you'll need to call this specific number on a designated day. Make sure to get up early in the morning. I promise you, if you get approved, it will make a significant difference. It will help you and your children immensely. As a young person, you need this assistance to stabilize your situation and start building a better future.' This neighbor seemed to have her life together, thanks to Section 8, which eased her financial burden by covering her rent and providing additional financial support. She had a nice car, a beautiful apartment, and she received clothing and other items for her children. She even shared clothes her kids had outgrown with me, as she had a total of six children and was married to their father.

After she provided me with all the necessary information, she said, "Make sure to wake up early and start calling. If you're unable to get through from your phone, you may need someone from the suburbs to make the call for you. But if you manage to get through, you'll be enrolled in the program." I replied, "Okay, that's great." On the day of enrollment, I began calling early in the morning, but I kept encountering busy signals.

Knowing that my older cousin Rome lived in the suburbs with my aunt Helene, I thought, "Let me see if he can help me." To my relief, he answered the phone at 8:30 a.m. I explained to him that I was trying to secure assistance through this program, and I asked, "Could you please assist me? You need to keep calling this number until you get through, and then connect me." Desperate to enter the program, I even offered, "If you manage to get through, I'll give you $50!" He agreed, saying, "Okay, that sounds good." About 15–20 minutes later, he called me back and said, "Cuz, I think I have them on the line." We remained on hold, eagerly awaiting the return of the agent to the phone.

When I finally spoke with the agent, they provided me with a thorough explanation of the program and the subsequent steps. I provided them with all the required information, and they scheduled an appointment for me. I expressed my gratitude, saying, "Thanks, cuz." That night, he came over, expecting to receive the promised $50. I thought to myself, "That's what I get for making empty promises." I had assured him $50 for the phone call. Despite feeling slightly bothered as it was all the money I had, I couldn't blame him. After all, nobody in my family had ever genuinely looked out for me. No one seemed to genuinely care about my well-being. I was slightly disappointed, but I understood his perspective. He had done what I asked him to do.

When I received the Section 8 certificate, I learned that it was part of a special program initiated under the Civil Rights and Equal Housing Project, which was established by Martin Luther King. To be eligible, I had to have lived in a housing project at some point in my life. Luckily, my birth certificate indicated that I was born at Henry Horner Homes. Additionally, I couldn't have a criminal background, which was fortunate since my record had been cleared of a warrant, thanks to divine intervention. The final requirement was to move into a community with a Black/African American population of less than 10% and reside there for a year before receiving the actual housing certificate.

Finding a place that would accept me and my certificate proved to be quite challenging. Most property owners were unfamiliar with this type of voucher and would say, "What is that? We've never heard of this before." I had to effectively explain the program, assuring them that their payments would be directly provided by the government, not me. I emphasized that they would receive their monthly check promptly on the first of each month.

By the grace and blessings of God, I stumbled upon a beautiful, newly constructed 2-bedroom duplex in Hanover Park, IL. It was an amazing home, featuring a master bedroom, two bathrooms, and a spacious living room with a fireplace. The master bathroom boasted his and her marble sinks, a jacuzzi tub with a walk-in shower, and a stunning kitchen with bay windows. To my surprise, the owner was a Black man married to a White woman. For some reason, he took a chance on me and offered me the opportunity.

He understood the challenges of the housing projects in Chicago and had managed to work his way up to become a real estate investor. The entire community was brand new, and I couldn't believe my luck. I was moving into this beautifully constructed home with just my children, and I didn't even have to contribute to the rent since I was solely relying on welfare at the time.

However, I found myself frequently traveling back and forth to the city because I was still deeply in love with LAW, and we continued our tumultuous relationship. He retained the basement apartment where we used to live, as he was reluctant to move all the way out to Hanover Park. He preferred the city. As I moved forward, he continued to engage in affairs with the woman who lived around the corner and had five children. She had five chubby little boys, and her license plate read "BEBEKDS," short for Bae-Bae Kids. She frequently visited him in the basement apartment we once shared.

I was sad about my situation. I was pregnant with LAW's child and still madly in love with him. My new place was a blessing financially, but it was so far from everybody. Everything was so different living out there. The area was so nice, bright, and clean, but it was so White. I was afraid to go to the store or be seen in public. I basically stayed in the house; I didn't feel right at all living in this predominantly White community.

When I went to the grocery stores, everything was very fresh and reasonably priced. The people shopping there would look at me strangely, as if they were saying, "What the hell is she doing shopping here?" It was an extremely uncomfortable situation for me. It was a total and complete culture shock: I didn't know anybody, I didn't have a car, and I couldn't be independent and get around to the stores or anything too easily. The buses didn't come remotely close to the area I lived in. I had to walk so far just to get home. And being pregnant with two small children made it seem like a mission impossible. So, the only time I could get around was when someone would come pick me up or come out to visit. Other than that, I was a sitting duck.

Strangely enough, that didn't bother me at all because I was a homebody anyway. But I kept coming back to the city to be around people I knew and to get to the grocery stores I liked to patronize, such as Moo & Oink and Aldi; they had the best deals on meat and food that I was accustomed to. The grocery stores in Hanover Park weren't my type of store; they had more expensive cuts of meat and name-brand grocery items.

When I would come, I would stay at my sister's apartment. Or I would go to Brenda's house. One day, while visiting her, I ended up going into labor, and LAW came to the hospital to help me deliver the baby. I gave birth to our daughter, whom we named Lawrencia. At this time, LAW and I were still struggling to be together because he was still fooling around with his daughter's mother and the lady around the corner. It was a messy situation. I just wished I could shake my feelings for him; he kept holding on to me, but I couldn't deal with him being involved with these other women.

So, I said to myself, "Forget it; forget him; forget it all." I ended up going back home, and I was just trying to make a life out there by myself for me and my three children. Around two months later, my dad came over with his wife one day because I had organized a little get-together. I invited my friends and my father. We all had a great evening. I cooked. We did the usual: eating, drinking, laughing, and talking. Everyone was saying, "Wow, your place is beautiful." I even saw that my father was a bit happy for me. We all had a lovely evening that night.

After everyone left for the evening, my children and I went to sleep. It was such a long night with so much company that I was happy and exhausted, all in the same breath. When I woke up the next morning, I decided, we're just going to go to the city. So, I sat Makeba at the kitchen table. I started getting our breakfast together. I was so hungry. Dell had gone back home with my dad and his wife the night before.

After I finished cooking, Makeba and I finished eating our breakfast, and I went to my bedroom to get my baby. As soon as I reached my doorway, something inside me said, "She's gone." I paused and tried to shake the premonition that had come over me. I said, "What?! I'm tripping, right?" I went over to her. I just had this terrible feeling. I went to touch her little feet, and they didn't move. Then I had this gut-wrenching feeling, and I said, "What the hell?!" It felt so weird; I could not shake this thought or feeling.

I kept trying to tickle her feet, but they wouldn't budge. So, I ended up gently grabbing hold of her by the sides of her chest and slowly picking her up. As I was lifting her, her body was stiff; her arms were folded upwards, her fists clenched tightly, and her head was turned to the right. I was afraid to look at her. Slowly, I turned her towards me, and I could see that rigor mortis had set in. When I saw her face, it took my breath away. All I could do was scream and cry. I went into hyperventilation. I laid her body back down and screamed for dear life. I immediately called 911, along with all my family. I was on the floor by the front door, crying.

All I could hear was my baby girl Makeba running around, playing, saying, "Mommy, why are you crying? The baby wants her bottle. Don't cry, mommy. She just wants her bottle. Do you want me to give it to her?" I screamed, "No! Baby, come here, come here; come sit next to mommy."

There were many police officers, EMTs, and firefighters there. I still don't know how the door opened for them to enter. I was in total shock. I felt numb, blank, and empty. Several detectives combed through the house, asking me questions about the previous night and what happened. They took pictures of everything, treating it like a crime scene. One of them pulled out a bottle of vodka they had drunk the night before when my dad and the others were over. "I don't even drink vodka," I exclaimed. I kept explaining everything repeatedly. Then, when I heard them zip my baby into that black body bag, the detective said, "You know she's gone, right?" I cried uncontrollably, begging them not to put her in that bag. I was crying, and I felt sick to my stomach.

My aunts, uncle, cousins, sister, and brother all came to be with me. I didn't have any life insurance for my baby. My aunt Tee-Tee kept asking me what I was going to do and why I didn't have insurance. I remember just sitting there, lost, stuck, numb, and crying. I was so lost. I didn't know what to do. I didn't know how to feel. I wasn't myself. I didn't want to be in the house anymore. I ended up going back to the city with my sister.

I finally got in touch with LAW, and we went to the funeral home to make the arrangements. They told me the funeral would cost between $3,000 and $4,000. I thought to myself, "I don't have that. How am I going to do this?" I told them I had been saving up to buy a car, and all I had was $2,000 in cash. LAW asked if he could use the phone. He called the woman he had been involved with. He put her on speakerphone and explained the situation.

With the nastiest tone I've ever heard, she said, "I'll just pay for the services because I know she don't got shit!" Her words immediately offended me, so I said, "No, thank you. She's not paying for anything for my daughter. I was woman enough to bring her into this world, and I will be woman enough to lay her to rest. I don't need a handout or any insults from your girlfriend." I got up and started to walk out. The funeral director gently grabbed my arm and looked at me with pride, saying, "Ma'am, please bring us the money you have and the clothes you want her to wear as soon as possible." With a smile, she said, "I've got you!"

I think I had a nervous breakdown because the next day, I remember walking from 69th and Campbell all the way to 103rd and Halsted. Mentally, I was gone. I was lost in some twilight zone. I wasn't present. I was so hurt. I was so hurt that my baby had died. I walked with her pretty little white dress in my hand.

I didn't know where my other kids were. I didn't know what was happening to me. I was completely out of my mind at that point.

I was just trying to bury my daughter, and when I arrived at the funeral home, they saw how broken I was and said, "Don't worry about the rest of the bill. We'll cover everything for you." I gave them all the money I had. She said, "It's all good. I'll never forget that while we were at the funeral home, they asked me, "Where would you like the car to pick you up?" I explained, "Well, it could just pick us up from in front of LAW's apartment." When I told my family about the funeral plans and where we would be picked up, they spoke about me derogatorily. They gossiped and called me all sorts of names. Honestly, I didn't care about the pickup location. I just wanted it to be over.

I organized a beautiful service for my baby. A few things stand out from that day. Firstly, my father was completely absent. He didn't even attend his own granddaughter's funeral. He hadn't come to my mother's funeral either, although I let that slide due to the issues with my mother's family before her passing. However, his absence at my baby's funeral was incredibly hurtful.

After the services had concluded and we were leaving the funeral home, my aunt Helen, my mother's sister, looked at me and said, "You'll be alright." Her words were devoid of empathy, cold, and heartless. It was as if my baby didn't matter, and she questioned why I was crying so much. Her delivery was entirely uncalled for, and I lacked the strength to respond.

As we were preparing to head to the cemetery, they initially attempted to place my baby's casket in the limousine with LAW, the children, and me. I couldn't bear it. I started screaming and crying, so they ultimately placed her in a hearse to transport her to the cemetery.

Once we finished the burial services and arrived at my sister Tia's house, I sat on the front porch, mourning silently, while they all gathered upstairs and spoke ill of me. The situation became so severe that my cousin Lily came out to check on me; she genuinely felt sorry for me. As we sat there talking, she could overhear their conversation upstairs, talking about me. She remarked, "This isn't right." I replied, "It's okay, cousin." She retorted, "No, I can't let this slide." She went upstairs and confronted my family. She said, "How dare all of you sit here and speak about this girl this way, knowing she just buried her baby? You're not providing any kind of family support. You talked negatively because she didn't have life insurance, because she still loved the man, she had her baby with, and because she had limited funds. But none of you offered any financial assistance or reached out to help her. You just sat there judging her. Give my cousin a break. You're going too far with her; she has already been through enough. She buried her baby; now, show some respect. You didn't even want to contribute or provide food for the repast, claiming she had nothing together. Who thinks about food when their baby has just died?"

# PART
# FOUR

# CHAPTER 12
# SURPRISE!!! - SURPRISED???

*"Nothing Is Predestined. The Obstacles of Your Past Can Become the Gateways That Lead to New Beginnings"*
**Ralph Blum**

Soon after, the autopsy results were released. I showed LAW the autopsy report, which indicated that she died of "sudden infant death syndrome" (SIDS). We discussed her death and how it affected both of us. That conversation led to discussing various aspects of our relationship. At that time, I wasn't particularly interested in getting back together with him. I was deeply disturbed and mentally exhausted. After burying our daughter, I had essentially reached my limit with him.

I was trying to move forward with my life and find my way, but I was consumed by heartbreak and depression. I felt incredibly sad, lonely, and miserable. I didn't have anyone to provide encouragement, uplift me, or support me through my grieving process. I was silently suffering. About a month later, a close friend from the neighborhood, who lived on the same block, happened to pass by while I was sitting on the porch with a despondent expression. She said, "Angie, girl, I'm so sorry about your baby. Get up from there and come on down to my house. I'm about to barbecue."

We started spending a lot of time together at her house, engaging in conversations about various topics. I opened up to her about how shattered I was after losing my baby and how my relationship with LAW had ended. Returning to my house in Hanover Park seemed impossible for me. All I could think about was my deceased baby lying there. I couldn't muster the strength to go back alone. Mentally, it was too overwhelming for me at that point.

I found myself always hanging out in the city, whether at my sister's or my friend's house. It didn't matter where I was; I remained miserable. One day, my friend said, "I want you to meet someone. I'm going to call my cousin over. He just broke up with his girlfriend and is looking for someone to hang out and have fun with. You'll like him. It's good to have someone take your mind off all this. You need to start going out and enjoying yourself." I replied, "Girl, I'm not interested in getting into a relationship anymore." She assured me, "Just have him as a friend; he's a cool guy."

So, she called him, and he came over that evening. He was tall, and I could tell he had some Hispanic heritage based on his complexion and hair texture. He had a long ponytail and went by the name Gee. He slightly resembled the actor, Steven Seagal. He had an impressive sports car with expensive tires and rims. He was dressed in sports attire, well-groomed, and wore pleasant cologne. However, I struggled to like him because he appeared to belong to a different ethnic background, and I was only accustomed to dating dark-skinned Black men.

As I walked into my friend's house, he looked at me with delight, and a wide smile brightened his face. We sat down and had a pleasant conversation. He shared details about his job and enjoying his favorite hobby as a DJ and talked about his family. He didn't have any children, explaining that his previous long-term partner had never gotten pregnant, consistently telling him that there was something wrong with him.

Despite his fine qualities, I simply wasn't attracted to him. He asked, "Do you want to go out?" I declined, explaining that I wasn't in the mood to socialize. I was so deeply depressed that I couldn't shake off the emotional funk I was in. Consequently, we ended up spending time at my friend's house, simply hanging out and enjoying each other's company. He mentioned, "I'll be back tomorrow. You know what? It's my mom's birthday soon, and I want to go shopping at the mall to find her a gift. Would you like to come along?" I responded, "Okay, that sounds cool." I asked my friend Londa if she could watch my kids, and she agreed.

The following day, we had a lovely lunch and went to see a movie before heading to the mall. While browsing at a perfume counter, he suggested, "Smell these perfumes. Which one do you think my mom would like?" I replied, "I'm not sure." However, there was one in a red bottle that caught my attention. I mentioned that his mom might enjoy that particular fragrance. Unfortunately, I can't recall the name of the perfume, but it had a pleasant scent.

He asked me, "Are you sure about this one?" I replied, "Yeah." With a smile, I added, "She's going to love it." He instructed the sales associate to package it, and he handed it to me. I said, "Do you want me to hold this or keep it hidden until her birthday or something?" Surprisingly, he said, "No, it's yours." I was taken aback. No man had ever done something like that for me. It really brightened my day, and I couldn't help but wear a big, happy smile.

We continued exploring the mall and made a few more purchases. Eventually, we got into his car and headed to dinner. During the drive, he glanced at me, and I thought he wanted a kiss. Instead, he handed me a tissue and said, "Look in the mirror. You have something in your nose." I felt so embarrassed; there was a large green booger hanging out of my nose. I mean, it was quite big. I kept apologizing, feeling ashamed. He smirked and smiled, saying, "Don't trip. It happens. We're only human. Everyone has a booger or two, or in your case, one really big-ass one, every now and then." We laughed so hard as I cleaned myself up. It had to be one of the most embarrassing moments of my life.

Spending that day with him made me feel incredibly good. It took my mind off all the problems I had been facing, and I wasn't as miserable as I had been since my daughter's death. It provided a temporary relief from the heavy burden I had been carrying. He took me out to dinner, and we had a wonderful time, laughing and talking while enjoying a glass of wine. He kept looking into my eyes and telling me how beautiful I was.

He opened up about his own situation, explaining that he had been with a girl since high school. He talked about why things didn't work out between them and expressed his desire for a good and faithful woman. He wanted someone who wasn't a gold digger or selfish, someone he could share companionship with.

They had recently broken up, and he was now looking for a friend he could get to know and see where it would lead. Meanwhile, I was trying to move on from my feelings for LAW. I had so much love for him, but I couldn't handle his constant cheating anymore. He was always driving around in that woman's car with her kids and still involved with his daughter's mother. Londa, my friend, and my sister lived just a few doors down, so I witnessed everything he was doing.

It was time for me to move forward with my life. Gee started coming to my house in Hanover Park, and he absolutely loved it. He kept questioning why I spent so much time in the city when I had such a beautiful home. I explained to him that I felt lonely in that house by myself and had difficulty getting around with my children. We had many conversations about it. He would drive back and forth every day, and we grew closer and closer. He adored my cooking, and I made sure to provide breakfast, lunch, and dinner. The house was always impeccably clean, and I took care of everything. He didn't have to worry about anything when he came over each day.

Before I knew it, we were in a relationship together. Shortly after, he moved in with me. I really needed his support at that time. He had a decent job and helped me with the bills, even though I was on Section 8. There were still bills to pay. He made sure my kids had nice clothes and the latest Jordans. He cared about appearances. He kept my hair done, placed a beautiful diamond ring on my finger, and insisted that I keep all my money to myself. He took care of all the bills.

He truly reminded me of my father. He had a strong desire for wonderful things. When he moved in, he furnished the house with expensive and stylish furniture, televisions, surround sound systems, and stereo systems. It felt like we were living the lifestyle of the rich and famous with how well-equipped our home was. I was incredibly happy. I told him about my aspirations to go to college and get a decent job. I just needed a car to get around, and I had to figure out where I would go to school and work. I could sense his hesitation because he had previously shared how he had spent years supporting his ex-girlfriend through college, only to be mistreated by her afterward. I was in the process of obtaining my moving certificate because, after my daughter's passing, I couldn't stay in that house any longer. The landlord agreed to let me move, but it was a process.

With Gee's support, I was able to focus on my life and work towards gaining independence and creating something for myself. However, there was a challenge with Gee's commute. He worked in the south suburbs while I lived in the northwest suburbs. He had to travel back and forth because he worked overnight shifts that ended around 6 a.m. Sometimes, he would fall asleep while driving home to me.

I remember one stormy night in particular. Gee woke me up from my sleep and brought me to the living room, where we ended up making love on the floor. It was a passionate experience, intensified by the raging thunder and lightning outside. I could see the glow of the lightning illuminating the house. It was a special and sensual night. To my surprise, I discovered that I was pregnant afterward. I couldn't help but exclaim, "Oh my goodness, not this fast. Come on now. Damn, we just got together." I wondered how Gee would react, especially since he believed he couldn't have children. I got pregnant very quickly with him. When I finally told him, he looked at me strangely and said, "Get the heck out of here!" I replied, "Yeah, I'm pregnant." He seemed shocked and started questioning himself, becoming paranoid about the situation.

Gee's cousin, Londa, who had introduced us, became jealous of our relationship. She didn't expect things to progress so rapidly and for Gee to take care of me and my children. She couldn't handle seeing me look good, be happy, dress nicely, and do so many things with Gee, including moving in together and now being pregnant. Her jealousy became apparent.

Londa began trying to make Gee insecure and suspect that I was fooling around with LAW when he brought me to the city. Londa lived two doors down from LAW, and I often visited the city to see my sister, who lived nearby as well. Gee started acting paranoid. He would leave work early in the early morning hours, attempting to catch me at my sister's or Londa's house, thinking I was up to something. I remember one night, around 3 or 4 a.m., Gee knocked on my sister's door while I was fast asleep. My sister woke me up and said, "Gee's here." I asked, "What is he doing here?" He came in and stayed the night, and we went home early the next morning. He would often show up unexpectedly, and Londa's behavior towards me became strange.

I wasn't thinking about LAW; he was still involved with the woman around the corner. I was genuinely happy with Gee. He took good care of me, and I believed we could build a future together. I admired his style and the lifestyle he lived. I wanted to achieve something meaningful in life, and he aligned well with the standards and aspirations I had.

I remember one day when Gee was opening the car door for me, helping me with the kids and groceries. Suddenly, LAW appeared, walking down the street. The tension between them was palpable. They despised each other's presence. There was something off about LAW that day, although I couldn't quite pinpoint it. Nevertheless, I brushed it off, thinking, "Not my problem." I was simply grateful to be living a decent life.

One day, Gee woke up and said, "My friends are coming over, and we need to take care of some things." He asked if I could prepare food and snacks for his company, and I agreed. I laid out a spread, including hors d'oeuvres, smothered cabbage, mac and cheese, fried chicken, and various snacks. Around four carloads of guys from the hood arrived, and to be honest, it was quite overwhelming. I felt a sense of fear as all these men entered my house, including one of my cousins from out west. I remained quiet, attending to the house while Gee tended to his business with his friends. They devoured the food, leaving no crumbs behind. They praised Gee, saying he was the man, complimenting my appearance and our beautiful house. Gee's confidence soared. He was proud and felt accomplished. Although I never inquired about Gee's personal affairs, I knew there was more to him than met the eye. He thanked me for catering to him and his guests, boasting about how delicious the cabbage was and asking how I became such a skilled cook.

A few days later, Gee said, "Get ready; my friend just got out of prison, and we're going to visit him. See if you can find a babysitter because we'll be away for the weekend." As we headed there, I noticed that the area looked familiar. We arrived, greeted his friend, and sat out on the back patio. Surprisingly, I discovered that one of my female cousins was next door, spending time with the neighbors. I hadn't seen her in over ten years, not since the day my uncle Bubba had severely beaten me at her mother's house, leading me to run away. It was a joyous reunion since she was one of my favorite cousins. We expressed how glad we were to see each other.

While I chatted with my cousin, Gee sat with his best friend. Eventually, I rejoined their conversation. Gee made sure I was comfortable, and I got acquainted with his friend's girlfriend, whose house we were at. Soon, Gee stood up and said, "I have to go to work. I'll be back tomorrow. We have a lot to do." I nodded, and he assured me that I was in good hands, saying, "I'll return in the morning as soon as I finish work. We'll spend the weekend here and go back to the house on Sunday." It was Friday night, around 8 p.m., when he left. We kissed each other goodbye, and I wished him a great evening at work, looking forward to seeing him in the morning. The friend's lady and I stayed up, chatting. Her partner had gone upstairs, drunk, and ready for bed. Suddenly, the doorbell rang. I could hear someone shouting through the door, "Angie, what the fuck are you doing here? You bogus as hell." Confused, I asked the lady, "What's happening? Who is that?" I glanced and saw that it was my cousin R.W from my mother's side of the family. He was furious, screaming at the top of his lungs, acting erratic towards me. I had no idea why he was so angry. I explained, "I'm here with my guy, visiting his friend." The lady tried to calm my cousin down while keeping him from entering, using her body weight against the door. I continued to question him, "What's wrong? Why are you yelling like this?

He kept demanding, "Angie, get your ass out of there now." I confusingly asked, "Why? I'm fine. Why are you yelling and acting like this?" I was genuinely confused. I didn't know why he was at this lady's house, making a scene about me. He sounded just like my uncle Bubba, my cousin R.W was his son. He continued to threaten, curse, scream, and yell at me, trying to force me to leave this lady's house. I swear I had no idea why. I just stood there, bewildered, confused, and terrified. Her partner heard all the commotion, came downstairs, and confronted my cousin, telling him to move the fuck around away from his door with all that bullshit. Eventually, she managed to get R.W to leave. I asked her, "What was all that about?" She proceeded to tell me that she and R.W had been in a relationship all year while Gee's friend was in prison. She said he couldn't handle her leaving him and going back to her partner, even though he knew she would return to him once he was released.

Now, mind you, I had no clue about any of this. It felt like I had just stepped into a minefield. I didn't know that she, Gee's friend, and my cousins lived in this housing project. It felt familiar when we arrived, but I had no idea she and my cousin were involved. I hadn't seen this cousin since I was beaten at my aunt's house as well. I couldn't believe he would come to someone's house and act so ignorant towards me.

After the confusion settled, Gee's friend called him, saying, "Dude, your lady is related to the guy who was involved with my woman while I was in prison." He explained everything that had happened and went upstairs to continue the conversation in private. I was still shaken up, and his girlfriend tried to console me. I repeatedly apologized to them. I swear, I had no knowledge of what was going on. I felt extremely embarrassed.

The next day, I sat there waiting for Gee to come, but he never returned to get me. I sat on the couch, pregnant, with cravings, and waited for him. Later in the afternoon, I asked if I could page him, but he didn't respond. I just kept waiting there. He never called me or anything. The entire Saturday passed without any word from him. I asked his friend if he had heard from Gee, and he said no. Eventually, I fell asleep. I was trying my best to figure out why he didn't come to get me, praying that nothing bad had happened. The next day, his friend said, "Come on, I'll drop you off at the bus stop so you can go wherever you need to." I responded, "But Gee was supposed to come back and get me." He said, "Well, I don't think he's coming, so there's no need for you to keep waiting here. Gather your things." He took me to the bus stop on Division and Western and gave me $1 for my bus fare. I caught the bus all the way back to the Southside and then walked over to my sister's house.

I went to my sister's house and continued to wait for Gee, just sitting there. I kept paging him but received no response. He didn't say a word and didn't call me back. I kept paging him throughout the day, but he remained silent. I couldn't believe it. By Tuesday, I finally asked my sister if she could please take me home.

I explained that I didn't know what had happened. I ended up going home. About a week later, Gee showed up with a U-Haul truck and his friend, who had just been released from prison that we went to go see. He had no excuse or explanation. He started moving all his belongings out. I kept asking him, "What's wrong? What did I do?" He calmly responded, "It's just not going to work out between us. I have to leave." I asked him, "What about the baby?" He didn't even want to discuss it. I honestly believe that he didn't think I was pregnant with his child. He couldn't believe

I had gotten pregnant so quickly, especially considering that he couldn't impregnate his previous girlfriend.

At that moment, after he loaded all his stuff, he said, "I'm going to need that ring back I gave you." I said, "Are you serious?" He surely did; that bastard took back the ring he had put on my finger. It was reminiscent of my father who did the same thing to me during my 8th-grade graduation. I simply couldn't believe he would do such a hurtful thing to me.

Here I was again, 20 years old, with two children, pregnant, and alone. There was no way I could consider aborting my baby, especially after losing Lawrencia just a few months prior to this pregnancy.

I found myself right back where I started. Pregnant and miserable, going through the same cycle again. I was at a lost as to why Gee had just up and left me like that. I couldn't comprehend how he could walk away from our seemingly beautiful relationship. Nor did I know what I had done wrong. I had been faithful, devoted, taking care of the kids, cooking, cleaning, and always being there for him. I believed I was doing everything a woman should do in a relationship. I took care of my appearance, maintained an immaculate home filled with food, and ensured his clothes were washed and clean. Everything was in order and up to par. Though I wasn't currently employed or attending school, I was in the process of getting my life together to return to work and enroll in college. As I worked on improving myself, I consistently made sure that Gee had everything he needed from a partner. I prepared breakfast, lunch, dinner, and snacks, and I took care of his sexual, emotional, and psychological needs. I ensured he was satisfied on every level.

I simply couldn't comprehend why he abruptly left me. But life went on. I told myself, "Well, I'm going to have my baby, and I'll continue doing what I've always done—carrying the load on my own." Soon, I developed a strong craving for watermelon. I longed for it so intensely that I would sit and cry, knowing I didn't have the means to satisfy my craving. It's important to note that I was still relying on public aid at that time. I kept paging Gee, hoping he would bring me watermelon, money, or anything to alleviate my longing. One day, he called me back and said, "Look, I'm not coming back, and I won't be sending you any money or bringing you anything." I cried, asking him what I had done for him to abandon me like that. I pleaded with him, expressing how much I craved his presence and the opportunity to discuss the baby and our relationship.

He said, "Stop calling me. It's over. I won't be coming back. If you have the baby, I'll see about it then." There was no explanation, no closure. He simply hung up, and that was the end of it. I thought to myself, "Oh my God." I sat on the porch of my sister's house, consumed by misery once again. I later came to the realization of the street code called bros over hoes... That was why he walked away because I was related to the enemy of his best friend. And he could not go any further with me no matter how good of a woman I was or how much of a good thing we had together. He simply was proving his loyalty to his best friend.

To my surprise one day as I sat there in misery, I saw LAW walking down the street. He looked at me with remorse and asked, "He, did you, uh...?" I snapped at him, saying, "Get away from me right now!" I thought he was teasing me, ready to mock me for being with Gee, thinking I was living some kind of fairytale life.

He replied, "Calm down, I just want to talk to you. I want to make sure you're okay. I still love you, girl. You mean a lot to me, Angie." I asked him, "What do you want? What do you want to talk about?" So, we talked for hours. He proceeded to explain how the woman he had been involved with had gone back to her children's father. I asked him about his baby's mother, and he mentioned realizing that she was a parasite who lacked ambition. He expressed how much he still loved me and regretted his past mistakes. He admitted that he didn't fully grasp the depth of his feelings until he saw me and the kids with Gee. That's when he finally understood the magnitude of his actions. He believed I would never speak to him again. I told him, "If you truly love me, you'd buy me some watermelon." He gave me a perplexed look and asked, "Are you pregnant?" I replied, "Yes," and he stared at me in disbelief. I looked at him and said, "You know how fertile I am, but I never anticipated having another baby this soon.

He went to get the watermelon, and we sat on the porch talking all night. I told him I had to try to figure this out. I explained why I could not abort the baby. He said, "No worries, I've got you." I craved and ate watermelon throughout the entire pregnancy.

LAW took care of me; he made sure I had everything I wanted and needed while I was pregnant with Gee's child. He accompanied me to my doctor's appointments and picked up all my prescriptions from the pharmacy. He even rubbed my feet when they swelled and made sure I had all the food cravings satisfied. He was determined to show me that he genuinely wanted to be back with me. We continued talking and praying, hoping to work things out.

One day, he suddenly said, "Look, let's go and get married." I responded reluctantly, saying, "No, let me think about that. You know you haven't been good to me; you've put me through a lot." He replied, "Angie, I'm going to marry you."

He assured me, "I'm here for you. We're going to work things out and raise these kids together." I exclaimed, "But this isn't even your baby." He responded, "It doesn't matter. I'm going to treat your baby as if it were mine." He spoke convincingly.

When I was about five or six months into my pregnancy, I was sitting on the front porch when Gee's older sister, Tricey, pulled up. She greeted me and began talking about her own children and what she had been up to. I told her I was trying to get myself back together. She asked, "Is it my brother's baby?" I laughed and replied, "Yeah." She then asked, "Are you sure?" She went on to explain that her brother didn't believe it was his child because he thought he couldn't have children. He later found out that his ex-girlfriend had been on birth control all that time and hadn't told him because she wasn't ready to be a mother, while he wanted children. Tricey shared that his girlfriend's education meant more to her than anything else. She asked about LAW, and

I explained, "Yeah, we're friends now. He has really been looking out for me during my pregnancy. Your brother just straight up ignored me." I told her how he had abandoned me and ignored every request and plea I made.

Tricey asked, "Do you need anything now?" I replied, "Could you go buy me some watermelon?" She bought me one, and we sat down and talked. She started coming over more frequently, almost every other day. However, being young and naive, I didn't understand the true reason for her sudden presence in my life. At that point, I was unaware of her ulterior motives.

She said, "Well, I'm going to be a part of that baby's life, whether he is or not." Every day, she would come over, buy me clothes, bring snacks and restaurant food, and plenty of watermelon. I believed she was simply being a genuine friend and a great auntie. I thought she genuinely wanted to be there for the baby and had been sincere with me. One day, she asked me, "How much would you sell your baby for?" I was taken aback and replied, "What? Excuse me, are you joking?" She said, "No, seriously, if you were to put a price on it." I responded, "Girl, stop playing around!" She explained, "I just wanted to make sure you love your baby." I asked, "Why would you joke like that with me?" I was young and naive, and I honestly thought she was playing around.

On March 5th, I went into labor, and Tricey accompanied me to the hospital, staying by my side until I gave birth. As soon as she laid eyes on the baby, there was no doubt in her mind that this was her brother's child. With excitement, she called her brother, exclaiming, "You have a daughter! It's a girl, and she looks just like you!" Shortly after, he arrived at the hospital, bringing me a single yellow rose—a gesture I will always remember. He complimented my radiant appearance, noting the growth and beauty of my hair. He saw his baby and expressed his desire for her name to be "De-De" without the final "e." Although I questioned the spelling, he insisted on his choice and soon departed.

Upon leaving the hospital, I returned home, and he began visiting me every day. Both he and Tricey showered me with various gifts for the baby, and he apologized for initially doubting the paternity. He explained that he never thought he could father children. He expressed his wish to be actively involved in his daughter's life and see her regularly.

I agreed, assuring him that I would never interfere with his relationship with his child. Deep down, I held onto the hope that our own relationship would work out, as I had desired all along. Despite our differences in lifestyles, I cherished everything about him. He possessed qualities that reminded me of my father more than any other man I had been with. He had a sharp sense of style, prioritized financial stability, and believed in enjoying the finer things in life. These similarities made me believe that we were highly compatible.

However, at that time, I wasn't living up to my full potential, although I was aware of my capabilities and aspirations. I genuinely wanted our relationship to thrive, but he remained solely focused on his child. Meanwhile, LAW persistently pushed the idea of marriage, fearing that I might return to Gee. It seemed like he wanted to secure our relationship.

After LAW proposed to me again, I agreed to marry him. We decided on the Fourth of July, following the birth of De-De. I believed it was crucial for me to enter into marriage, as I was tired of repeating the same mistakes—having children with different men. I didn't want to be that person. My desire was to become a virtuous woman, someone who had all her children with one partner and lived happily ever after. I acknowledged the mess I had created with my past relationships and pregnancies. Dependent on welfare, I despised the state of my life and recognized that I was falling short of my potential. It was time for me to get my life together, and marrying LAW seemed like the right step to break the cycle.

So, on the Fourth of July, we exchanged vows. On our wedding day, Gee arrived to pick up De-De. As he entered and caught sight of my dress and bouquet in hand, his expression conveyed a mix of disgust and anguish. He was deeply hurt and angered by my decision to get married—not only had I married, but I had chosen LAW. He stood there, staring at me in complete disbelief. I handed him the baby and returned to my wedding. I vividly remember the way he walked away, consumed by frustration and resentment towards me.

I was dealing with a lot emotionally that day. I had invited everyone I knew, but none of my family was there to support me. My father didn't come to walk me down the aisle, my sister didn't come, and none of my aunts and uncles showed up. LAW and I didn't care; we decided to proceed with our vows anyway. I walked down the aisle to the song "I Miss You," which was dedicated to our daughter, Lawrencia, who had passed away. Surprisingly, I got pregnant on our wedding night. Yup, I got pregnant on our wedding night. LAW and I were confident that we could handle it together. He continued working every day and hustling on the side, fixing cars.

Meanwhile, I was at home taking care of the kids and trying to figure out my next steps. I was ready to pursue my career. Soon after, we had a little girl named London. I was fully invested in my marriage and the idea of us being a happy family. I was looking forward to getting our lives in order. Unfortunately, we soon found ourselves caught up in arguments and fights once again. LAW started cheating again with his daughter's mother. She had found out about our marriage and the birth of our baby, which made her extremely jealous. She made it difficult for LAW to see his daughter. This happened when our daughter London was just a little over seven months old, on Thanksgiving Eve. LAW surprised me by asking me to get dressed and leave the kids with my sister. He took me out on a date, fulfilling all the things I had been complaining about—whining and dining with me, and spending quality time together. He bought me everything I wanted, including chocolates, flowers, and a teddy bear.

We had dinner at a nice downtown restaurant, and it turned out to be the best time we had ever spent together. When we returned home, he had prepared a hot bubble bath for me, with soft music playing in the background. He gave me a relaxing body massage and we made passionate love. It was an experience like no other in my life. Afterward, I fell into a deep sleep, and when I woke up the next morning, he was gone. I wondered to myself, "Where is he?" It was Thanksgiving morning, and he had gone to my sister's house the previous night to get the children and put them to bed. I was so exhausted from all the fun and festivities that I didn't hear him leave or put the children to bed.

We had recently bought a brand-new van with the help of my godmother, Rev. Rosie Wilson. I asked the kids if they saw him leave, and they said he had kissed them goodbye and left. I tried paging him repeatedly but received no response. Days went by, and I grew increasingly worried. His family hadn't heard from him, and his workplace confirmed that he hadn't shown up for work on Monday. I was lost and didn't know what to think or do. I felt completely bewildered. Eventually, after about a year, I had to find a way to move forward with my life. That's when I started working odd jobs and riding with my sister, Tia, and her partner. We applied to a company that manufactured casings for hot dogs and sausages, which paid well and provided me with the flexibility to be at home with my children. I was working 12-hour overnight shifts 4 days a week on, 3 days off, so I could be at home with my children.

Despite earning good money, I was often exhausted from working long hours. I felt like I wasn't fully present for my children. I lacked the energy to cook for them, clean the house, or spend quality time with them. I would briefly see them, kiss them, and ask if they were okay before going straight to sleep. I would sleep until it was time to go back to work. Although I enjoyed the factory job, I knew I wanted to work in a more professional environment. I desired a more relaxed position and still wanted to pursue my college education.

I eventually landed an even better job at Merrill Lynch, a prestigious brokerage firm in downtown Chicago. It was a perfect fit for me, as I had always aspired to work for a reputable company with excellent benefits. I was working towards establishing a career for myself. At Merrill Lynch, I gained valuable skills in software systems such as Word, PowerPoint, Excel, and more. While working in an operations management role, I also had the opportunity to learn accounting practices, which sparked my interest.

However, my progress was limited due to my reliance on Section 8 housing assistance. I was hesitant to work too much overtime or strive for significant promotions because I wasn't financially stable enough to support myself independently. I lacked confidence in my ability to thrive in the competitive professional world, especially given that I only had a GED. I didn't want to jeopardize my Section 8 voucher or food stamps. Additionally, I needed the medical card because private medical insurance would consume a substantial portion of my paycheck.

The fathers of my children were not providing any child support. I attempted to pursue support from Dell's father, but they repeatedly claimed they couldn't locate him. Makeba's father had been ordered to pay me $25 a month, but he consistently refused to make payments. Occasionally, I would receive a check for $2 in the mail. Very rarely, he would send $20 or $25, but those instances were exceedingly rare. Most of the time, I received nothing from him. At that time, I was engaged in a custody battle with Gee regarding De-De. I tried explaining to the judge that I would be able to do much more if I received child support, but it was never ordered. I was still legally married to LAW, but I didn't know his whereabouts in order to file for a divorce. Child support services advised me that support would have to be included in the divorce decree for them to enforce it.

During this period, I was still struggling to provide for my children and make ends meet while trying to rebuild my life. My brother Buck would often visit my house seeking assistance with his social security application and handling mail correspondence.

I helped him with various tasks, ensuring that his paperwork was organized, and all the forms were properly filled out. To his surprise, he discovered that Social Security owed him benefits dating back to his childhood. Despite previous denials when my mother applied for benefits on his behalf, he eventually received

## Surprise!!! - Surprised???

a substantial settlement of over $200,000 for the years he was wrongfully denied, extending into his thirties. I advised him to be cautious and make wise decisions with his money, suggesting that he consider investing in a building. My suggestion was to rent out the first two floors to Section 8 recipients while occupying the basement unit himself. I also recommended seeking an affordable foreclosed property as an investment, providing him with a source of income and a place to reside once his funds depleted. He expressed his agreement with the idea.

He called my sister, my little brother, and me to meet him at Tia's apartment. We were all expecting a significant blessing. I will never forget that we waited all day for him to arrive. When he pulled up that evening in his brand new shiny black Oldsmobile, which he had foolishly financed, he mentioned something about getting his credit in order. I knew it was a joke because he was not financially responsible at that time. He was dressed impeccably in a new outfit, sneakers, and a full-length leather trench coat. We were all standing outside, eagerly anticipating our blessing from him. He handed me and my sister a white envelope, and our little brother received a $100 bill. The envelope he gave me was filled to the brim, and my sister looked in her envelope and said, "Buck, I know you're playing right?" He replied, "What?" He looked, and as I was opening my envelope, I discovered a stack of hundred-dollar bills. He quickly snatched it from me and switched the envelopes between my sister and me. He had given my sister Tia $5000 in cash and bought her a car. Meanwhile, he only gave me $200 in my envelope.

I could only stare at him in utter disbelief. I remember my sister trying to smooth things over and talking about how they were real brother and sister. I couldn't even express my hurt in words. I was so disappointed by my brother's actions towards me. I felt that after all the help I had given him, filling out paperwork and explaining the meaning of his mail from Social Security, I couldn't believe he only gave his little sister $200 out of the over $200,000 settlement that I had literally helped him obtain. He gave generous amounts of cash to both our aunts and spent a lot of money on our cousins and drugs. I took it with a grain of salt, and to this day, I have forgiven him. However, I have never forgotten what he did to me, especially considering that we both needed cars and I was in desperate need of financial assistance. It taught me a valuable lesson on how to treat people, especially when you have been blessed, and they have been a blessing to you.

After going through so much at that point in my life, I was content with living by myself. I started having many friends and family members come over to the house to spend time with me and keep me company. I remained single for quite a while. My best friend Brenda would often come over, and we would dance, sing, cook, and watch movies together. Life was just cool. I was in a place of contentment.

One day, when my cousin Myron got married, it had been a long time since I had gone out anywhere. I walked up to that wedding wearing a sharp all-white pantsuit, hazel contacts, a white brim hat, and extra-sharp white stiletto heels. I was as sharp as a tack! My bust was accentuated and alluring in my bustier. I confidently strutted into that wedding. The attributes of my well-dressed father were evident in me. I will never forget sitting there when my cousin made his entrance, walking down the aisle. Two best men escorted him, and one of them was incredibly handsome. I had never seen a man look that fine before in my life. Jokingly, he gave my cousin a playful push down the aisle, and everyone laughed. He had the most beautiful smile, a ponytail on top, and his sides and back were cleanly tapered. He was incredibly attractive, I must say!

As we all left the church and made our way to the reception, I noticed him stealing glances at me as I got into my car. He had a look of admiration on his face. Once we arrived at the reception hall, he continued to sneak glances at me, and I would shyly return them with a newfound sense of confidence. It's important to note that at this point, I hadn't been in a relationship for a couple of years. Going through the trauma of losing LAW without any knowledge of his whereabouts, whether he was alive or not, had led me to give up on relationships. I was focusing on healing myself from that painful experience. It was a confusing and hurtful place to be for someone who had no idea where their beloved husband had disappeared to.

As I sat at the reception table, a guy named Go, caught my eye. He was Puerto Rican and approached me while I was chatting with my cousins. He said, "Hey, how are you doing? Nice to meet you. I've never seen you before. What's your name?" I introduced myself as Angie and asked for his name. I told him how I noticed that he was my cousin Myron's best man. He seemed puzzled and asked, "Your cousin?" I confirmed that Myron was indeed my cousin, explaining that his father was my uncle, and my mother was his aunt, making us relatives. He mentioned how he and Myron had grown up together, being best friends and neighbors. He found it amusing that he thought he knew the entire family, only to discover me. We laughed as he jokingly remarked that they had saved the best for last. We continued to exchange pleasant looks and found it hard to look away.

Although it was difficult for me to remain composed, I couldn't let him see me flustered. We ended up having more conversations, and he invited me to the dance floor. And boy, did we have a blast! We danced with wild abandon, even performing some embarrassing moves. I told myself, "He's not going to outshine me on this dance floor."

I have no idea how we ended up in a 69-position dance, but we did. He was wild and acting like a fool, and I was out there, matching his energy and acting just as crazy. We had an incredible time. We all hung out that night at the reception and enjoyed ourselves. Eventually, I went home. As soon as he got home himself, he called me, and we talked on the phone all night. The next day, he called again, suggesting, "Come on, let me take you out for breakfast." I didn't have any other plans, and it felt good to have someone to spend time with. I was strongly attracted to him. He was simply the most attractive man I had ever met. There was an indescribable chemistry between us, and his presence took me to another level. He awakened something within me, and I found myself completely infatuated.

Over time, I discovered that he was a member of a fraternal organization as well as I was member of a sorority, so we had that in common. We frequently attended various social events and functions together. I felt that he was proud to have me by his side whenever we went out. He would come over, pick me and my kids up, take us for drives, and spend time with us.

He even took my eight-year-old son and me to the Monster Car Show at the Rosemont Horizon, which was incredibly exciting. This gesture touched me deeply because no man had ever done something like that for my son before. Davis had not shown any interest in being a part of my son's life, and the others hadn't paid much attention to him either. I believe it was because Dell had a lot of feminine energy and didn't fit into the typical mold of boys his age. He was more interested in things traditionally associated with girls.

As time went on, Go and I started spending more time together. He was living with his parents out west, working as a truck driver, while I was still employed at Merrill Lynch during this phase of my life. After work, we would often go out for meals and watch movies. I would usually cook dinner, but we also enjoyed dining out occasionally. He would visit me every day, and I cherished our time together. His presence never failed to make me laugh and smile. He had a genuinely joyful and positive spirit.

Even though we spent a lot of time together and he frequently stayed at my place, we never officially moved in together, which turned out to be a good thing. I was content with the arrangement because, despite not living together, we considered ourselves a couple. I believed we were taking our time to build something meaningful.

During this period, I was taking birth control pills as a precautionary measure to avoid another pregnancy. Go had recently become a father, and I had just gone through the turmoil of a failed marriage and the mystery surrounding my missing husband. Despite the challenges, we enjoyed our time together, regularly socialized with friends, and embraced the joy of each other's company. We were living life to the fullest. For more than a year, we went out together, talked every day, and he frequently spent the night at my place. Then, unexpectedly, he vanished without a trace.

It was devastating. I couldn't believe it was happening again. Weeks passed, and I hadn't heard a word from him. I was bewildered and hurt. We had spent an entire year together, seeing each other every day, and suddenly he disappeared. I couldn't comprehend what was going on. I tried reaching out to Go's parents, but they provided no information. I contacted my cousin to inquire about him, but he hadn't heard anything either. I was at a loss, unsure of whom else to turn to for answers.

During this time, some of my female cousins were frequently by my side. They witnessed my increasing stress and sadness as I struggled to comprehend Go's disappearance. I had already experienced this pain with LAW, and now it was happening again with Go. I was deeply affected by the trauma. I assumed that Go had returned to his son's mother since she had recently given birth to their child.

My cousins attempted to console me, telling me not to dwell on him and that it was his loss. But I couldn't help feeling like there was some curse upon me. I was unsure how to process my emotions. Every man I had been with had hurt me and left without what I considered a justifiable reason. After experiencing the departures of LAW and now Go, I was truly devastated. However, my cousin urged me to lift my spirits and move on. She insisted that I deserved so much more and that I deserved to be happy. She mentioned that her child's father would be coming over, accompanied by his brothers, and suggested we have a fun and relaxing time together. If Go was willing to walk away so easily, then I should let him go. I agreed, eager to clear my mind, laugh, and engage in conversation. I didn't want to fall into a state of depression because of this.

They arrived, and among them was Payton, my cousin's baby daddy's brother. I couldn't help but notice how attractive he was. He had a great physique and an athletic appeal. We all walked to the park together, and they indulged in drinking and smoking weed while I remained distant and disinterested. My mind was preoccupied with Go's sudden absence. Payton noticed my demeanor and asked if everything was alright. I replied that I had a lot on my mind. Surprisingly, he asked if the house we had been at earlier belonged to my mother. I chuckled and clarified that it was, in fact, my own house. Payton expressed his admiration, saying, "Wow, it's a nice place." I thanked him, to which he responded, "If that's your place, why did we come to the park?" I replied, "This is where you all wanted to go."

He said, "Let's go back to your place and hang out if you don't mind." I replied, "Of course, that's cool." We all went to the store, bought more drinks, and returned to my apartment. We spent the time laughing, joking, and talking. Later, as the late hours approached, I laid down on my bed. Payton knocked on my door, and we both sat on my bed, fully clothed, engaging in a friendly conversation.

Around 2:00 a.m., my doorbell rang, and my little brother knocked on my bedroom door. He whispered, "Sis, come here." I asked, "What's wrong?" He replied, "You won't believe who is at the door." I nervously responded, "Who?" He said, "Go!" I sighed and said, "Oh, Lord." I opened the door and stepped out onto the porch. I greeted him, saying, "Hey, what's up, stranger?" He asked, "What's up?" and reached in for a hug. I pushed him back and questioned, "Where have you been?" He replied, "I went to Puerto Rico with my dad." I asked, "You didn't think it was necessary to let me know?" I proceeded to express my frustration about not hearing from him for three weeks. He explained that he couldn't call because it was a long-distance call. Angrily, I said, "But you couldn't have given me a fair warning, heads up, or anything before you left?" He responded firmly, "Let me go inside and lie down; we can talk about it later. I just got off the flight, and I'm tired. I came straight to you as soon as we got back." I stopped him as he tried to enter the house and angrily told him, "No, you can't come in." He asked, "Why not?" I replied, "I'm busy, and we can talk later." He looked bewildered and sarcastically asked, "You're busy?" I sternly said, "Yes." He then said, "Come on, don't play games with me." He forcefully tried to push his way inside. I pushed him back and repeated that he couldn't come in.

I told him, "No, Go, you can't come in. You hurt me; you abandoned me out of nowhere. I thought you loved me, but I haven't heard from you, and you haven't been around for almost a month. I thought you had moved on." He asked, "So you're not going to let me in?" I responded, "No, I'm busy." He became angry, as if he wanted to force his way into the house, but he reconsidered, turned around, walked down the stairs, and headed towards his car, furious with me. As he opened the car door, I could see the anger and pain on his face. It was as if he suspected someone was inside the house, but he didn't know who, and he couldn't believe that I was there with someone else. We locked eyes, filled with hurt and heartbreak, as he got into his car and drove away.

# CHAPTER 13
# RIDICULOUS EXCUSES

*"Sometimes You Don't Need to Hear Their Excuses or What They Have to Say for Themselves…Because Their Actions Already Spoke the Truth."*
**(Unknown)**

I paid no more attention to it, and suddenly, a couple of days later, my phone started ringing incessantly. I wondered, "Who's constantly calling me?" It was my cousin Myron, another one of my uncle Bubba's sons, yelling in the same aggressive voice his father Bubba used to have. I answered, "Hello," and he said, "What the hell you got going on?" I responded, "What are you talking about? What's wrong? What's going on?" He said, "Man, you got my boy Go caught up in some bullshit over here!!! They are about to get into it! They are over here in the park arguing and pulling guns out on each other and Go has his kids in the car with him!!!" I asked, "Who is pulling guns out on each other?" I didn't know what or who he was talking about—no more than the man on the moon! I asked him again as he was screaming and yelling at me, "Myron, what in the hell are you talking about?" Myron calmed down enough to explain the situation to me. It all started when Payton saw Go at the park near their house out west and confronted him. He walked up to Go and said, "Don't come over to my girl's house anymore. That's over. She's mine now. Don't let me catch you back over there." Go angrily responded, "Dude, what the fuck are you talking about? Who's your girl?" Payton

## Ridiculous Excuses

answered, "Angie. Don't come to her house anymore; she is mine now. I saw you when you came over to her place the other night. Don't let me catch you at her house again!" They had gotten into a huge argument. Go couldn't fight the dude because his small children were in the car. But somehow, it got so bad that guns were drawn, and my cousin was called. Payton called his brothers. It got really serious. They were threatening to kill each other and everything.

It all made sense to me now; I recalled that night when Go returned from Puerto Rico. Unknown to me that night, as I was standing out on the porch trying to stop Go from coming into the house, Payton got up and looked out the window to check on me to ensure I was okay. He saw I was out there talking to Go. He didn't come out then but did mention it to me when I returned to the room. He asked, "Oh, so you know Go? That's the guy you are hanging out with." I replied, "Yeah, how do you know him?" He told me they grew up around each other. I said, "Small world." Payton remembered Go from around the way! They grew up in the same community and went to school together.

I explained that we were cool, but he hadn't been around lately, and life went on. It is what it is. We finished talking that night, and I didn't think twice about it. We ended up falling asleep, and he and his brother left the next morning. We didn't sleep together or anything that night. We just talked ourselves to sleep. I woke up lying on his chest, but that was more for comfort than romance.

A couple of weeks later, I went to the doctor for a regular checkup. The doctor informed me that I was pregnant. Yes, I was pregnant with Go's child. I couldn't believe it because I was taking my birth control pills on time every day. When I got home, I called to tell him. He sternly said, "What the fuck are you calling me for? Who's the father? You better go find that nigga." I responded, "Come on. Quit playing with me. You know darn well that this is your baby." Go told me to go to hell. He felt I wasn't pregnant by him, and he would not talk to me anymore. He honestly thought I had slept with Payton. Even though I didn't, he thought I did, and I honestly couldn't blame him. But he also knew I had been with him every day since we had met until he unexpectedly left to accompany his dad to Puerto Rico. He knew he was the only man I had slept with since LAW went missing.

I was 25 years old and pregnant with my 6th child, still dependent on low-income programming to help support my children with housing, food, utilities, childcare, and medical care. I was married but single because I still didn't know what happened to LAW; he'd been gone for over 3 years. I was employed throughout my pregnancy. I wanted to become self-sufficient, but it was going to take far more than the money I was making for me to take care of all of us alone. I didn't have a real support system. My family was using me a lot at this point in my life. My aunt Tee-Tee & my sister Tia would borrow money from me but wouldn't pay me back. My brothers Buck & Slick would get into trouble with the local drug dealers, and I would have to pay the drug dealers off to stop them from hurting or killing my brothers. My father would stop by and take a lot of my food out of the freezer and pantry and take it to his house to feed his family. I was helping and supporting just about everyone in some shape, form, or fashion. I would do just about anything for my father, sister, brothers, and my aunt, Tee-Tee; they were all I really had to hold on to for me to call family. I allowed them to use me just so I wouldn't lose them. That was all I felt I had. I truly feel like they totally took advantage of my being young and kindhearted, my vulnerability, and my instability.

Go would not acknowledge me throughout the entire pregnancy. I constantly kept calling him. I simply could not bring myself to get an abortion, considering what I had gone through before. I said, "Come on, Go, you know this is your baby," and he just didn't want anything else to do with me after that incident with Payton. He wouldn't talk to me. He wouldn't come around me anymore.

I thought to myself, "Okay, so I'll just take care of myself through the pregnancy." I was not going to abort my child. I went on about my business. Soon, my baby boy, DJ, was born on April

23rd. I called Go and told him our son was here. He wouldn't acknowledge him. He wouldn't come to the hospital. I went on about my life. I was taking care of myself and my children the best I could.

One day, we got the call that my uncle Bubba had passed away, and we were all at the funeral. My entire family, Go and his family, were there as well. By this time, our son was about 2 years old, and he was running all around the church. As DJ was running around playing, everyone talked about how cute he was and how much he looked like his dad. Go played it off. It was inevitable that our son was going to run into him. He wouldn't look at or acknowledge our baby.

Go's parents, sister, nieces, nephews, and his entire family were there. My friends and family were there. And he would not even look at our son—this precious, sweet, innocent, 2-year-old handsome little boy. His father's ego would not allow him to look at him. I was so damn embarrassed. I just kept looking at him with a disappointed look, thinking, "You cannot be serious right now, dude." People were whispering and gossiping. It literally made me sick to my stomach. I became so full of anger and rage against him. I was so ashamed that I just wanted to go somewhere and hide. I could not believe he would treat me and my son like that in public.

There was absolutely no way I was going to sit there and allow him to keep doing this to me and our son. The very next day, I called him and told him, "Look, Go, we're going to have to figure this out because this is getting beyond ridiculous. I know you don't wish to claim our son. But you mean to tell me you won't even look at him? What you are not going to do is treat me as if I were a prostitute. Whatever happened between us happened; we are going to have to get over it. I'm fine with going on with our lives separately as we have been. But at the end of the day, this is still your son. Now, I have been more than patient with you, allowing you time to get over it and come to see him. But if you simply refuse to respect us, continue to not acknowledge him, or even look at him for that much, what the hell else am I to do? I cannot continue to allow you to put me in these embarrassing situations. Look, I can't avoid my family. My son has to grow up around them. And you know this isn't right of you to continuously come around and ignore us like we ain't shit. If you don't come over and start acknowledging your son, you leave me no other alternative than to have to take you to child support and get a DNA test done so you can stop it with the BS. I'm going to have to let them deal with it from there."

He said, "Well, do what you've got to do then." I angrily replied, "Oh, really? Okay" and I definitely did just that. I marched my way down to that child support office and filed those papers against him the very next day! They ordered us to come to court for child support. Go ordered a DNA test. A few weeks later, Go called me, saying, "I just got the results showing he is definitely mine. Is there any way we can meet up so I can get to see and know him?" I responded, "That's fine." We ended up meeting at one of the little kiddie's amusement parks, and we had pizza and played games. He got to know a little about his son. He found out little things about him and asked, "When can I come to get him and take him to meet my family?" I had absolutely no problem with that.

We ended up resolving our conflict. I apologized to him for what Payton had done and explained that I honestly was not in a relationship with Payton. And I hadn't a clue as to why he did that. I did explain that Payton thought we were going to be something, but we weren't, and I told him Payton was at the house the night he came, but we were not doing anything. I explained that my cousin had a baby with his brother, and his brother brought him over to meet me. I didn't want Go to think anything funny, so I didn't let him in. I told him that Payton and I had been talking all that evening, and I did not know they knew each other or that Payton would have done such a foul thing as to confront him so baselessly like that.

But I wouldn't lift that child support order off of him. I surely wasn't. And so, we went on from there. He decided to be a dad and come pick him up and spend time with his son whenever he wanted to. I never stopped him from seeing his son or being a part of his life. I didn't mind any of the children's fathers being actively involved in their lives. Dell's father came around once when Dell was around 10 years old or so, and we all went out to dinner; it was Davis, Dell, me, my aunt, sister, and cousins. Davis paid for his and my cousin's plates but did not pay for Dell. Makeba's father and his family would pick her up a lot, and she would spend lots of time with them in the summers and on weekends with her granny on her father's side. De-De's father had run off with her, and I didn't know where he was. And, of course, LAW had walked out of London's life.

One day, there was a knock on my door around 8:00 p.m.; it was LAW. I couldn't believe that was LAW! He had come to inform me that his stepfather had passed, and he was in town for the funeral. He'd come to see if he could see London and take her to the funeral to see his mom and family. I was confused and shocked. I yelled, "What the fuck, dude? Are you serious?" She was almost 4 years old at this time. I asked, "Where in the world have you been?" He said, "I moved to Missouri." I said, "Missouri?" He said, "I went down there because my daughter's mother had gotten Section 8, and she was taking my daughter from me. I couldn't tell you I was leaving because I knew it would've hurt you. I chose to go down there because I knew my daughter needed me. I knew you could hold your own and care for yourself and London." I said, "So you just took it upon yourself to walk out on your wife to be with your daughters' mother, and you just up and abandoned me unexpectedly? No warning, no reason, no help for our newborn baby! Do you realize your daughter was only 6 months old when you walked out? You didn't send me a penny for her all these years!" I was so angry and hurt. I couldn't believe the excuse he gave me for walking out on me. "To say you knew I was strong enough to hold my own and you knew she needed you is sorry as fuck!" I stood there in total disbelief. That did not register with me in any way.

# CHAPTER 14
# IT'S TIME TO TAKE CONTROL OF MY LIFE

*"I Am Taking Control of My Life and Demanding Better...I Am No Longer Controlled By Those Who Tried to Hurt Me."*
**(Shaneel Lai)**

I was essentially still juggling work every day, raising my children, and looking after them. At this point, I attempted to return to school. At Merrill Lynch, my interest in accounting spurred me to pursue a bachelor's degree in the field. I enrolled at Robert Morris University in Downtown Chicago. I was thrilled; finally, I had the chance to attend college. I was confident that I was on my way to success. On my first day of classes, I felt like a child eagerly packing their school bag with supplies and choosing their outfits. You couldn't tell me anything! College represented a return to the joy of learning and reading. I was excited to sit in the front row, ready to participate in class discussions. I was rehearsing my introduction, thoroughly pumped! The fear of student loan debt no longer bothered me; I was willing to make this sacrifice to improve my education and provide a better life for myself and my children. I yearned for more from life than what I was currently experiencing. I wasn't content; I felt an urge to excel, to reach greater heights, and to build a fulfilling career.

All my children were still young at this time. I believe Dell was around 11 years old, the eldest among them. They were all quite young. Returning to school turned out to be more challenging than I had anticipated. Every five minutes, it seemed someone was calling me, reporting, "You need to come home and tend to your kids. Makeba fell and injured her head; Dell fell off his bike and hurt his arm, possibly even broke it; London has a fever; DJ is sick and vomiting." There was always something with the children that required my attention. Thankfully, I managed to obtain my associate degree despite these challenges. I got a taste of higher education, and it was exhilarating. I continued to work towards my bachelor's degree, but the pressure from my kids became overwhelming, leading me to drop out. It was a heartbreaking decision, but I promised myself that once my children were older and more independent, I would return to school. It was always on my mind. I kept telling myself, "I know I'm capable of completing college." Getting my bachelor's degree was a deeply personal goal, one I was determined and destined to achieve.

For some time, I remained alone. I focused on my job, absorbing as much knowledge as I could, then I went home to cook, clean, launder, and care for my children. I helped them with their homework, combed their hair, and spent time teaching them about God. While I couldn't take them to church every Sunday, I ensured we tuned in to church programs on television, singing and worshiping from home. I imparted lessons on prayer and reliance on God. I found myself instilling strength and independence in my children, teaching them to make wise decisions, lest they find themselves lost or stranded in this world without guidance.

On Mother's Day, my sister Tia called, urging me to step out of the house for a change. "We're going out for dinner and drinks to celebrate Mother's Day; we deserve it," she said. So, we dined out and then headed to Sexty Sex, a club on 66th and Western in Chicago, for cocktails. As I sat at the bar, laughing, and chatting with my sister, I felt someone's gaze fixed on me. He sent over a drink, and I thanked him. He nodded shyly. When I returned from the restroom, he was on the dance floor, grooving to some house music. I could see he was a talented dancer. He gestured for me to join him, and we danced a bit. I observed him; he observed me. "He's quite the dancer," I thought to myself. Indeed, he had some moves. His name was Dane; he was 42 years old, while I was 26 at the time. He had a brown complexion, a bald head, and stood about 5'6" tall – notably shorter than my 5'9½" height. He was quite amusing, cracking jokes. We hit it off, enjoying each other's company. It was refreshing to laugh and converse with someone new. Eventually, we exchanged numbers. Interestingly, the bartender that night happened to be one of his childhood friends. My sister knew the bartender, and we all laughed and chatted. Shots were poured, toasts were made. It felt good to socialize a bit, considering I had been alone, focused on work, and raising the kids.

He called me that night, and we began talking. He asked if he could take me out on a date. I explained that my schedule was tight due to work and managing a small business. He agreed to come over. I had a little candy shack where I sold snowballs, chips, nachos, and candy. It was initially owned by my godmother, Rev. Rosie Wilson, who passed away. She had a home on 72nd and Claremont, with a vacant lot next to it. She had a small candy shack built on it, along with a playground for local children. After her passing, my friend Diane and I decided that I would move into her home and rent it on my Section 8. I reopened the candy shack to help with expenses, as owning a house incurred greater bills compared to renting apartments. This marked my first venture into entrepreneurship. I obtained a business license and insurance, naming it Rosie's Candy Shack. I felt proud and excited to have something of my own and looked forward to its growth.

Initially, things went smoothly. However, Diane started increasing the rent as she saw the candy shack prosper. She demanded payment for using the shack, despite my modest profits. The disagreements escalated, and tensions rose as she became overly controlling and demanding. Unable to afford the additional expenses, I decided staying there was becoming untenable. Consequently, I had to close the candy shack and move out.

Around this time, Dane began visiting frequently. He worked as a local truck driver for FedEx and offered to help with rent and bills. This assistance was crucial as I had lost my job at Merrill Lynch due to downsizing. While disheartened by the loss, I was grateful to maintain my Section 8 and welfare benefits, which provided a roof over our heads and food on the table. These benefits proved invaluable during this challenging period. Reflecting on the situation, I realized the importance of pursuing higher education to improve my circumstances. I understood that having only an associate degree wouldn't suffice for financial stability in the long run.

At this juncture, I found myself in a financial bind with renting the house and the Candy Shack from Diane. Dane and I discussed it, and he moved in to assist me. He worked diligently, contributing to all the bills, and even giving me some extra money for personal grooming. Meanwhile, I relied on the Depo-Provera shot for birth control, despite experiencing weight gain and hair loss as side effects.

While Dane was supportive and great with the kids, his frequent outings to nightclubs became a point of contention. Despite our affection for each other, his recurrent clubbing habits strained our relationship. I confronted him, expressing my frustration at his excessive socializing. I said, "Look, you cannot keep running these streets every weekend. This is getting ridiculous. You are going out way too much to be in a relationship." His response, "Well, that's where you met me, in a club, so what would make you think that just because we're together, I would stop doing what I enjoy?" That only fueled my exasperation.

Gradually, Dane's behavior escalated to infidelity, causing further strain. With his much-needed financial support, I felt caught in a losing situation.

With him being older, Dane's infidelity left me feeling disheartened. Despite our plans for marriage, his repeated cheating, including an affair with an older woman that lived in the projects, led to intense arguments and his eventual departure.

Heartbroken, yet hopeful, I invited him to my birthday party, expecting his presence despite his infidelities. Disappointed by his absence, I drowned my sorrows in alcohol. Eventually, seeking comfort, I left the party with a male friend, craving emotional support amidst the turmoil.

He was one of the guys from around 69th Street, where LAW and I used to live together. We'd known each other for years. His name was Milk, we called him Milk because he drank milk all the time. We were talking about how he got into ministry. He had been hit by a Metra train and received a huge settlement, which he said changed his life. He mentioned that he was married but separated from his wife, who preferred the streets and left with half of his settlement along with their kids.

I found myself at his place, pouring my heart out about Dane and the struggles I was facing. Before I knew it, we ended up kissing, and things escalated quickly. He expressed his desire for me over the years, and in the heat of the moment, we engaged in passionate intercourse. While it was enjoyable, it didn't fulfill me because deep down, I still longed for my relationship with Dane to work.

The next day, Dane unexpectedly showed up at my door. We talked, and he pulled me into the bedroom, where we made love. I couldn't resist him; I missed him terribly and was deeply in love. Regardless to my previous encounter with Milk, I was determined to make things work with Dane, despite his infidelity.

A few weeks later, to my surprise, I discovered I was pregnant again. I felt overwhelmed, realizing it would be my seventh child. At 27, unemployed with an associate degree, relying on Section 8 housing, food stamps, and medical assistance, I knew something had to change. All I could say to myself was, "Angie, this must stop!" But there was absolutely no way I could abort my baby.

I was just stuck. I seriously thought that by being on the Depo shot, I was good and well-protected. I just had to figure this out. I couldn't bring myself to abort the baby; like all my other children, I loved and wanted this child. I also knew I needed to confront the reality of my situation.

When Milk came by to check on me, I excitedly shared the news of my pregnancy, convinced it was Dane's child. He sat on the couch, looking at me, and asked, "Is that my baby you're pregnant with?" I said, "Nah, this is Dane baby; I'm sure of it." However, Milk's questioning gaze made me pause, and we discussed his efforts to reconcile with his wife and raise their children, she wanted him to move down to Georgia. That was the last time I saw him.

I went to Dane to share the news of the pregnancy. While he initially promised to be there for the baby, our relationship deteriorated over time. He distanced himself, refusing to sign the birth certificate or come to the hospital when our daughter, Day, was born. I put him on child support, and despite his financial contribution, he demanded a DNA test, which ultimately revealed he wasn't the father. Devastated, I was left grappling with the truth and uncertain about the paternity of my child. I thought to myself "Oh my God, no, there's no way this could be Milk's baby." I was so messed up over this. I didn't know what to do.

He was deeply hurt because, before we underwent the DNA test, he had returned and was providing support for her. She fell ill as a newborn with viral meningitis, and he stood by us throughout her hospitalization, spending every day and night with us until she was discharged. We even discussed the possibility of marriage again.

He had begun showing immense love towards her and me. I was devastated when we learned she wasn't his daughter. I had to come to terms with the situation and continue with life. I realized I had to take full responsibility for this baby on my own. I felt guilty because I genuinely believed she was his. I was deeply in love with him and couldn't believe I had conceived a child with Milk. To this day, I still doubt that she is his daughter, but I haven't been able to find him to inform him of the possibility. So, I bore the burden alone with her.

I made a firm decision to put an end to this cycle of having children. It had spiraled out of control and become unsustainable. I approached my OBGYN, Dr. Alston, who had delivered all my children; I jokingly told him that if he didn't tie my tubes, I was going to take him to child support. We shared a laugh and signed the necessary paperwork, scheduling the procedure at the earliest convenience. On the day of the surgery, I woke up at 5:00 a.m., caught the bus to the hospital, and underwent the tubal ligation. I was too sore to take the bus back, and the hospital required that I have someone pick me up due to the anesthesia. I called my aunt Tee-Tee, who sent my uncle Lamar to fetch me. Getting my tubes tied felt like a significant step towards taking control of my life.

# CHAPTER 15
# WHAT HAPPENS IN VEGAS, STAYS IN VEGAS

*"Lack of Love Often Motivates Their Children to Go Searching for Love in Other Relationships. This Search Is Often Misguided and Leads to Further Disappointment."*
**(Gary Chapman)**

Reflecting on my circumstances, I pondered my next move. My father and his wife, Roxanne, had relocated to Las Vegas, NV, enjoying newfound financial stability after my father became a 100% service-connected disabled veteran. They had invited everyone to visit except me and my children. Feeling a sense of exclusion, I decided to show my father that I was deserving of an initiation by moving to Las Vegas with my kids. Ike, a friend from the old neighborhood, expressed interest in joining me.

I found a house in Las Vegas using my Section 8 certificate and thought, "This is it." I packed up our belongings and embarked on a new chapter in Las Vegas. Initially, things went well. The kids were involved in various activities, attending excellent schools, Girl Scouts, and Boy Scouts. I was employed, and life seemed promising. However, one day, two Mormon missionaries knocked on my door, and my encounters with them led me to join the Church of Jesus Christ of Latter-day Saints. I embraced the idea of having my children baptized, believing it was essential for their spiritual well-being and upbringing in the church.

The church provided significant support to help me stabilize and settle into my new home, but I refrained from sharing details about Ike because I didn't want them meddling in my personal affairs or passing judgment. Unfortunately, Ike's behavior took a troubling turn when I discovered he had a severe alcohol addiction. Our arguments escalated, and he would often come home intoxicated and aggressive. I vividly recall one incident where, as I was getting out of the shower, he entered the house drunk, and we engaged in a physical altercation. He caused injuries, including kicking my bottom teeth through my lip and forcibly ejecting me from the house while I was unclothed. Alone in the bushes, I wept and prayed for deliverance from this situation, questioning how I had become entangled in such abuse. When he allowed me back inside, he issued menacing threats, instilling profound fear within me. He said, "Bitch, I will kill you and your kids, and no one will ever know I did it."

I became very afraid of him. Despite my attempts to maintain focus on work and church, I recognized the danger I faced and couldn't jeopardize my safety and that of my children. Desperate, I reached out to contacts in Chicago, pleading for assistance from Go, Dane, or anyone who could help us relocate.

Gradually, I became disillusioned with the church's teachings, finding their beliefs and practices unsettling. Their doctrines, including exclusionary criteria for salvation and rituals performed in the temple, seemed cult-like to me. I sensed an urgent need to extricate myself and my children from this environment. Moreover, the wealthy man I worked for, a fellow Mormon, seemed to harbor intentions of polygamous marriage, adding to my discomfort. Determined to escape, I resolved to abandon everything in Vegas and return to Chicago. Packing my belongings into my car, I embarked on the journey back home, leaving behind all my possessions.

En route to Chicago, I confided in my sister about the threats and abuse I endured from Ike, seeking refuge until I could secure housing through Section 8. She graciously welcomed us into her spacious four-bedroom house with a basement. Shortly after our arrival, Ike followed me back to Chicago. One evening, he arrived at my sister's home and demanded access to my car despite his inebriated state. Refusing his requests, I faced his violent outburst as he physically assaulted me. As he was beating on me, my sister intervened; she came down with her gun and cocked it. She told him that if he didn't get the fuck off me, she was going to blow his brains out. He got up slowly, said he was sorry, and left. That marked the last time I encountered him, bringing closure to that tumultuous chapter in my life.

That was a pivotal moment in my life when my sister stood up for me, and I felt immensely grateful. I promptly began searching for both a place to live and employment while awaiting the transfer of my Section 8 papers back to Chicago. Eventually, I secured a four-bedroom house in Richton Park for myself and the children. However, despite having a roof over our heads, I couldn't shake off the feeling of fear and insecurity. The specter of Ike's potential return loomed large, haunting me with the dread of possible harm to us. Thus, I found myself grappling with the aftermath of an abusive relationship, hesitant to embark on any new romantic endeavors.

During this period of solitude, I conversed with the gas man who came to hook up the gas in my new home. Our conversation delved into life's complexities, and I expressed my disillusionment with relationships, resigning myself to a solitary existence. His response, "For you to say there are no good men out here is like saying there's no Creator." That struck a chord with me. As a believer in God, I recognized the truth in his words and resolved to abandon my pessimistic outlook on love.

With my focus primarily on caring for the children and seeking employment, I encountered significant challenges in securing a job, compounded by the aftermath of the 9/11 tragedy, which had plunged the world into crisis and stymied employment opportunities for many. Thankfully, I received unemployment benefits after leaving my job at the mortgage company in Las Vegas.

# CHAPTER 16
# NEW LOVE, NEW LIES & NEW GROWING PAINS

*"If You Ignore the Red Flags, Embrace the Heartache to Come."*
*(Amanda Mosher)*

Subsequently, at the urging of my children, Makeba and Dell, I explored the concept of the party line—a platform to connect with others for amusement and laughter. Intrigued and partly motivated by curiosity about my children's activities, I reluctantly decided to give it a try. Little did I know that this decision would introduce me to DC, with whom I struck up a conversation. To my surprise, I discovered a familial connection; DC's uncle was a close friend of my sister's husband, Miguel, whom I had known for years. This familiarity put me at ease, despite our initial interaction being solely over the phone.

DC shared details of his life, portraying himself as a successful physical therapist at Northwestern Hospital, a homeowner with a Range Rover, and a former football player with promising prospects until injuries intervened. His extensive knowledge of physical therapy jargon and his apparent success lent credence to his narrative, and I found myself believing his every word. Our conversations became a regular occurrence, providing me with companionship without the complexities of a committed relationship. The way he presented himself as a physical therapist portrayed a man with promising prospects, and I felt I had finally encountered someone worth pursuing. Given my low self-esteem, particularly after enduring a tumultuous relationship with an alcoholic, I viewed this as an opportunity to connect with someone decent. Throughout my life, I had grappled with the challenge of sustaining relationships, leaving me with diminished self-worth and confidence.

I questioned whether anyone of value would desire a connection with me, burdened as I was with multiple children. I felt akin to the old woman who lived in a shoe, overwhelmed by the responsibility of caring for so many offspring. With six children from six different fathers, I carried a heavy emotional load; making my options for finding a suitable partner seem limited.

Despite my reservations, I decided to explore the possibility of a relationship with him. We engaged in extended phone conversations, during which I endeavored to ensure he appreciated me for my intellect rather than my physical attributes. Proceeding cautiously, I sought to establish a deeper connection based on mutual understanding.

Although I had not actively sought companionship, I found solace in our conversations. He differed from previous partners in his meticulous grooming and adherence to propriety—a reflection of his upbringing in a prestigious family with stringent behavioral expectations. This aspect was appealing to me, particularly as I navigated the challenges of parenting adolescents. Recognizing the need to provide a stable environment for my children, I was determined to break free from the cycle of tumultuous relationships, mindful of the dangers posed by individuals like Ike who threatened to kill us again.

When discussing red flags and warning signs, it is crucial to pay attention to unusual indicators. I will never forget the night when DC and I had planned our first date. Our intention was to go downtown to Navy Pier, have dinner, and enjoy live music at a jazz bar he knew. However, there were some concerning signs that emerged.

On that evening, DC informed me that his truck was currently out of commission and asked if I could pick him up. Despite being located far away in Richton Park, I agreed to drive to the Southside of Chicago to get him. Unfortunately, I was significantly late due to going shopping with my sister and getting our hair and nails done. By the time I arrived at his house, it was already 10:30 p.m., making it too late to go out.

I apologized for my tardiness upon arrival, and DC invited me inside. He explained that he had given the rest of his house to his mother and sister, as he rarely stayed there due to his demanding work schedule. He simply wanted his mother to be happy and comfortable. We went to his basement area, where we engaged in conversation, enjoyed music, and watched a television show. It was around midnight when he excused himself, went upstairs, and returned with a glass of ice water. Strangely, he didn't ask if I was thirsty or if I wanted anything. Although I felt thirsty, I chose to ignore it and pretended to be shy.

Despite the enjoyable conversation, music, and laughter, this incident served as the first warning sign. I reassured myself not to overreact, thinking that perhaps he had forgotten to offer me a drink or that he might have been nervous as well. We ended up talking throughout the night, unintentionally falling asleep. Early in the morning, I abruptly woke up and informed DC that I needed to leave and pick up my children. He then asked if I could take him to a nearby McDonald's before I left. Although I was in a rush, I agreed, thinking about the urgency of getting back to my kids. At McDonald's, he selfishly ordered breakfast for himself and an orange juice without even considering if I wanted a cup of coffee or anything else. I sat in the driver's seat, feeling incredulous about his behavior. However, I chose not to confront him and remained silent. He paid for his meal, and I dropped him off at his house before speeding away.

As I drove home, I couldn't help but think, "He seems okay, but he clearly has some issues." I decided not to call him, feeling that his selfish behavior was a major turnoff. About a week later, he unexpectedly called me, questioning why I hadn't reached out to him after our last encounter. He asked if I didn't like him. In response, I asked why he hadn't called me, and he claimed to have lost my number while doing laundry. I found his excuse dubious. I candidly expressed my dissatisfaction with how he had treated me—specifically, not offering me a drink during our conversation in the basement and failing to ask if I wanted anything when we went to McDonald's. I made it clear that I was not interested in a man who behaved that way and that it was a complete turnoff.

In response, DC immediately began apologizing, admitting that he hadn't been thinking. He assured me that if I had expressed my desires, he would have gladly fulfilled them. However, I emphasized that offering refreshments should have been a matter of common courtesy, and I shouldn't have had to ask. I firmly communicated that his behavior was entirely unacceptable. He then asked if we could give it another try and promised to make it up to me. He sounded genuinely remorseful and apologetic.

We decided to see each other again and started going on dates while discussing our issues. We engaged in long, stimulating conversations, as DC proved to be highly intelligent and knowledgeable about various subjects. One night, during one of our dates, things became intimate. It had been a while since I had been with anyone, and I was in the mood. DC passionately kissed me and performed oral sex on me like no one ever had before. It was an experience different than what I had ever encountered. Although he may not have been well-endowed, he more than compensated with his cunnilingus skills and made sure to please me in every way possible.

Despite enjoying our physical relationship, I exercised extreme caution and refrained from introducing him to my children. I didn't want to repeatedly introduce different men into their lives, only to have those relationships not work out. It took several months before I felt comfortable enough to let him meet my children.

One night, he came over and spent the night with me. He had to get to work early the next morning, so I suggested that he could drive my car and bring it back when he finished his shift. He had been telling me that his Range Rover was being repaired and taking longer than expected. On Valentine's Day, I called to inquire about the progress, and his mother informed me that he wasn't there but had left my keys at her house. She said I could come and retrieve my car. I was surprised and asked why he would do that. She seemed curious about our relationship and mentioned seeing me pick him up on several occasions. I explained that he had been coming to my place because we didn't want to disturb her, and I would drop him off at home before he went to work at the hospital every morning. She seemed taken aback and asked about his job. I told her he had told me he was a physical therapist, which she vehemently refuted. She revealed that he was actually a manager at a store called Work and Gear, and his responsibilities included taking care of his paraplegic uncle, whom he would take to Northwestern Hospital for therapy every other day.

This revelation explained the phone calls from the hospital and his knowledge of physical therapy, paralysis, and sports medicine. She went on to tell me that DC's uncle had become paralyzed because of an incident when DC was a teenager. His mother had sent him to live with his uncle in Alabama, where he faced harassment from gang members. His uncle intervened on his behalf, which led to a confrontation and his uncle being shot in the back. DC carried immense guilt and regret for what had happened.

As I listened to her, I was in shock, wondering why he would fabricate such a complex web of lies. It became clear that his mother was also involved in the deception. She told me that he was trying to impress me and that the broken-down Range Rover parked outside her house actually belonged to the tow truck driver next door. I expressed my confusion and disappointment, unable to understand why he would lie like that.

Later that afternoon, I went to retrieve my car. DC called me and offered explanations, claiming that he didn't want me to think less of him and that he felt the need to present himself as someone successful. He professed his love for me and expressed his fear of losing me. Despite the lies, we continued to see each other and grow closer. He was working and financially supporting me, taking care of the bills, and contributing to the household. He also took on tasks traditionally associated with masculinity around the house. However, I recognized that I couldn't continue living together without being married, especially with my children witnessing the situation. I confronted him about this, and his response was straightforward: "Well, let's get married."

I agreed, and two years after we first met, we had a small and intimate backyard wedding with close family and friends. I reached out to my father to attend, but once again, he didn't show up. I was hurt by his neglect, but unfortunately, it wasn't a new experience for me. Shortly after our wedding, DC lost his job, and he started receiving unemployment benefits. Although he assured me that he was actively looking for work, he spent most of his days at home, collecting unemployment and not making much effort to find new employment. At that point, it didn't raise any red flags for me since he was still contributing financially to our household.

After a year into our marriage, he was still unemployed, so I never saw a lack of assistance from him. However, I started noticing that he was spending all day sitting in the house. We ended up moving to Romeoville, IL, which was far out in the western suburbs. We settled into a newly built, spacious house with five bedrooms, two baths, a master suite, on a large piece of land. I was ecstatic; it was the best house I had ever lived in. Despite being on Section 8 and welfare, I found job opportunities readily available in that area. I was quickly hired at Nicor Gas Services, and remained there until we were laid off. Having him at home on unemployment and the kids entering their teenage years turned out to be beneficial because it helped keep the kids out of trouble. While I was able to go to work, build a career, and support our family, I was also focused on self-improvement. Eventually, I landed a job at BP US Headquarters, which made me incredibly happy. However, I knew that accepting this position would mean earning too much money and losing my low-income assistance.

Despite the potential consequences, I saw this job as an opportunity to finally get my life together. It paid a significant amount at the time, nearly $60,000 per year, with excellent benefits. It was the highest-paying job I had ever obtained at that point in my life. I realized that if I accepted this position, I would no longer be able to rely on Section 8 assistance and welfare benefits. I wanted to become a homeowner and provide a stable life for my children.

So, I took a leap of faith and accepted the job at BP US Headquarters. It was terrifying for me, but I kept asking myself, "If not now, then when? When will I challenge myself to a better way of life?" I had to make a move and commit to this job to have something substantial for myself. I was tired of not living up to my full potential.

I had intelligence, youth, professionalism, and beauty. In every job I worked, I learned various skills and trades, mastering anything I found valuable or useful for my next job. I became proficient in typing, computers, programming, software, accounting, record-keeping, managerial, technical, and administrative duties. I was a quick learner and taught myself these skills because I couldn't afford to attend college. I wanted to be more valuable and knowledgeable in any organization I worked for.

I emulated my father, learning by observation and practice. I relied heavily on my memory. The only difference between my father and me was that I could read. And all my efforts had finally paid off. I had reached the big leagues in terms of my career and salary. With just an associate degree, I couldn't envision earning much more than what I was making.

As my children grew older, I faced many challenges with them. My oldest daughter, Makeba, who was 12 at the time, began exhibiting rebellious behavior, being promiscuous and stubborn. She engaged in sneaky and mischievous activities. I remember attending my cousin's baby shower when I suddenly realized Makeba was missing. I searched the entire house for her and eventually found her having sex with my cousin's girlfriend's son in the bathroom. I was furious and confronted her about it.

Makeba started associating with the wrong crowd and became increasingly argumentative with me. She had always been loud and argumentative, but her behavior was getting out of control. She was even arrested by the police for being in a car with an adult woman, intoxicated and behaving erratically. When I went to the police station to pick her up, she showed disrespect towards me. In frustration, I grabbed her by the throat and scolded her for disrespecting me.

Makeba began meeting people online and running away from home. She got involved in various troubles and started engaging in sexual activities with multiple boys and men. Her rebellious and stubborn behavior escalated, and she frequently talked back and complained. I would impose punishments on her, sending her to her room, but she would respond by screaming and complaining loudly, saying nonsensical things. It had reached a point where her behavior was out of control. At the age of 12 to 13, I had three pending cases with the Department of Children and Family Services (DCFS) simultaneously because of her calling them on me and making all sorts of false allegations. She constantly roamed the streets, staying out all night. To protect myself, I had to report her as a runaway multiple times since there was nothing else, I could do, and I feared for her safety.

Around the age of 13, Makeba met a man on the social media site Myspace. While I was at work, he came and picked her up. Unfortunately, he took her to Chicago and forced her into sex trafficking, moving her in and out of cars. She ended up in a vacant apartment on the east side of Chicago, near 71st and Cottage Grove. They kept her drugged and trapped in that place. One day, when they left, she managed to escape by climbing down a fire escape, completely naked. In a drug-induced state; she stumbled into a Midas Muffler shop, desperately asking for food.

They called the police and an ambulance, who took her to the University of Chicago hospital. I received a call at work, informing me about the situation. When I arrived, I found her lying there, heavily under the influence of drugs. They had kept her sedated for weeks. She recounted being trapped in the building, subjected to continuous beatings, rape, and drugging. After her release, she was transferred to a psychiatric hospital. Witnessing my daughter being taken away in an ambulance and committing her to the psych ward for evaluation and detox was an incredibly painful experience as a mother.

I had to take numerous days off work during this period. It's important to note that I had recently started my job at BP and had relinquished my Section 8 certificate. DCFS was closely monitoring my situation, questioning my neighbors, and interviewing my other children. I had to deal with psychiatrists calling from the hospital, discussing treatments and medications. Detectives also called and visited me at work. Additionally, I had to interact with school counselors and therapists. The pressure was overwhelming as I tried my best to excel in my job and make a positive impression on management. I had to meet with management multiple times to explain the situation and justify my frequent absences.

One day, my boss called me into her office when I arrived at work. She praised me as a great employee and expressed how highly they thought of me. However, she conveyed that my priority should be to go home and be a mother. While they understood my circumstances to some extent and had tried to be accommodating, the number of days I had taken off work due to my daughter's issues had become unacceptable. They emphasized the importance of meeting deadlines and fulfilling crucial responsibilities in the workplace. With a heavy heart, I stood there in shock and disbelief.

It felt as if something inside me had shattered. The fear and panic of losing the protection provided by Section 8 overwhelmed me. I had genuinely loved that job and was proud of the progress I had made. It felt like a significant achievement to have a real career and be financially independent. Standing there, I felt the pain ripping through my soul, and all I could think was, 'My Lord, my God, what am I going to do now?

Makeba consistently caused trouble for me, lying, and running away. I faced numerous problems with her. A caseworker from DCFS visited my home and advised me to save myself. She suggested that if Makeba wanted to live with her father so badly, I should let her go and sign the guardianship papers over to him. The caseworker believed that Makeba would eventually drive me crazy, and it would be better for me to focus on my other children who needed my attention. Although I didn't want to allow Makeba to live with her father, Hook, she had made life so difficult for me that I felt I had no other choice. It was incredibly hard for me to drop her off at her grandmother's house so she could go reside with her father. I knew she wasn't ready to be out of my care, but her behavior had become uncontrollable.

Makeba moved to Peoria with her father, which turned out to be a disaster. She got him evicted from his low-income housing. She lied, claiming that he was abusing her and selling drugs from his apartment, forcing her to work. DCFS contacted me and asked me to come and get her. We had to drive down there to bring her back home. Trust me, this was just the beginning. I started experiencing a form of depression, dealing with all the stress she put me through. I was trying to figure out what to do and how to handle her challenging behavior. The doctors eventually diagnosed her with manic-bipolar disorder, and the medications prescribed were potent and strong. She kept going in and out of psychiatric wards because she continued to act out.

Then Dell, my oldest son, began acting out as well. Throughout his childhood, he had shown feminine and gay-like tendencies. I went through a lot with Dell. His actions were often peculiar, and it was evident from a youthful age that he would be gay. He displayed little interest in traditionally masculine activities such as sports or playing with typical boys' toys like trucks, footballs, basketballs, etc. Instead, he preferred his sisters' Barbie dolls, jumping rope, styling hair, and playing dress-up.

He would engage in activities that the little girls wanted to do. Dell had no interest in playing sports, hanging out with other boys in the neighborhood, or engaging in activities like throwing rocks or riding bikes. He preferred staying indoors, helping me cook, and getting dressed. He loved picking out my outfits and giving me advice on how to apply makeup. Dell had a passion for dancing and was a loving, sarcastic, strong, and high-spirited child. He had boundless energy and was incredibly helpful with his siblings. While I went to work, he would do anything he could to take care of his younger brothers and sisters. He would help with cooking and keeping the house clean, ensuring that everyone left for school on time since I had to leave early every morning. He was a fantastic kid, but as he entered his teenage years, things started to change.

I remember when Dell began attending high school; he wanted to work, so I allowed him to get a job at KFC. He would go to work after school every day. However, the principal called me and informed me that Dell was failing in school. This alarmed me because Dell was a math genius with dreams of becoming an architect. Reading was always a challenge for him, but he knew enough to get by. This sudden drop in his school performance was out of character, as he would usually come to me for assistance whenever he struggled academically. I was supportive of my children's education, and I didn't allow them to miss school unless it was a critical situation. They had to complete all their homework, and I limited their video game and television time to avoid distractions from their learning. I would often give them impromptu quizzes and engage in educational activities with them. I told the principal that I had allowed him to have a part-time job at KFC, but I would address his failing grades and insist that he quit his job to focus on his studies.

After hanging up with the principal, I immediately called KFC to inform the management about his academic struggles and the need for him to stop working in order to prioritize his education. The manager reluctantly informed me, "Ma'am, I regret to inform you that we are familiar with Dell; we know him quite well. He was hired here and given a uniform, but he never showed up for work." This happened almost a month ago. Around the same time, he was telling me that he had started working there, even wearing the uniform, and pretending to go to work every day. I couldn't believe what I was hearing on the other end of the line. I was furious with him and didn't know what to do.

Now, mind you, both DC and I were dropping him off at KFC every day, thinking he was working there. DC became increasingly suspicious after some time and kept telling me, "Angie, that boy isn't working at KFC. I'm telling you; he would have received a paycheck by now. Every two weeks, he would ask me for money, and when I inquired about his paycheck, he would come up with excuses like, 'Oh, mama, there was a delay,' or 'I'll get paid next week.' And when that week passed, he would say, 'Oh, I meant it's going to be another two weeks.'"

So, I asked myself, "Where is he going if he's not going to work every day?" That night, we decided to stay up and hide in the car. We said, "We're going to catch him red-handed; I want to know what's really going on." And sure enough, there he came, pulling up in a car with a white boy from the area. They kissed each other, and then Dell got out of the car and started walking toward the house. I got out of the car and shouted, "Excuse me, sir!" He looked terrified. I asked him, "Where have you been?" He replied, "I've been at work." I said, "You're a damn liar; you don't even have a job. I went to KFC today, and they told me everything about how you never showed up for work over a month ago, even after they gave you the uniform. Now, I'm going to ask you again, and you better not lie." He continued lying to me, insisting that he was working and had just left KFC.

That's when my anger escalated, and I started fussing and confronting him. I berated him for lying to me and failing in school. I made it clear that such behavior was completely unacceptable and that I would not tolerate him underperforming academically. Failing was not an option in my household. I demanded to know who the person in the car was. He remained silent. I informed him that he was grounded and couldn't leave the house until he told me the truth about who he was with, where he had been, and how he planned to improve his grades. Yet, he continued to ignore me. I kept pressuring him, following him around the house, using strong language to express my frustration about his lies, academic failure, and sneaking around in the streets with who knows whom, engaging in who knows what activities.

Sure enough, after I went into my bedroom to calm down, the next thing I knew, I heard the front door slam. I got up and looked; he had packed some of his belongings and left. Yes, Dell packed his things and walked right out the front door. It really hurt me, but all I could do was call the police and report him as a runaway. I went into my room and started praying. I said, "Lord, I have to give it to you. I don't know what else to do."

Now, mind you, I did not physically discipline him. But I did reprimand him and tell him he was on punishment. At that time, he was 14 years old and in his freshman year of high school. I didn't hear from him at all. I didn't know where he had gone. I was just sure he was going to come back home the next day or so. But nope, no word at all. I called all his friends' houses. No one had seen him. I still didn't know who the white guy he was kissing in the car that dropped him off that night was. I completely overlooked getting the license plate number to help the police locate him. I believed he would come back. The rest of the school year passed without a word, and then the entire summer.

I told myself, "I'm not going to worry about it. I have to keep moving forward." I was hurting over my firstborn walking out and not knowing where he was. But I had to keep going. So, Makeba was 13, and Dell was 15, and both of them were acting out and gone. I was extremely worried about both of them. But I still had to keep pushing ahead. I had to continue searching for a job because I was still unemployed after Makeba's actions led to me being fired while I was dealing with all her issues.

We ended up moving because I started paying rent out of my own pocket. The home we were living in back then cost $1,850 a month, which was a significant amount for rent. I was shouldering this expense alone. DC was still unemployed at that time, but he stayed at home and took care of the house and made sure the younger kids went to and from school. Makeba was constantly getting into trouble and ended up being placed in group homes by the Department of Children and Family Services (DCFS). We tried to work things out so she could be at home, but it was difficult because she was misbehaving. We moved from Romeoville to Bolingbrook, into a townhome.

Makeba was associating with older men and friends in the neighborhood. DC would go to the men's houses and tell them, "Look, get my daughter out of there." He would remind them that she was underage. This led to a lot of conflicts between Makeba and DC. She was angry because he was keeping a close eye on her, and she couldn't get away with anything.

I realized that I needed a job in the federal government because with so many children and various issues to deal with, I needed job security. I had heard that working for the government was great because it was challenging to get fired unless you did something extreme. I believed that if I could secure a good government job, I would have stability and a long-lasting career. This was especially important since I no longer had Section 8 assistance. It seemed like the best path to establishing a solid and secure future. After an extensive search and numerous applications, I managed to secure a position at the Social Security Administration. I felt a huge sense of relief. I could take care of my bills and start organizing my life. I constantly urged DC to find a job to support me. I felt he wasn't putting in enough effort. It had been a while since he last worked, and his unemployment benefits had finally run out.

He eventually found employment, so he couldn't be there as much to watch the kids. Then we started experiencing more problems with Makeba. She would lock the younger children in the garage and invite boys over while we were at work. My younger children would call me at work, saying, "Mom, Makeba wouldn't let us into the house to eat. Makeba locked the doors, and we couldn't get in. She told us to sit in the garage and do our homework." There was a lot of back and forth; she kept running away from home. I had to deal with her and with the other kids growing older.

It was the beginning of the new school year when I received a call from the Carbondale, IL, police department inquiring if I was Dell's parent. Confirming my identity, they informed me, "Well, ma'am, we have your son." Eagerly, I asked, "Where is he?" They replied, "He's down here in Carbondale, IL." Anxiously, I inquired, "Is he alright?"

They assured me, "Yes, he is fine. We received a report that he ran away, and his cousin is here attempting to enroll him in school." I was taken aback and exclaimed, "WHAT?" To my surprise, it was my cousin Bree, another daughter of my Aunt Tee-Tee. Throughout the entire time my son was missing, my cousin never bothered to inform or contact me.

Apparently, Dell had called her the night he ran away, expressing that we were having family problems and he wanted to live with her. Without consulting me or keeping me informed, she purchased a bus ticket for him to come down to Carbondale. I was furious. I immediately told the officer, "No, I did not grant permission for him to be there with her. I had no knowledge of his whereabouts all this time." Dell did not know my family as well as I did; she simply wanted a built-in babysitter so she could have her freedom. He would soon realize that.

Dell was supposed to be at home attending school. I refused to tolerate this situation. It was utterly outrageous. They had a caseworker present, attempting to mediate the situation. I grew increasingly upset as Dell spoke on the phone, expressing his unwillingness to return home. He claimed he couldn't be himself at home and wanted to remain with my cousin. Filled with anger, I exclaimed, "I can't believe this." I demanded to speak with Bree.

When she got on the phone, I confronted her, saying, " Bree, why would you take my son down there without informing me? How could you do such a thing? He is just a child, only 15 years old. It's not right." She responded, "Well, he called me and said you two were having problems. He's my little cousin, and I'm looking out for him." I retorted, " Bree, my child is a minor. You can't just take someone's child because they make a phone call and say something is wrong. Kids go through challenging times, and parents discipline them from time to time. That doesn't give you the right to send a bus ticket for someone's child to come all the way down there without informing them or attempting to discuss the situation."

In the background, I could hear Dell talking back and making threats, saying, "If she makes me go back, I will just leave again."

It felt as if I was talking to a brick wall. Bree told me, "Now isn't the time or place to discuss this. He's here, and I'm willing to let him go to school. Are you willing to allow him to attend school down here with me?" Feeling overwhelmed, I decided to let him stay; there was no need for me to further stress myself over it. I recalled what the DCFS lady had told me about Makeba and said, "He can stay. Yes, let her enroll him in school." However, I knew it wouldn't work out for long.

Soon enough, I started hearing all sorts of things about my son. Bree was encouraging him to fully embrace his sexual orientation and come out of the closet. She urged him to act out and demand attention from everyone. She would say, "Well, if you're going to be gay, then be extravagant about it!" She was manipulating him in the worst possible way, making him put on a show and behave foolishly. Subsequently, she would call and laugh about it, discussing him with the rest of the family.

Sure enough, that only worked out for two or three months from when I allowed him to stay with her. He had gotten into a car accident, damaging her car, and was verbally abusive towards her. They ended up having a major fight, and he eventually left.

London, on the other hand, was doing really well in school, so I was rewarding her a lot. I thought, "Okay, just because the others are struggling, I can't ignore the ones who are doing well and behaving. I can't neglect my other children." I focused my attention mainly on them while still trying to take care of the others.

I couldn't neglect the rest of my children, so I started giving them more attention and rewards, especially to encourage London to continue doing well in school. She was intelligent, remarkable, and respectful. As long as London was meeting her responsibilities, I made sure to acknowledge and reward her accomplishments.

Despite the challenges with my children, I was also trying to maintain my job. When I was hired at the Social Security Administration (SSA), it was on a temporary basis. I started as a summer hire, and the office couldn't offer me a permanent position due to low productivity numbers of their office or similar reasons.

Unfortunately, they had to let me go, which was tough because I loved working at SSA. Serving the public gave me a sense of fulfillment. When clients approached me for assistance, I made it a point to look out for the elderly, disabled individuals, and those who were illiterate. I could easily identify their needs and treated them with the utmost respect. I often thought, "What if this was my illiterate father, my disabled and sickly mother? How would I want them to be treated?"

Working at the Social Security Administration was a source of pride and honor for me. I was deeply saddened when I served my last customer at the office, uncertain about my career's future. But I knew I couldn't give up; I had to keep pushing forward. My colleagues threw me a big going-away party and expressed their appreciation for my service. They assured me they would provide the highest recommendation for any future endeavors.

I actively sought new job opportunities by sending out numerous resumes and applications. I had to take the first job offer that came my way because I needed to cover the rent. During this time, DC was working at Aaron's Furniture, but he eventually got fired after arguing with the manager over a missing frozen White Castle burger. He became upset because someone had eaten his burgers from the freezer on his day off. He confronted the manager, criticizing the lack of control in the workplace. Despite the manager's attempts to calm him down, DC continued complaining and obsessing over the missing burgers, resulting in his termination.

I managed to secure a job at the US Census Bureau Chicago Regional Office, which, in my opinion, was the worst agency to work for. They lacked a union, and the work environment was extremely stressful. It felt like being in a factory where workers were pushed to their limits, constantly pressured to produce more. The management was unsupportive, and job security was always at risk.

I knew this job wasn't the right fit for me. It was merely a temporary solution to keep me financially afloat until I could return to the Social Security Administration. While at the Census Bureau, I continued applying to other agencies, particularly SSA. I couldn't understand why I wasn't getting promoted or being offered jobs I was more than qualified for. I later discovered that the manager at the Census Bureau was intentionally blocking my transfer requests to other agencies. She didn't want to lose me and would dispute any attempts from other agencies to hire me.

Eventually, I interviewed with a manager in Evanston, Illinois, and explained the situation with the promotion blockage at the Census Bureau. I expressed my frustrations and how they were preventing me from leaving. The manager told me, "Angela, I want you to write a letter of resignation and turn in your equipment. Once you do that, give me a call, and you can start working with us the next day."

With a scared and trembling voice, I repeated after her, "You want me to write a letter of resignation?" She replied, "Yeah, write a letter of resignation. And you'll start here immediately." I agreed, putting my trust in her to hire me, despite the anxiety of leaving my current job. But I took a leap of faith and followed her advice and promise. When I returned home, I typed up a letter of resignation. The next morning, around 6:00 a.m., before management arrived, I nervously entered the census office. I turned in my laptop, keycards, and credentials, feeling a sense of wrongdoing as I had never written a letter of resignation before.

I contacted the manager at the Evanston SSA office, and she informed me, "Okay, you'll begin tomorrow. Come in, and we'll do your fingerprints and get you processed." I asked, "Do you need to inform my previous employer?" She confidently replied, "Nope," chuckling a little. She reassured me, "You don't work for them anymore. Come on. We're bringing you on board here. We'll get you going."

"I got the job!! Back at the Social Security Administration! On a permanent basis!" I couldn't contain my excitement. I felt invincible. Working in the Office of Disability Adjudication and Review (ODAR) was a departure from my previous role at the regular Social Security Field Office. In the SSA offices, I interacted with customers, assisting with printouts, filing claims and social security cards, answering benefit inquiries, and conducting interviews. I thrived on the opportunity to help people and listen to their problems; working with the public brought me immense satisfaction. It was an honor to serve the American people.

My position at the Social Security office specialized in hearings. I worked in the legal division, processing evidence and cases for Administrative Law Judges (ALJs) to review in hearings. As a legal assistant, I played a role similar to a clerk of the court. I found fulfillment in the work involving hearings and appeals, although it was more demanding, considering the lengthy waiting periods for benefits decisions. I began at a GS 5 level, which was a positive starting point given my educational background. When I applied for the government position, I went through testing. Interestingly, my second cousin, once removed on my mother's side, was also testing for the same position. Surprisingly, I outperformed him in the testing, leaving him and his mother bewildered. They couldn't fathom how I secured the job despite his master's degree. In my view, having a degree didn't necessarily equate to superior intelligence, and this experience proved that point.

Working for the federal government brought me a sense of job security that surpassed corporate America. That's why I was determined to maintain a job in the federal government, particularly with the challenges of raising multiple children and dealing with various issues. I wanted to avoid the pain and constant threat of being swiftly fired due to problems with my kids. I needed a job that offered flexibility as a mother while also allowing me to build my career and progress within an agency. Working for the Social Security Administration turned out to be an excellent fit for me. I experienced professional growth, acquired numerous new skills, and expanded my knowledge during my time there. I advanced swiftly through the ranks without encountering any major obstacles. Prior to obtaining this job, my family and I had relocated to the south suburbs of Richton Park, IL, far south from our previous location on the south side.

Despite the challenges of transitioning from Section 8 housing and adjusting to paying regular rent out of my own pocket, I persevered. Managing the expenses and bills on my own without any support was undoubtedly challenging. Though I was married to DC, his inability to maintain a job meant I couldn't rely on or consider his income at that point.

I wasn't receiving much child support at all. Occasionally, I would receive small payments from Go or Hook, but it was never consistent or substantial enough to make a difference. Their fathers were not providing any assistance in raising them. To say that Makeba's father was giving me the bare minimum would be an overstatement; he would occasionally send me a $2 child support check, but it was sporadic. What can I do with $2 in child support? Dell's father never paid me any child support because they said they were not able to locate him. LAW got off from paying child support for London because the child support office told me that I was unable to pursue it legally because the child support order wasn't included in the divorce decree; there was nothing they could do. I wasn't aware that I could have included the child support order during the divorce filing. I just wanted to be done with him after the way he left me, so I opted for a clean divorce with full custody of our daughter. I never received any financial support from him for London. And as for Dane, we all know how that turned out, so I was prepared to bear that burden alone. I was willing to accept the consequences of the mistake I had made.

There I was, still trying to rebuild my life. I was managing the household responsibilities on my own. However, the frustration of having to go to work every day while DC lacked consistent employment started to wear on me. Something had to change. I desired more from life. I repeatedly told myself, "Once these kids are old enough, I will return to complete my college degree and earn my bachelor's." As I strategized my future, I found myself facing another round of challenges with my children. Guess who was starting to act out towards me now?

# PART
# FIVE

# CHAPTER 17
# DEFIANT DISORDER

*"When Oppositional Defiance Disorder Is in The Picture, None of The Traditional, Logical Parenting Models Seems to Work, And That Feels Maddening."*
**(Anonymous)**

At this point in my life, I found myself caught in a whirlwind of struggle. I was transferred from working at the Social Security office in Evanston, Illinois, to an SSA office in Oak Brook, IL. Upon arriving at the Oak Brook office, I was greeted by a pleasant office environment that had a completely different vibe and atmosphere compared to my previous workplace. Situated in a prestigious and affluent community, the learning style there was distinct. I quickly acquired a wealth of knowledge in this new setting, which resulted in a promotion not long after. My confidence and self-esteem soared, and with an increasing salary, I yearned for more in life. I was able to provide better for myself and my children during this time.

However, as I focused on taking care of my children, I began to notice concerning behavior in London, who was in her freshman year of high school. She started displaying a smart-mouthed and disrespectful attitude. I observed that she would frequently retreat to her room, shutting the door behind her. I grew suspicious of her behavior and decided to investigate. One day, while she was in the shower, I felt compelled to go through her phone and computer. To my astonishment, I discovered something alarming. I couldn't believe my eyes when I saw the explicit pictures, she had been sending to someone through text messages on social media. She had been communicating with an individual whom she believed was a girl her age from another state. This person was attempting to persuade her to take a Greyhound bus and meet them.

I confronted London in a state of shock, emphasizing the danger of the situation and highlighting the fact that she had no knowledge of who she was communicating with. I questioned, "Why would this person be trying to influence you to cross state lines?" Something felt profoundly wrong about the whole situation. I repeatedly voiced my concerns, suggesting that this person might be a predator. The individual had even informed London that they could legally marry without my consent once she turned 16, instructing her to keep their relationship a secret until then.

The messages contained explicit sexual content, and I confiscated London's phone and laptop while grounding her as punishment. She responded with screams and insults, expressing her hatred towards me. A heated argument ensued, leading to me retreating to my room and slamming the door. Eventually, she fell asleep. Throughout the night, I wrestled with the decision of whether to involve the police and worried about my daughter's well-being. It was evident that she was in a dangerous situation with this individual, and it deeply troubled me. I couldn't find any peace, and sleep eluded me. I resolved, "Once I'm at work, I'll seek advice from one of the judges regarding this matter."

The following day, while seated at my desk, I received a distressing call from one of the school officials at London's school. The female counselor urgently informed me that London had been admitted to the hospital, and I needed to come as quickly as possible. Calmly, she explained that London had gone to the school counselor and confessed that she had taken a bottle of pills with the intention of ending her own life. I immediately got into my car and embarked on the hour and a half drive to the hospital. Although I felt concerned and prayed for the safety of my daughter, I remained composed and steadfast. I believed that London's actions were a result of her anger towards me for confiscating her phone and laptop. When I arrived at the hospital, I was greeted by a case worker from the Department of Children and Family Services (DCFS), a school counselor, a hospital social worker, and a police officer. They proceeded to ask me a series of questions about my relationship with London, the events of the previous day, and possible triggers for her suicide attempt. After providing them with answers, I finally spoke with the doctor. He explained that they had pumped London's stomach and found only one Excedrin pain pill. There was no evidence of her having ingested multiple pills.

Essentially, she had lied about the incident. I felt immense anger towards my daughter, but I was convinced that she was attempting to manipulate me and assumed I would feel sympathetic and revoke her punishment. This only strengthened my resolve to stand my ground and continue with her disciplinary measures. The following week, she returned to school, claiming to the nurse's office that she had attempted suicide again, this time by cutting her wrist.

When I arrived at the hospital, the doctor informed me that she had scratched her wrist until it began to bleed. I was taken aback by her extreme behavior at this point. Since this was her second claim of wanting to commit suicide, she was admitted to the psychiatric ward for further evaluation. It was a difficult and unsettling experience to go through with my child. Once at the ward, she expressed her desire not to return home with me. She insisted on going to live with her father in Missouri, even though I knew it would likely end in disaster.

It seemed that she was acting out against me because I was firm in maintaining her punishment and not returning her electronics. I remembered what the previous DCFS worker had told me about Makeba, and I made the difficult decision to let her go and live with her father in order to preserve my sanity and be there for my other children who needed me.

# CHAPTER 18
# DEVIL, YOU WON'T DEFEAT ME!!!

*"God Allows Difficulties to Happen So That Your Strength, Faith, and Power Can Multiply"*
**(Tee-Teeette Coron)**

During my marriage to DC, I started noticing a recurring pattern. He had become extremely lazy and dependent on me. I constantly urged him to find a job and contribute to the bills, but he showed no real effort to help. He would only go to work when I pushed him hard, resorting to yelling and screaming at him to get up and assist with the bills. He would find temporary jobs and work just long enough to receive one or two paychecks before quitting or getting fired.

I remember one incident where he was employed at a department store but refused to bring in shopping carts, resulting in his termination because he argued with management. He claimed he wouldn't go out in the rain to retrieve the carts, despite it being part of his job description. Then he would return home and remain unemployed until I started fussing again. This cycle persisted for months, with him pretending to search for work. I recall one instance where he found temporary employment, but after a month, he called me from the emergency room, claiming that mop water had splashed back on him and caused poisoning. His story was not believed, and he was fired. This pattern continued for years. The most unbelievable part was when he was even fired from driving for Lyft and Uber due to his attitude and road rage. It's rare for someone to be fired from those platforms since drivers have flexibility and control over their schedules. I was left shouldering all the rent, bills, and utilities without any assistance from him.

Despite receiving promotions and cost-of-living raises, I found myself becoming increasingly stressed, depressed, and feeling used and neglected. Although I had successfully transitioned off welfare and food stamps, I gradually accumulated more debt. I had to cover school fees, expenses, and cash for my children's lunches, as they were no longer eligible for free meals, tuition, and fee waivers due to my income.

I was buying groceries with cash and shouldering the burden of rent, utilities, food, household and personal care supplies, clothes, shoes, car maintenance, and expensive taxes, medical, vision, life, and dental insurance for my family. Balancing all these obligations was a tremendous challenge, particularly on a GS salary, with me being the sole provider for my household.

We were frequently moving from place to place due to DC's lack of support, which made it challenging for me to keep up with everything on my own. Adjusting my life without relying on Section 8 and welfare assistance was an arduous process.

My son DJ was going to great lengths to prove his masculinity because he didn't want people to think he was gay, considering his brother's sexual orientation and the resulting embarrassment and scrutiny. He faced teasing due to his brother Dell's flamboyant behavior as a gay individual.

DJ went above and beyond, engaging in extra activities to prove his masculinity. His brother's mother owned a sandwich shop and made every effort to make DJ work for her. He essentially built her business by himself. She convinced him that the life she and her son lived was everything. It became challenging to get him to come home as he started working for her at the age of 12. I was unaware that his father was picking him up and dropping him off at her shop. She exploited my son to the maximum. As he reached high school age, she encouraged him to argue more with DC, telling him he could just come with her and didn't have to listen to a man who wasn't his father.

She also emphasized that she didn't have any men around her son. She remained single, waiting for his father to return, and received support from her father and extended family. Her son had all the name-brand clothes, shoes, and video games. I tried my best to make my son see how she was manipulating him, but he wouldn't listen. I attempted to get him a job at Menards, but she convinced him that he would be working for the White man and that every Black man should work for himself. She constantly inflated his ego, making him believe that working for her meant building a family business. He eventually realized that wasn't the case as he grew older, but I had to deal with his disrespectful behavior. He ended up moving in with her, dropping out of high school, and assisting her in building her business.

One morning, while lying in bed and crying due to the overwhelming pressure to become self-sufficient and independent, I made a decision. I said to myself, "I'm going to push even harder!" I committed to giving it my all, surpassing the efforts I had already been making. I refused to give up or succumb to thoughts of weakness and incapability. I had come too far to surrender and fall into depression. I thought about my mother and how she stayed in that house, worrying herself to death, dealing with a useless husband she depended on, and stubborn, difficult children. I declared, "Not today, devil, you won't defeat me." I got out of bed, put on the whole armor of God, and pushed myself even further in life.

I began proactively managing my finances, learning how to budget and pay rent and bills on time. It was challenging to learn on my own and discipline myself to become independent and responsible. I balanced my checking account and made timely bill payments to avoid late fees. I had to file for Chapter 7 bankruptcy to eliminate payday loan debt, clear my record of mismanaged credit card debt, and regain control of my utilities. I started maximizing my 401k savings contributions. I made every effort to restore my credit and improve my score so that I could purchase a home for myself and my children. I believed that if I was already paying high rent and bills, it would be better to invest in my own house and establish some stability. This was my ultimate dream—to provide a secure living environment for me and my children.

When my youngest daughter, Day, graduated from junior high, I told myself that it was the moment to seize. I had made a promise to myself long ago when my children were very young, and I was determined to fulfill it. On the day that my daughter Day walked across the eighth-grade stage, I registered at DePaul University to pursue my bachelor's degree. I was overwhelmed with happiness because I knew that nothing could hinder my progress. This time, I was determined to go all the way, regardless of any challenges that may arise.

As time went on, I experienced personal growth and maturity. I reached a point where I wanted to break free from the bond between DC and myself. Divorce was never something I desired, but it had become an option in my life. I continued to pray and offer DC chances to get his life together. I began to realize that not everyone could change as quickly as I did, considering the time it took me to transform myself. I attempted to motivate DC to strive for better. I emphasized how his own son, Jay, looked up to him and needed him as a role model. I genuinely cared for Jay and treated him as if he were one of my own children. Unfortunately, DC failed to demonstrate genuine love and attention towards his son.

Although I had reservations about buying a home in Illinois due to high taxes, crime rates, and cold winters, Day, who was in high school at the time, pleaded for us to remain in Evergreen Park. I felt guilty because we had moved frequently throughout the years. Eventually, I decided to stay a little longer to ensure Day had stability through high school. I believed that I owed it to her, as she was the child who never caused me any trouble. During high school, Day participated in numerous activities such as band, acting, chess club, dance, and theater, all while maintaining excellent grades. I expressed my gratitude towards her. She never talked back or attempted to run away, and overall, she was an exceptional child. We cherished our quality time together.

Unfortunately, we had to move due to our landlord's marriage and his need to sell the house in order to provide for his new family. The mother of one of Day's classmates owned a house nearby and was renting it out. It made sense to rent this house so that Day could have stability throughout her high school years. Meanwhile, I was contemplating ending my relationship with DC because I was tired of his laziness.

DC had moved back in with his mother, while I prepared to settle into the house I was going to rent from Day's classmate's mother. However, when the day came for me to move in, there were unexpected obstacles preventing us from signing the lease. Despite this, I proceeded with the move and called the movers to transport my belongings to the new house. The house itself was a small two- or three-bedroom property with a finished basement, a modest living room, an eat-in kitchen, and a two-car garage. I believed it would be suitable for me and Day.

As we were in the process of moving in, the owner of the house arrived and began behaving strangely when we were about to place items in the basement. She suddenly declared, "Oh, no, you can't use this part of the basement." I was taken aback and asked for clarification. She explained that she had intended to rent the house for $1800, although we had agreed on a maximum of $1500. However, she firmly stated that she would retain the basement area. In that moment, I told myself, "Okay, I won't let this bother me. It is what it is. Maybe she is in the midst of settling into her new home and lacks sufficient space. She will probably collect her belongings later." I was willing to compromise, accepting access to only half of the basement.

However, as the movers were bringing in my belongings, we encountered a problem. My living room furniture set was too large to fit through the door of the house. As we explored the garage, we discovered that it was filled with the owner's belongings. I explained to her that I needed access to the garage. Once again, she responded, "No, you can only use half of the garage." Once again, I was taken aback and asked for more clarification. She proceeded to explain, "You are not paying the full rent that I requested for the house. I wanted to rent it for $1800, but you can only afford $1500. Therefore, you will only have access to $1500 worth of the house. Additionally, I want you to know that only you and Day are allowed in this house. Your other children cannot visit on a daily basis, and your husband cannot return. You will have to find another arrangement for them."

She continued, "We don't want too many people using our hot water tank and furnace or causing wear and tear on our house. I will have the neighbors watching, so your children can come for visits, but they cannot stay overnight. I will be monitoring the situation closely." I was shocked and asked, "Are you serious?" She replied, "I will have people watching you."

Realizing that the situation was unreasonable, I decided to ask the movers immediately for them to move my belongings back out. We completed the move the following morning. I was relieved that I had not signed a lease with her. I told her that she must be insane to expect me to live under such restrictive rules and conditions. It was absolutely outrageous for her to agree to the proposed rent amount and then attempt to manipulate me with these demands. She had gone too far.

Fortunately, the homeowner and his wife were understanding and allowed us to move back into the house temporarily until I could find a new place. DJ returned home to assist me, but he and DC had been having frequent conflicts.

During the moving process, my son DJ came back home to help us. I had decided he could come on back home to stay now that DC was gone and praying that things would get better, and he had learned his lesson about his brother's mother manipulation and influencing him to work for her. As we were returning for the evening after moving back in the house. DC stopped by as he was driving past to make sure I was good. The kids were in my room with me eating. I asked them to excuse us as we talked. DJ was looking at DC with serious hatred in his eyes. I told DC we were good and thanked him for stopping by to check in.

As he proceeded to leave the house, DJ was standing by the front door and in a rude way he purposely stood in the way of DC being able to walk out. I told DJ to move over so DC could leave. He just kept looking at DC like he wanted to fight him. DC proceeded to walk out the door with a little laugh off at DJ and as he was walking towards the car, my son flew out the house and ran up behind him and punched DC in the side of his face, as DC turned around; DJ hit him with a few more punches to the face.

Me, Day, my daughter De-De was all screaming to the top of our lungs for it to stop. DC started chasing DJ up the block; my son was teasing and taunting him as they were running, and DC was angrily chasing my son. Somehow DC managed to catch my son and wrestled him down. By that time, the police pulled up and arrested DC. I was so angry with DJ because I told him I had the situation under control, but he refused to listen to me. I told him I could not have him in the house being that disrespectful and hardheaded, and how someone could have really gotten injured. He kept talking back and being argumentative and disrespectful with me. I made him leave and go home with De-De because I could not deal with his mouth and disrespect. I felt so bad for DC, my son had blacked his eye, and busted his lip, and his face and hands were swollen. I knew my son had gone entirely too far. DC knew how bad I felt for him, and he managed to work his way back in, saying how we had to stand together and how the children were growing up and becoming too disrespectful. I really felt bad for DC, and I felt like I wanted us to work it out and I was praying this would make him come on and act right so we could live happily ever after.

I had reached my limit with DC. To supplement my income, I began extreme couponing. I collected coupons from local newspapers and purchased bulk quantities of various items like toilet paper, paper towels, dishwashing liquid, soap, and laundry supplies. I networked and advertised on Facebook, meeting potential buyers, and selling these items for extra income.

One day, while I was advertising on Facebook, I came across someone promoting the same items I was selling. To my surprise, it was DC. He was selling my supplies on Facebook and using the money to buy weed and clothes for himself. That was the final straw for me. I was tired of living with him and being taken advantage of. After work, I went home and told Day, "We need to move, and I don't want to stay in Illinois." She cried, begged, and pleaded with me to stay in the Evergreen Park community to complete high school. So, we embarked on the search for a new place to live. I was constantly looking for an affordable rental, but it was extremely challenging and frustrating. Many places had high rent requirements and preferred applicants with excellent credit and minimal financial setbacks. It was particularly difficult for me with a Chapter 7 bankruptcy on my credit report.

I came across a house that caught my attention. It was available for lease with the option to buy. There was a program that allowed your rent payments to be applied towards the closing costs or down payment on the home. Intrigued, I decided to check out the house. It was exactly what I had envisioned for my first home—a comfortable three-bedroom house with a full-finished basement, a family room, a beautiful living room, a charming kitchen, a two-car garage, and even an office space. It reminded me of my Aunt Helene's house in the suburbs when I was younger.

As I spoke with the sales associate about the house, he explained the program in detail. He assured me that they could help me become a homeowner, giving me enough time to improve my credit and providing assistance along the way. Owning a home had always been a dream of mine, but I lacked the knowledge and guidance to make it a reality.

The salesman's convincing explanations and answers to my questions and concerns made me believe that I could indeed accomplish this goal. Although I was still in the process of rebuilding my credit after filing for bankruptcy two years earlier, I was approved for the house, and we moved in.

Day was thrilled, and DC ended up moving in with us as well. We were attempting to work on our marriage, and he promised to find employment, which he failed to do. Before long, we found ourselves back at square one. DC worked at a few temporary agencies but kept getting fired for trivial reasons. He didn't put in any effort and would complain about every job. Once he thought he could get away with it, he would retreat to the basement with the remote control, enjoying life while I worked tirelessly.

I was working nearly seven days a week, twelve hours a day, and taking on all the overtime I could get. I didn't miss a day of work or take sick leave. I was fully committed to achieving my dream of homeownership and had to enter grind mode. I needed to save up enough money and position myself to finally become a homeowner. I wouldn't let anything, or anyone stand in my way.

Fortunately, I found a program that provided guidance on managing my credit cards and ensured I made my car note payments on time. I prioritized paying all my bills promptly and exercised even greater self-discipline than before. My credit score skyrocketed, and I felt incredibly proud of my self-sufficiency and independence. Eventually, I was able to purchase my first home. I was filled with excitement and pride. The mortgage payments were significantly lower than what I had been paying in rent all those years. It felt like I had overcome all obstacles and was living the American dream. I had a successful federal career, owned a home in a wonderful community, had excellent credit, furnished my house with nice things, owned two new cars, and could afford my daughter's education. I was finally living my best life.

# CHAPTER 19
# I CAN SHOW YOU - BETTER THAN I CAN TELL YOU

*"A Woman Who Knows What She Brings to The Table Is Not Afraid To Eat Alone"*
**(Unknown)**

I confronted DC, expressing my frustration and urging him to step up and support me. I simply wanted him to be a husband and help me. When the time came for my graduation from DePaul University with my bachelor's degree, he didn't attend the ceremony. I was deeply hurt and embarrassed. It was difficult to fathom that I had been with this man for so many years, and he couldn't be there to witness this significant milestone in my life.

I felt deeply hurt and heartbroken, completely shattered. At this point, I was extremely disillusioned with him and ready for him to leave my life. After everything I had gone through, I couldn't understand how any husband wouldn't be there for their wife. I stopped talking to him altogether, and he started behaving in a hostile manner towards me. I couldn't comprehend what he was going through, but it had become unbearable. We had countless arguments, yet he still refused to get up and find work. I repeatedly threatened him, telling him that if he didn't start working, we would have to get a divorce.

He responded defiantly, saying, "Well, I'm not going anywhere until I feel like it, and that won't be anytime soon!" I kept telling him, "So you're going to force me to take care of you?" We went through these motions, and I eventually made it clear that this was not how our marriage was going to end. I told him he had to leave, but he didn't want to go. He had become so lazy that he wouldn't even take care of basic household tasks like cutting the grass, so I had to hire Lawn care services. He wouldn't clean, do laundry, or help with groceries. He simply refused to assist me in any way.

I was incredibly frustrated, to the point where I completely cut him off. I stopped buying food and ceased giving him money for personal items such as hygiene products, haircuts, shoes, and clothes. I disconnected his cell phone, and the cable television services, and changed the internet password so he couldn't spend his days idly watching television, playing games on his phone, or engaging in social media. I did all of this in the hope that he would finally get up and make a positive change in his life.

Meanwhile, I continued to pay the mortgage and all the bills on time. My frustration stemmed solely from him, and I declared, "I am no longer going to take care of this man." I consulted with attorneys, and they informed me, "If you initiate the divorce now, you may end up having to pay him alimony." I responded angrily, "I refuse to pay him alimony. This man has done nothing but sit around on his ass and force me to take care of him all these years. I won't do it."

I provided Day with a daily allowance so she could have meals at McDonald's. She would go with her friends on their way to school and have breakfast together. I also gave her lunch money for school. In the evenings, when I finished work, I would pick her up and grab a bite to eat. If I had to work late in the office, I would give her money so she and her friends could go to Culver's, a pizza place, or anywhere else in the neighborhood, and she could have whatever food she desired.

However, I refused to provide a single grain of rice for him to sit around and eat. I was extremely agitated and beyond irritated. At that point, I didn't care anymore because I had repeatedly asked him to get up and help. As a husband, all I expected from him was to contribute his share by taking care of and assisting in paying the household bills.

As I continued with my actions, starving him to exert pressure, his anger grew. He resorted to malicious acts, such as cutting the Internet wires outside the house because he no longer had access. I immediately contacted the police and began documenting his actions, creating a paper trail. Dane, Day's father, started sending money to assist with my daughter's college expenses. Even though my daughter wasn't his biological child, he still cared for us deeply and wanted us to reconcile, but I refused to go back to him. I allowed my daughter to maintain a relationship with him.

After all, she was named after him, and he promised to always consider her his daughter.

One day, he attempted to send money for her so that we could purchase college supplies. He called and asked, "What does she need?" My daughter then called upstairs and said, "Mom, my dad asked, 'where should he send the money?'" I instructed her to tell him to send it to my bank account. DC rushed upstairs, yelling at me, "Was that her dad? Why is he sending you money? If I find out, I'm going to fuck you up." We argued, and I firmly stated, "This is it. You won't control me! He is sending money to support her education, and I need the assistance. You're not doing anything to help us."

I told him, "I'm not playing games with you, but I won't allow this. I need help. I've begged you for help. And if Dane wants to contribute, then I'll accept it because I need assistance in getting our daughter through college. This is not for me. He's sending the money for her."

Now, here's the important part: I had a checking account for Day, but since she was under 18 at that time, we also opened a separate account for her. I always linked it to my bank account specifically because DC was behaving dishonestly and taking advantage of me. I would tell Day, "Listen; if something happens to me, I want you to go to the ATM, withdraw as much money as you can, and hide it. Make sure you change the PINs." I didn't have anyone I could trust; my other children had disappeared and weren't speaking to me. They were just doing the most at this time. Day was the only child I felt I could trust with the money I was trying to save. I had multiple credit cards that were in excellent standing because I had worked hard to improve my credit in order to buy the house.

I was truly doing everything necessary, but I feared what would happen if something ever happened to me. Remember, my mother passed away at the age of 47. It was always one of my greatest fears that something would happen to me at a young age, and DC would simply walk away without providing anything for my children, just as my parents had left me with nothing. So, I wanted to ensure my kids would be taken care of. I made sure to list only them as beneficiaries in my life insurance policy, with equal shares, and I intended to create a will designating all my possessions directly to them.

I shared all the necessary information and instructions with Day in case something happened to me. I made sure she knew where everything was, but remember, she was still underage.

DC continued to argue and curse at me regarding Dane's intention to send money to my daughter. My daughter, Day, told him, "Stop yelling and cursing at my mom. My dad only wants to help me by sending money. You need to calm down." He started threatening both of us, making violent threats and telling her to mind her own business. The situation became extremely ugly. I warned him that if he didn't calm down, I would call the police.

Day had a scheduled job interview for the summer, so I told her, "Let's go." We got into my car, and DC angrily got into my other car and started chasing us. Both Day and I were screaming in fear as we drove at high speeds down 95th Street. I called 911 while driving and explained, "He has become violent and is threatening me like this. He threatened to harm me and my daughter. I need assistance."

The operator responded, "Ma'am, you are driving through multiple towns, so I cannot dispatch assistance. You will have to go to either Evergreen Park, Oak Lawn, or Chicago Ridge police departments for help, unless you pull over and allow me to dispatch someone to your location." We were still speeding down 95th Street, and there were no police officers in sight to assist us, so I decided to keep going. I was genuinely afraid to pull over.

DC continued to chase us relentlessly. Finally, when we reached the mall, both of us were trembling with fear. We quickly got out of the car and ran inside. I managed to calm Day down, and we hid in a corner of the mall where I could still keep an eye on him. I reassured her, saying, "We will be okay. Let's focus on your interview."

While she was being interviewed, I remained seated, constantly watching out the window to ensure he didn't leave the car in the parking lot. Eventually, he drove away. I felt relieved, thinking he had calmed down and that we would be safe. However, I still had concerns and thought to myself, "What am I going to do?" When Day finished her interview, we returned to the car without any issues. I said, "I'm going straight to the police station to file a report." We got in the car and drove off, but he started following us again.

So, I pulled into the parking lot of the Evergreen Park Police station. I called and asked if they could send an officer to escort us inside to file a report, explaining that we were being chased and feared for our lives. DC sat there and watched us but left once the police officers emerged from the building and approached my car. I suppose he realized what I had done and that he had gone too far. I had no intention of dealing with him any further. I provided the police with a detailed account of everything that had been happening, including the paper trail I had been keeping of his actions, as well as my previous calls to the police. I informed them about his threats against our lives, the internet wire cutting, his demands for me to take care of him, and my exhaustion from enduring such abuse.

The police responded, saying, "We will escort you to the house so you can gather some belongings. Tomorrow morning, you can go to the courthouse and obtain a restraining order against him." It was a Thursday, and Father's Day was that Sunday. They asked if we had somewhere to stay. We quickly retrieved a few items from the house, finding DC absent upon arrival. We swiftly gathered our things and left. We went to my cousin's house; I was simply tired of dealing with the situation. I declared, "I want out of this marriage." The next morning, we went to the Bridgeview Courthouse, where I obtained a restraining order against him. They advised me, "If he comes to the house, call the police. We will come to serve him." They also recommended changing the locks for added security. If he needed his belongings, he could request a police escort to retrieve them.

So, I called the locksmith, had the locks changed, and tried to stay focused on getting my life back together. The entire Father's Day weekend passed, and he didn't come to the house. I said to myself, "He's going to come back, and there will be trouble." True to my prediction, the following Monday, at around two or three o'clock in the morning, I heard him ringing the bell. I woke up and went into Day's room to wake her up. He began banging on the windows and all the doors. I immediately called 911 and explained, "I have a restraining order, and he's here. I need help now, please." I could hear him getting angrier, and the police on the line could hear all the banging on the doors and windows.

Suddenly, there was a brief moment of silence, and then I heard the doors being kicked in. Boom! Boom! Boom!

He kicked in all the doors and tore down the wooden gate in the back. He ripped through the screen door and busted through the office door. Then he kicked in the kitchen door. I was shouting, "Oh my God, police, please hurry; we need help." The operator told me, "Ma'am, please stay on the line." I was in a state of panic as he got closer and closer to entering the house. I could hear the sirens outside, somewhere nearby, but they hadn't arrived yet.

I started to panic even more, screaming, "Oh my God, what are we going to do?" Day grabbed a set of curling irons, and the dog ran under the bed. I stood there with my daughter behind me upstairs in my bedroom because it was the farthest from the back of the house. We stood there in the darkness. I was praying, and Day was shaking uncontrollably. I said, "God, please give me the strength to beat his ass if he comes up here and tries to hurt us."

I could hear the police approaching. DC stood at the bottom of the stairs, glaring at me, and said, "I told you I wasn't going anywhere until I felt like it!!!" Day screamed at him, saying, "Do you really have to do all of this, DC?" I yelled, "Why are you doing this?" He yelled back, "I told you I wasn't going anywhere until I felt like it. And that's what I fucking meant! Well, your little friends are outside." I could see the flashing sirens and police lights outside. He went downstairs to the basement and started playing loud rap music by Scarface. Day and I remained upstairs, huddled in a corner, trembling with fear. I heard numerous police cars outside. Their lights were flashing everywhere as they tried to figure out how to enter the house. They noticed the broken gate at the back and the kicked-in doors. I could hear the police storming into the house, asking, "Where is he? Where is he?" They were all around. We both shouted, "He is in the basement."

They quickly rushed to the basement and arrested him. Oh my God. All the doors had been kicked in. They said to me, "He entered with so much force. We understand how terrified you must have been." I replied, "Yes, we were scared for our lives." I had to prove that I was the homeowner and explain everything that had been happening—why we were going through a separation, how I had obtained a restraining order against him, and how tired I was of his mistreatment.

They told me, "Regardless of the circumstances, this level of force used to enter someone's home is unacceptable. We can only imagine how frightened you were." That was my get-out-of-jail-free card with DC. I was so relieved to finally be free from his abuse and the way he had used me for all those years. Eighteen years of suffering in that marriage with him. I was happy, but also fearful. They served him with the restraining order while he was in custody. I refused to look back; I couldn't look back. I was never going back. I made a firm decision to never subject myself or my children to his behavior ever again. No matter what happened, I was never going back.

I was feeling joyful, relieved, and in high spirits. My focus was on preparing for Day's college departure and gathering her belongings. Finally, I would have freedom from parenting and could dedicate my life to myself. Simultaneously, I had enrolled in a master's degree program and was determined to continue pursuing my education. I cherished being a student, engaging in learning, and accomplishing so much. This was the time for me to rebuild my life, achieve new goals and dreams, and establish a legacy for my children and future generations.

Despite these positive emotions, Day and I still experienced some fear as we remained alone in the house. I took the necessary steps to repair the damages caused by my ex-husband's forceful entry, including installing security doors. It's important to note that his actions had deeply traumatized me on a psychological and emotional level.

# CHAPTER 20
# A TINDER SCAM

*"Ignorance Might Be Bliss,
But it's Irresponsible & Dangerous Too"*
**(Robyn Carr)**

During this period, we were preparing for Day's trunk party, which celebrated her upcoming college journey. She had been accepted to Tuskegee University, an HBCU in Alabama, and I couldn't have been prouder. As I busied myself with cooking, grilling, and organizing the decorations for the party, I unintentionally neglected my phone. Engrossed in my tasks, I was completely absorbed in the moment. Meanwhile, Day had connected with a guy on the dating app Tinder, who claimed to be a student at the University of Illinois. They began communicating, and the guy eventually called her.

Day never told me about meeting the guy and did not inform me that the guy had asked for her account number to send her a gift for the going-away celebration. Trusting him, she obliged and provided her account information for a transfer via Zelle. However, the guy was playing a scam and informed Day that it hadn't worked. He then requested her online user ID and passcode to manually deposit the money into her account. Deceived by his lies, Day went outside without my knowledge and handed her debit card to this stranger she had never met before. Throughout the day, he kept telling her that her bank wouldn't accept a check. It's worth mentioning that Day's bank account was linked to mine as a precautionary measure against my ex-husband accessing my funds in case something happened to me. At this point, Day had recently turned eighteen and had access to everything I had.

Once Day handed over our online banking information, chaos ensued. Unbeknownst to me, I was being systematically robbed while I cooked and readied the house for the trunk party. Amidst all this, Day remained silent, and I had no inkling of her actions. We all had a wonderful time in the backyard, enjoying the party and spending quality time with our loved ones. As I retired upstairs to get ready for bed, I glanced at my phone and was shocked to find numerous emails and text messages. Confused and alarmed, I wondered what was happening.

The notifications were filled with phrases like "Withdrawal," "Order confirmed," and "Purchase confirmed." I exclaimed, "Oh my God! What is this?" I couldn't comprehend the situation. Frantically, I called out to Day, desperately seeking answers. "Day! DAY! Where's your debit card? Day, what have you done? What did you do?" She proceeded to explain, "Mom, my friend said he would contribute some money for my trunk party." Distraught, I probed further, "But Day, what did you do? What did you do?" Regrettably, she replied, "Well, he asked for my debit card." I implored, "Day, how did he access my account?" She clarified, "Mom, he asked for the password because he needed direct access to deposit the money. So, I gave him the online user ID and password." Overwhelmed with emotions, I cried, panicked, and struggled to catch my breath. Day stood there, sensing the panic in my voice, fully aware of her grave mistake. I immediately contacted the police, berating her, and simultaneously attempted to reach the bank for assistance.

This person took advantage of me in a major way. All of my credit cards were linked to my bank account, which meant that my mortgage payment and savings were all connected to it. This person knew exactly what they were doing and hit up every ATM they could find, withdrawing thousands of dollars from my account. They were relentless in taking money from me. On top of that, they also maxed out my credit cards and had items shipped to various abandoned houses throughout the city. The damage they caused was extensive, and I was completely lost and devastated. It was a financial catastrophe that turned my life upside down in a matter of moments. I was furious with my daughter. I didn't know what to do. I was hurt and overwhelmed, crying uncontrollably, and feeling sick to my stomach.

I managed to get in touch with the bank, and they immediately cut off all access to my account. They informed me that the day's activities would be investigated. By the time this person was done with me, I had nothing left. My bank account was destroyed, all my money was gone, and my credit cards were a mess. I was left with absolutely nothing. The police conducted an investigation that night, but instead of focusing on the culprit, they kept asking my daughter if she was okay and if she wanted to press charges against me for reacting angrily when I found out what she had done. I couldn't believe it. She had caused so much damage, and they were more concerned about her well-being than holding her accountable. I was furious with the police at that point.

The police provided me with a report number, and I contacted the bank to explain the situation. Their response was disheartening. They apologized for the inconvenience but stated that since my daughter willingly gave this person access to my bank account and she was over 18 years old, they couldn't help me. They classified it as a willful act rather than fraud, so I wouldn't be reimbursed for anything. I was left in a tremendous amount of debt. On top of that, I had to send my daughter off to college within the next two days, but I didn't have enough credit or money to rent a car to drive her there. I was constantly debating what to do. Should I still send her to school? Could I trust her to be responsible on her own? It was a difficult decision because if she had been so irresponsible in this situation, how could I trust her so far away from me?

I kept asking myself, "Should I send her to school or make her stay home?" It was a tough call, but I wanted her to have a chance at success in life. I wanted her to become someone and avoid being trapped in a cycle of welfare dependency or low-paying jobs due to a lack of education. I was worried about what would happen to her if she stayed in Chicago without going away to college. I considered sending her to a community college, but I felt that she really needed the full college experience. She was my first child to attend a university, as her siblings had struggled and not accomplished much when it came to graduating and pursuing higher education. I believed that Day had the potential to succeed, so I made the decision to take her to school.

I drove my daughter to Tuskegee by myself, even though the original plan was for my aunt and family to accompany us and help us settle into college. However, due to the financial devastation caused by my daughter, I couldn't afford to make that happen. So, I packed everything I could in my car and made the trip alone. I managed to borrow money from the VFW hall since I was on the Women's Auxiliary Board, which helped cover the expenses for her transportation and my return trip home. That was my top priority. I drove all the way to Tuskegee, got her settled in, and then immediately headed back home. I couldn't even afford to stay at a hotel and rest. With the little extra money I had, I took her to Wal-Mart to buy snacks and other essentials to hold her over until I could send her some money for supplies once I got back.

# CHAPTER 21
# FROM 18 YEARS TO 18 WHEELS

*"A Journey of a Thousand Miles Begins with A Single Step"*
**(Lao Tzu)**

On my way back, the lawn guy called me and informed me that someone had broken the windows in my living room. I couldn't believe that DC had resorted to attacking my property again while I was away in Tuskegee. I guess he thought I was out with someone else. This individual had shattered my large bay windows. It was devastating to come home after a long trip to Alabama only to find myself in such a terrible situation. I didn't know what to do. Reluctantly, I ended up taking out a payday loan to get the windows fixed. I strongly suspected it was DC who had done it, but I couldn't prove it since I wasn't at home. I had no choice but to get the living room windows repaired and install security cameras, as I couldn't substantiate his involvement in breaking the windows.

DC did attempt to come back a couple of times, but I refused to let him in and go down that road again. I had filed for divorce and was waiting for our court date. He even tried to say goodbye to me at my workplace, but I avoided him and didn't utter a word. I heard he had moved to Atlanta, and a warrant was issued for his arrest because he missed his court date related to our domestic violence case.

During this time, I was under immense pressure to regain control of my life as I was drowning in debt. I resorted to taking out payday loans and personal loans in an attempt to stabilize my situation, but I found myself sinking deeper and deeper into debt once again. I started talking to a guy who lived in North Carolina just to have someone to chat with and alleviate my worries. He was a celebrity bus driver, and we became good friends.

He expressed interest in having a long-distance relationship. He would visit me when he was in town with one of the celebrities he was touring with. He spent months on the road working for various artists like Steve Harvey, R. Kelly, Keith Sweat, Janet Jackson, and the Temptations, to name a few. It was somewhat exciting being with him because he wasn't around the house, and I felt like I could experience life on the road through his stories.

He expressed a desire to pursue a career in trucking, stating that he didn't want to work for a company his whole life and desired something of his own. We discussed the possibility of getting him a truck and his intention to eventually come off the road. He was tired of being away for extended periods of time. Meanwhile, I shared my aspiration to leave Illinois as I was planning to pursue a master's degree. I expressed my dissatisfaction with remaining in Illinois, and he suggested making future plans together. Eventually, he purchased a spacious and beautiful home in Atlanta.

Although we discussed the idea of entering the trucking business together, I had reservations about him. I always felt that he wasn't entirely honest with me for some reason. I had a gut feeling urging caution in the relationship, reminding me not to become too emotionally invested since we primarily had a long-distance relationship. While we had met in person a few times, most of our interactions consisted of daily phone conversations.

During this time, one of my Facebook friends, Anthony Brown, posted about being the owner-operator of a newly purchased eighteen-wheeler. It's important to note that I was trying to rebuild my life after experiencing financial devastation caused by DC and Day, which led me to file for bankruptcy. I had just acquired a new home and was determined to keep it. However, I had a car loan, significant credit card debt, as well as payday loans and personal loans.

I had managed to secure an excellent job and was focused on finding ways to regain financial stability. Becoming an owner-operator seemed like a viable option, especially if things worked out with my partner. It would provide me with the opportunity to travel and become a business owner. Therefore, I decided to educate myself about the owner-operator business since I had limited knowledge about the trucking industry. Anthony seemed like the ideal person to ask given his experience.

One evening, I reached out to Anthony via Facebook Messenger, expressing my interest in buying a truck and seeking information about his own purchasing experience. I explained that I wanted to educate myself about the trucking business before committing to it and investing with my partner. I was particularly interested in verifying the earnings potential he had mentioned, as he claimed there was significant money to be made as a trucker, ensuring he could provide us with a comfortable life.

I also asked if there were better deals available for purchasing a truck since I lacked familiarity with the trucking industry. Anthony responded, confirming that he was indeed an owner-operator. He enthusiastically shared his love for the profession and the income he generated. We engaged in an extensive conversation, discussing various aspects of the industry. Our conversation continued throughout the night via text messages.

We delved into topics such as our past marriages, children, jobs, finances, travel, religion, and bills. Our conversation flowed seamlessly, and we found pleasure in each other's company. We laughed, engaged in serious discussions, and shared our thoughts and concerns. Eventually, he mentioned that he had reached his destination and needed some sleep. We agreed to talk soon, and we hung up. The following day, he called me back, and we spent the entire day engrossed in conversation. It was a delightful experience to indulge in such engaging and fulfilling discussions. We shared laughter and delved into serious topics and issues. He mentioned that he would be back from the road by the upcoming weekend. I said, "Okay." So, here's the interesting part about him: when he first returned from the road, I was eagerly waiting for his call because I really wanted to meet him. However, the next thing I knew, he posted on Facebook, supposedly alone at home, enjoying a bottle of wine and a dinner he had cooked.

I thought to myself, "He's not being truthful. There's probably a woman with him." But I decided not to make a big deal out of it; I just saw him for who he really was. As expected, I didn't hear anything else from him that night.

The next day, he told me he had spent time with his kids. I didn't let it bother me anymore and carried on with my own affairs. I had a feeling that he would be with another woman that night. I really wanted him to call me; I really wanted to hang out with him. He seemed like such a cool guy. So, the following day, I got up and went to my Aunt Helene's house, where I spent time laughing and enjoying the company of my family. Suddenly, my phone rang. It was Anthony. I answered with a "Hello," and he asked, "What are you doing?" I replied, "Nothing, just chilling with my family." He said, "Oh, that's cool. Would you like to go on a date?" I smiled and asked, "When?" He responded, "Do you want to hang out tonight?" I said, "That's possible." He suggested, "Well, meet me at the casino."

I met him at the casino, and when we saw each other, we exchanged a warm embrace. He looked me up and down, and I gave him a look that said, "Okay." He was quite attractive—short, dark-skinned, with an absolutely stunning smile that lit up the room. He was bald-headed and had this laid-back aura about him. We headed to the roulette table where he was playing, although I usually preferred playing slots. He accompanied me upstairs to a slot machine. After about an hour, he joined me and asked, "Hey, do you want to go to the movies?" I replied, "Okay." It felt good to get up, go out, and do something because I had been feeling stressed and preoccupied with the DC and Day situation. I was alone at home, and the solitude was overwhelming. So, we went to the movies, and during the film, he was quite touchy. I playfully resisted his advances throughout the movie. We ended up laughing about it, but I must admit it felt nice to receive all that attention. Later, we went to a karaoke bar. I sat on his lap, and we laughed and enjoyed a few beers. While we were there, he kept trying to convince me to go on stage with him and sing, but I bashfully declined.

He asked if I wanted dinner, and I told him, "No, I just ate at my aunt's house." He then mentioned, "Well, I drove my eighteen-wheeler to the casino. Do you mind giving me a ride back home? You can stay at my place for a while." I politely declined his offer but agreed to drop him off. He insisted, saying, "I really want you to come in; I want you to see my place. Besides, it's late, and you have such a long way to drive home all by yourself. I promise I won't bite." He was a genuinely sweet and charming guy.

When we arrived at his house, we sat on his couch, embraced, and shared kisses. Before I knew it, I asked him if he had something I could sleep in, and he gave me one of his wife beater t-shirts. He said, "You can sleep in my room. I'll crash on the couch in the living room." I responded, "That's fine." He had a cozy little three-bedroom house in Indiana. We hung out for a little longer, and then he handed me the t-shirt. I went into his room, got all settled in, and was ready for bed. He entered and gave me a long kiss goodnight. Next thing I knew, we ended up making love. It was an incredibly pleasurable experience! I had been with the same man for the past 18 years, and there was no comparison to Anthony. I was completely shocked that a man could take me to such heights. It was the most amazing encounter I had ever had. We engaged in passionate intimacy repeatedly. It was a deeply romantic and gratifying experience.

The following morning, I dropped him off at his truck. Upon returning home, I couldn't help but think, "Oh my goodness, what have I just done?" Whatever it was, it served as a genuine stress reliever. It completely blew my mind. I thought to myself, "Wow, so this is what I've been missing out on." I chuckled to myself and resumed focusing on getting my finances back on track. I was diligently managing my bankruptcy affairs and striving to organize my bills.

For the first time in my life, I found myself alone at home, contemplating my situation. What was I going to do? How would I regain my footing and rebuild my life? I had come so far only to find myself in disarray once again. Anthony started calling me regularly. I discovered that the guy I had been talking to in Atlanta had been lying to me on several occasions. I decided to cut ties with him as I realized he was simply trying to deceive and take advantage of me. Consequently, Anthony and I began talking daily, and as luck would have it, my birthday was the following week. He proposed, "I have a delivery to make in California. Would you like to come with me? We'll be on the road for a few days, maybe a week. We can make a stop in Vegas, spend the night, and have an exciting time there.

Then I can take you back home in a few days." I told myself, "You know what? I've been under tremendous stress and working tirelessly for years. I haven't had a vacation in ages because when I was with DC, he never helped me with anything. During our marriage, I was solely focused on survival and purchasing my home. It's been years since I've been anywhere, and no man has ever taken me on a vacation."

I thought, "You know what? A vacation would do me good right now. What the hell?! Forget it. Come get me!" I handed my keys to my Aunt Tee-Tee and asked her to watch the house and the dog for me. I also gave a set of keys to my cousin. And lo and behold, he arrived in that truck, parked in front of my house like a knight in shining armor. He came in and spent the night with me since he had driven all the way from Detroit to be with me on my birthday. The next day, we woke up early and hit the road. It felt amazing.

At this point in my life, I was incredibly happy. I felt a sense of freedom, liberated from the pressures of raising children and enduring the psychological stress and drama that came with it. I had dealt with numerous behavioral and mental issues with the kids, as well as family problems, stress, strain, and failed marriages. I had overcome so much during my academic journey. The time on the road was exactly what I needed. It felt therapeutic being in the truck, observing the vast landscapes. The conversations I had with Anthony along the way were profoundly healing for me.

It provided me with an opportunity to reflect on my life—where I was and what I was doing. I was able to acknowledge my accomplishments, identify what I lacked, determine my desires, and recognize what I didn't need. It allowed me to reassess my life from that point onward. To my surprise, Anthony and I made it all the way to Las Vegas, Nevada. And guess what? Just as we reached Las Vegas Blvd. on the highway, the truck broke down.

I couldn't believe it. We eventually exited the highway and got out of the truck, only to be informed that the clutch and transmission had failed. Fortunately, I had accumulated a considerable number of points as a rewards member with Caesars Entertainment due to my previous residence in Henderson, Nevada. This tier status enabled me to secure free hotel rooms, and we took care of each other. We went into survival mode together, as the repair schedule for the truck kept getting delayed.

I had just received my paycheck when we went down there, so I had some money in my pocket. He also had some money, so we took care of each other. We went to all the shows and dinners, all over the place. We were simply enjoying ourselves; we ended up being there for two weeks. We engaged in passionate lovemaking every single day; we didn't watch a second of television. We shared numerous jokes. He ended up going on stage at a hypnosis show we attended. They told him he was a stripper named Tony the Tiger and he had a blow-up doll with him on stage. It was incredibly hilarious; he became a mini celebrity in Vegas for a couple of days. People who were in the audience would see us on the street and say, "There's Tony the Tiger!"

It was adorable; he was such a good sport about everything we did together while we were there. We laughed, drank, ate well, danced, gambled, and partied. I felt so youthful and free. It was wonderful. I had never experienced the kind of feelings I had with Anthony. It was like a breath of fresh air. It felt good and right, and we supported each other financially. We were a perfect match. We fell in love with each other in Vegas. We had a small mock wedding ceremony in the garden at the Flamingo Hotel. It was incredibly special between us. We smiled and laughed so much. We were just so happy together. Unfortunately, I eventually had to return home after those two weeks because I needed to get back to work. When I got back, we discussed the prospects of being in a relationship together. I was at a responsible point in my life. He resided in a house in Indiana, but the rent was really expensive, and he was rarely there because he was an over-the-road truck driver and was away most of the time.

He had various other bills and child support payments to make. Moreover, his children were in private school, which he was paying out of pocket. Then we started considering the fact that he had a heart condition, and as a private owner-operator, he had no medical insurance, hospitalization coverage, medication coverage, dental or vision insurance, or even life insurance.

I told him, "Anthony, this is not how I live." We started figuring out what our life together would look like. One thing I never wanted to do again was cohabitate with another man for the sake of my children. I simply wouldn't do that. I have always valued and respected marriage. Despite having many failed relationships in the past, I couldn't just live together with a man for survival's sake.

"We must be together; I believe it's better to marry than to burn." We continued discussing our financial situation as well as our past experiences with marriages and relationships. Now, keep in mind, I was in the midst of divorcing DC. I knew without a doubt that I would never go back after what I had been through with him.

I was completely done with that chapter of my life. I had chosen to move forward without any regrets. Anthony had been divorced from his ex since 2012. We decided to get married, and the wedding was scheduled for the following year in September. That would give us a year to plan. My divorce date from DC was set for December 12, 2018. Anthony and I got married on December 31, 2018. Just like that, that's what happened. We moved on, got him out of that house, and sold all his belongings. We moved in together and said, "There's no turning back now; let's do this. We're going to raise these kids, live our best lives, build something solid, and enjoy plenty together." And that's exactly what we were doing.

Let me tell you about this journey. We went through numerous difficulties with the mother of his children. He had experienced a great deal of emotional and psychological turmoil due to her constant disputes over their kids. It was unjust. This situation often led him to leave home frequently. It caused me to develop a dislike for truck drivers because he would always escape and live in his truck. He was torn and conflicted about his love for his children. She would constantly call and guilt-trip him, treating him as if he were an inadequate father who put everyone else before his kids.

Soon after our marriage, he encountered further heart complications and had to be readmitted to the hospital. I stood by his side throughout. His heart condition prevented him from continuing his career as an over-the-road truck driver due to the medications he needed to take. He attempted to work a few local gigs, but his heart couldn't withstand the physical strain. His heart was only functioning at 15% capacity, an alarmingly low level that posed a life-threatening risk. He was on the highest dosages of medication available for heart failure.

Anthony started experiencing depression. He expressed his concern, saying, "I can't spend the rest of my life relying on Social Security. I can't leave you burdened with all these bills." I wasn't worried about the bills. I knew I had to support us, even though the timing was unfavorable since I was already struggling due to the financial ruin caused by DC and Day. However, I couldn't turn my back on my husband.

# CHAPTER 22
# ANT & ANGIE'S, REAL GOOD AZZ SANDWICHES

*"People Find It Difficult to Let Go of Their Pain, They Prefer Familiar Suffering Because They Fear the Unknown'*
**'(Thich Nhat Hanh)**

At this point, I began praying even more fervently, asking the Lord, "What can I do to help him?" God inspired me with an idea. I am someone who loves giving thoughtful and practical gifts. On a previous Father's Day, I had bought Anthony a Blackstone flattop grill to cook family tacos and breakfasts on our home deck. One day we made some grilled steak and potato sandwiches, almost like Philly cheese steaks, but they were far better than Philly cheese steaks. They were so good with my secret special homemade "Big Daddy Ang" sauce. Suddenly, I felt compelled to make those sandwiches. I called him and said, "Anthony, God wants us to sell those sandwiches." He responded with surprise, asking, "What?" I repeated myself, and without any hesitation, he said, "Alright, let's try to sell them." So, on that Friday, after he finished work, we made a few sandwiches and decided to hit the streets and see how they would do.

I think we had around 25 sandwiches with us. Would you believe that within two hours, we had made over three hundred dollars? I couldn't believe it. I was like, "This is unbelievable. Did we really do that?" The very next day, we went out again and sold out. I asked him what we should call our endeavor, and he replied, "I don't know." I said, "Well, I don't know either, but those are some real good azz sandwiches!" He excitedly responded, "That's it, that's the name!"

And so, we named the business "Real Good Azz Sandwiches." I immediately registered it as an LLC. We worked hard to get the business off the ground, and we were thrilled to see our fan base and social media following grow rapidly. He became a local celebrity, known as "Sandwich Man!" Everyone on the streets knew him. My daughter, Makeba, was incredibly proud of us for our business. She had come into a significant amount of money and called to say, "Mom, I want to buy you a food truck, so you don't have to sell out of your car anymore. Find one and let me know the cost."

True to her word, we traveled to Detroit, Michigan, and found our first food truck, marking the birth of Real Good Azz Sandwiches. Life was looking up for us. I began feeling a sense of fulfillment and happiness. Money was flowing in, and we were on our way to building an empire with our new brand and delicious products.

However, during this time, I started facing difficulties at my job. It was the Trump era, and the new leadership in our office exhibited clear biases and racism. The director began terminating Black employees left and right, treating us with disrespect.

We were aware of the personal issues she was dealing with. She was a white woman married to a Black man who held a high position in the agency. However, they divorced, and he moved on with someone else. Despite my years of experience at the agency and my expertise in my role, she made my life difficult. She expressed envy towards my pursuit of higher education and acquiring multiple degrees. She boldly stated that she wouldn't dare do the same because she didn't need higher education to advance in the ranks. Furthermore, she asserted that it wouldn't benefit me in any way within the agency.

Every day, I endured immense stress at this job. My career at the Social Security Administration meant everything to me. I took extraordinary pride in my work and considered it my means of survival. However, working under this racist woman became unbearable. The more I pursued my education, the more she targeted me, harassed me, and made my job a living nightmare. It felt as though she was punishing me for striving for higher education.

I aspired to become an administrative Law judge, and she belittled my ambitions, questioning why I was trying to do so much. She made me feel unworthy of a higher education and created an atmosphere of competition. She treated me poorly in the office, accusing me of racism and hiding case documents. Her actions were profoundly disturbing to me.

Eventually, I had to undergo surgery, which allowed me some respite from the pressure at work. I was able to focus more on the food truck business, but I prioritized building our business credit. Managing the food truck became hectic as demand grew rapidly. We received catering orders and invitations to various public events. People wanted us to vend in the south suburbs, the south, and the west side. We were in high demand everywhere, and our customers frequently asked about our location.

After careful consideration, I made the decision to resign from the federal government and fully invest in our dream and future. I used my 401k savings and other funds to invest in the business. The food truck was thriving, and my cooking creativity was exceptional. We had a strong market presence and a devoted following. I believed we had the potential to achieve great success. Investors were interested in us, and opportunities to expand our brand and products arose. We had so much going on at that time.

I thought, "Why not take the chance to build something for ourselves?" Anthony was an excellent salesperson, and we were blessed with our first restaurant, which we promptly opened. Now, we faced a challenging situation: Anthony's son was involved in drug experimentation during this time. His son's behavior was spiraling out of control. One day, while Anthony was selling in a club, he allowed his son to ride on the food truck with him. Unfortunately, his son attempted to purchase drugs from a crack head on the street. Given that the restaurant was located in a neighborhood with high drug and gang activity, I strongly disagreed with having Anthony's son work in the restaurant. I knew it would inevitably lead to significant problems for us. We agreed that Anthony should not disclose our personal business to his ex-wife, and as a result, his children should not be aware of our business affairs, including our ownership of a restaurant.

His ex-wife continuously tried to extract money from us in any way possible. It was disheartening to witness the extent to which she would go to swindle money from him and our marriage. Over the years, she persistently took him to court, attempting to acquire more and more money. The situation deteriorated to the point where the judge ordered her to undergo a psychological evaluation due to her extreme psychological abuse, manipulation, and control over both Anthony and his children.

She constantly sought out ways to generate income, which was the reason I registered the business in my name. I had to maintain control over our affairs. However, despite my intentions, Anthony, in his excitement, revealed the business to his children without my knowledge. To make matters worse, he brought his son into the restaurant. I expressed my concern, emphasizing how dangerous it was and the precarious situation it put us in. I explained that if his son were to buy drugs from one of the local dealers and they subsequently entered our establishment, we could be forced to pay a substantial amount of money for his drug purchases. I stressed that his son's behavior had the potential to create severe consequences for all of us and put our lives at risk. Consequently, we found ourselves engaged in constant arguments, day, and night, regarding this matter. Eventually, Anthony walked out on me just two weeks after we opened the restaurant doors because I opposed having his son, with his drug problem, present in the business. The pressure from his son and others had pushed him to make an agonizing choice between me and them.

I had invested everything in my relationship with Anthony, believing in our joint creation as husband and wife. When he left, he left me with nothing. He completely cut off contact, ignoring my calls and blocking me on social media. He treated me terribly. I was utterly heartbroken and devastated, unsure of what to do. The food truck was at a standstill since I had no reliable driver or salesperson. Business was slow, particularly because it was right before Christmas. I found myself unable to afford anything—products, supplies, staff—absolutely nothing! I struggled immensely with the weight of these responsibilities on my own. He provided me with no prior warning and no opportunity to prepare for his departure, no chance to plan, save, or make alternative arrangements.

He simply walked out, leaving me stranded and solely responsible for holding down the fort. In addition to managing the restaurant, I was no longer employed. The income generated from the restaurant was insufficient to cover the expenses for both the establishment and our mortgage, as well as other bills. I had no one to turn to for help and found myself in a dire situation. I had depleted all my savings, including my 401K and thrift savings, in an attempt to support our business venture. It left me devastated, ashamed, and heartbroken. Anthony's sudden departure left me alone to manage the business, and it was an uphill battle. We were nearing the end of the COVID-19 pandemic, and people were gradually emerging, but I lacked the funds for advertising, proper signage, and other essential expenses.

The restaurant owner, who happened to be Arabian, was highly demanding when it came to rent and utilities. He treated me disrespectfully and degraded me as a woman. He showed no regard for how he spoke to me and frequently threatened to cut off utilities and change the locks if I failed to make timely payments. The pressure was immense, and I found myself in a state of panic, wondering how I would overcome these challenges. Despite having a master's degree, I felt lost and unsure of my next steps. In desperation, I resorted to taking out personal loans to cope with the overwhelming debt left by Anthony. However, many people rallied behind me, offering support and encouragement for my Black-owned business. They were appalled by what my husband had done to me, abandoning me, and leaving me in such a vulnerable state.

My son, DJ, also stepped in to assist me as much as he could, despite the hardships he faced with his own financial responsibilities and two children. He would work as an Uber driver during the night and dedicate his days to helping me. Witnessing his mother's struggle weighed heavily on him, but he drew strength from my determination and resilience. I knew it was unfair to burden my son with my troubles, so I resolved to take action. Anthony and I had investors who had supported us in getting the food truck business off the ground, and we still owed them money. However, his abandonment made it impossible for me to meet these financial obligations.

Consequently, I found myself facing yet another financial crisis, while still recovering from the consequences of previous failures with Day and DC. I was drowning in bills and on the verge of losing the house. I could barely afford assistance at the restaurant, and I worked tirelessly every day, hoping Anthony would return and provide the much-needed support. I clung to the belief that if I could hold on a little longer, he would see the error of his ways and come back to help me.

Eventually, the house faced the threat of foreclosure, and I had no choice but to file for bankruptcy once again. I had to relinquish the restaurant, leaving me with nothing. I found myself sitting in an empty house, desperately seeking employment opportunities wherever I could find them.

# CHAPTER 23
# MORE THAN A CONQUER

........................................................

*"God Is Going to Work It All Out for The Good. All The Pain, Frustration, Heartbreak. Somehow, And in Some Way, He Is Going to Use All of The Broken Pieces To Make a Beautiful Masterpiece."*
**(Ashley Hetherington)**

The COVID-19 shutdowns had severely limited job openings, but I refused to give up. I was determined to survive and rebuild my life. While a few catering orders trickled in, DJ supported me by contributing to gas expenses and other necessities. I wasted no time and immediately registered for my PhD studies, determined to pursue my dream of becoming a psychologist. I believed that obtaining a doctorate would equip me with lifelong tools to empower individuals and help them reach their full potential. Moreover, it served as a trailblazing example for my children and grandchildren, becoming a role model and source of inspiration for my entire family. This was an opportunity to reshape the course of history for my family. Pursuing a higher level of education was a personal challenge, a testament to my intelligence and my unwavering determination to achieve educational success. I told myself, "I won't let life hinder me, no matter the obstacles." I remained focused and continued to pray, seeking guidance from God.

Anthony had filed for divorce, moved into his own apartment, started trucking again, and driving for Lyft, and he was treating me poorly. Months later, when I heard from him after he left, he asked if I would sign the divorce papers. I replied, "It is what it is. Come on, that's fine." So, we met up at TGIF on a Friday; we sat down, ate, and had a cocktail. He then said, "No, we're not going to do this right now. We're going to wait." Eventually, we ended up in the car, and we made love in the back seat. Despite the fact that he had left me feeling hurt and abandoned, I never cheated on him, nor did I want our marriage to end. I just wanted him to get his act together.

I believe he saw how tough life was out there on his own and how hard he was working to survive. I think he seemed surprised because I had completely let go.

I had to allow him to go through what he needed to go through. I wasn't there to tell him what was wrong with his children or how he was being taken advantage of. I didn't try to make him see how he was being used. I simply let him go and allowed him to see the truth for himself. I had let go of the relationship because it was causing me too much pain due to his ex and children. But when I let go, I stood still and trusted God. I kept crying out to God, asking Him to fix it.

I remember standing in the restaurant, and early in our marriage, Anthony had told me, "If I ever die, I want Zebediah White to preach my sermon." I asked, "Who is Zebediah?" He replied, "I went to school with him, and I want him to preach my sermon if I ever die." One day, while I was in the restaurant, broken, hurting, lost, and under immense pressure, a man walked in and asked, "Is Anthony in?" I responded, "I'm sorry, he's not here. How can I help you?" He said, "Okay, I just wanted to support you guys. Please let him know Zebediah came through." I questioned him, asking, "The pastor?" He replied, "Yeah," and I said, "Oh my goodness." I opened the door, walked out, and reached out to hug the pastor. I broke down, crying and crying. He confusedly and concernedly asked, "What's wrong? Did something happen to Anthony?" I replied, "No, he's fine; he walked out on me and left me." As I stood there, still crying uncontrollably, I felt like I let all the pain out on that man's shoulder. I don't know why I felt so comfortable speaking to him, but I told him everything. I told him how bad everything was. He prayed for me and said, "I'm going to reach out to Anthony to see what's going on. I'll see if there's something I can do to help," and I replied, "It's okay."

We sat and talked in the lobby for a long time until customers started coming back in. He invited me to visit the church. I told him I would be there the following week, and I joined the church that Sunday right then and there, on the spot. I was so broken when I walked up to that altar. I felt like I had the weight of the world on my back.

I was broken, and I gave myself to God that day. I just asked God to fix it because there was nothing, I could do to make things right. I went home. Anthony and I talked more. I kept going to church every Sunday, praying, reading my Bible, and giving everything to God—all my worries, burdens, struggles, marriage, kids, bills, and debts—I gave it all to God. I had to break free from all the stress, strain, and worry I was under.

Pastor White was a great spiritual guide for me. He truly helped me out of the darkness I was in. I was lost, torn, miserable, and truly broken. He prayed for me and guided me through. He took all my calls and helped me understand where I was and how to reconnect with God.

And things just started getting better and better for me. I actually got hired as an administrative Law judge. I was going to have to go to DC for two and a half months, but they ended up retracting the position. I informed Anthony about my plans to go to DC; we were constantly working on reconciling our marriage. Anthony had given up on church due to the ordeal he went through with his ex, who had an affair with a member of the church they attended and lived with. He had been praying to the universe and seeking solace for a long time. I honestly believe his ex's infidelity played a role in his disillusionment.

Eventually, we started attending church together and worked through many of our problems. We began praying together every day and prioritizing God in our lives. Anthony gained a better understanding of the true meaning of marriage, the Laws that govern it, and the divine order of marriage and family. He started comprehending the spiritual order of life: putting God first, then the husband, followed by the wife, and finally the children. He learned the dynamics of divine order, and once he realized that everyone had their rightful place, he refrained from disrupting the order to which they belonged. That's when our life began to improve. Our communication and mutual respect grew, and he started treating me as his wife in front of everyone, including his children and his ex.

Anthony eventually moved back home and resumed working on the food truck. I found an excellent job at the Veterans Administration, and as I write this book, I am close to completing my Ph.D. studies with distinction! I am excited to embark on establishing my own organization called "The Blueprint of Success: The Bridge from Welfare Entrapment to Self-Sufficiency." I am writing these memoirs in the hopes that they can serve as a beacon of hope, a survival guide, or a roadmap to a better life for someone. I pray that all the trials and tribulations I have experienced can assist someone on their life journey. Please learn from my mistakes and take inspiration from the good I have accomplished in this life. As my children, grandchildren, and future generations read this book, I hope to have left them something to be proud of.

The underlying meaning and purpose of this story is to help you all understand and realize that no matter what challenges you face in life, you can overcome them if you make an effort and strive to do your best! Trust me; life will take you through trials and tribulations. You will experience heartaches, pain, disappointments, and confusion. There will be numerous obstacles, difficulties, highs and lows, family trauma, drama with children, failed relationships and marriages, and the loss of loved ones. I have personally endured some of life's most difficult situations. Now, I can reach out and attempt to teach others, while also raising awareness about the systemic issues we encounter.

Just look at how I managed to overcome them. All I can do now is express my gratitude to God for His wisdom, the time I had, and the lessons I have learned. We must learn to heed the lessons we encounter in life.

Anthony and I are still married, and we have eight adult children. We continue to face trials and tribulations as we care for, love, and guide our grown kids.

Life presents challenges for everyone, even the wealthiest individuals. It's part of the game called life. The key is to learn, live, grow, and be comfortable with who you are! It's perfectly acceptable to pursue your dreams, to be intelligent, and to embrace your uniqueness. The important thing is to learn from your mistakes, strive for improvement, aspire for more, and put in a little extra effort. And above all, never give up on your dreams!

Place your trust in God and make Him the priority in every aspect of your life. Maintain your faith, no matter how difficult it may seem. Never give up on yourself. Continuously strive for personal growth, set higher goals and expectations, and learn from all your experiences. Seek wisdom, acquire knowledge, and aim for understanding in all things. These are the elements that contribute to becoming a better version of yourself.

Continue to seek the best within you, while also blessing those around you. Never abandon love, faith, or life. Most importantly, never give up on yourself! Never tell yourself "No." Life is a journey filled with trials and errors, love and happiness, joy, and pain.

What we must understand is that there is purpose behind everything we go through, even the most painful experiences. Those are the experiences that shape us into resilient individuals. Never forget these lessons.

Strive to become the best possible version of yourself! I am signing off as Dr. Angela Sherelle Brown. I am somebody; I am a survivor; I am the woman who emerged from a life filled with pain, shame, abuse, neglect, abandonment, embarrassment, and hurt, yet maintained love for everyone throughout it all. I came from failure, from the depths, from circumstances that had the potential to mentally break people. I encountered negative influences and trusted individuals who wished me harm.

But guess what? I still stand. I stand as a determined woman, committed to doing the best I can for others while living on this Earth. My goal is to assist those who are in the position I once was, helping them find a path to a better life. I am still here, striving to make a difference for those who desire to make a difference in their own lives. I am here because I move forward without regrets, armed with strength, courage, endurance, and wisdom! That's why my husband refers to me as the modern-day Harriette Tubman. Thank you for reading this book. I pray that you find the strength to persevere through whatever challenges you are facing! Remember, no matter what, this too shall pass, and that's the Bible.

# ABOUT THE AUTHOR

## Angela S. Brown
*PhD (c)*

Empowering Lives, Building Bridges from Welfare Entrapment to Self-Sufficiency

Angela S. Brown is a beacon of hope and resilience, dedicated to breaking the chains of welfare dependency and poverty-stricken cycles. As the founder and CEO of "The Blueprint of Success: The Bridge from Welfare Entrapment to Self-Sufficiency," she leads an agency aimed at empowering individuals trapped in the clutches of low-income and welfare systems.

## About the Author

Born and raised in the tumultuous neighborhoods of Chicago, Angela's journey has been fraught with adversity from the start. Following the untimely demise of her mother and grappling with a father burdened by illiteracy, psychological trauma, and alcohol abuse as a 100% disabled Vietnam Veteran, Angela found herself navigating a world of hardship alone from a tender age. With over 20 years of experience working for the US Federal Government, Angela brings a wealth of knowledge and insight to her endeavors.

Enduring homelessness, shelters, and harrowing experiences such as child sexual exploitation and teenage pregnancies, Angela's early years were marked by trials few could fathom. Yet, fueled by an unyielding spirit, she refused to succumb to despair. At 12 years old, with scant familial support and lacking stability, Angela embarked on a quest for survival, determined to carve out a better future for herself.

Her pursuit of education became a cornerstone of her journey. From earning her GED to pursuing an associate degree in accounting at Robert Morris University while raising seven children as a single mother, Angela exemplified unwavering resilience. Her professional journey saw her contributing to esteemed organizations such as Nicor Services, BP US Headquarters, and Merrill Lynch.

Undeterred by her tumultuous past, Angela continued her educational odyssey at DePaul University, graduating with distinction with a bachelor's degree in Disability Law and a master's degree in Applied Professional Studies. Currently on the cusp of completing her Ph.D. in Community Psychology at National Louis University, Angela's academic prowess has garnered accolades, including the prestigious "Woman of the Year" award at DePaul University in 2015.

Angela's multifaceted endeavors extend to the realm of literature, where she shares her insights and experiences with the world. As the author of "It Takes a Fool to Learn," she imparts invaluable wisdom gleaned from her journey of resilience and redemption. Through her written word, Angela continues to inspire and uplift others, offering a roadmap for navigating life's adversities with grace and tenacity.

Angela's commitment extends beyond academia; she is deeply entrenched in community service and advocacy. As a board member of the American Legion of Evergreen Park and the Women's Auxiliary, she actively champions causes close to her heart. Her involvement with organizations like the NAACP and the Rainbow PUSH Coalition underscores her dedication to effecting systemic change.

Recognized as a member of the Golden Key International Honor Society and a leader in academic circles, Angela's influence extends far beyond the realms of education. Her brainchild, Shells of Success (S.O.S), serves as a beacon of hope, offering charitable deeds to communities in need. Additionally, her role as a board member at New Eclipse Church underscores her commitment to faith and community.

Angela's tireless efforts in mentoring, motivational speaking, and community engagement have earned her the moniker of "The Modern-Day Harriet Tubman." Through her transformative work, she endeavors to empower individuals from underprivileged backgrounds, equipping them with the tools to break free from the shackles of poverty and dependency.

In her personal life, Angela is a devoted wife to Anthony Brown, her childhood sweetheart from the Englewood community. Together, they impart invaluable lessons of compassion, hard work, and civic duty to their eight children and four grandchildren, nurturing a legacy of empathy and social responsibility.

Angela's vision for the future is one of systemic change. She aims to revolutionize the distribution of low-income programming, ensuring recipients are equipped with the knowledge and resources to thrive. With "The Blueprint of Success" poised to become a cornerstone of welfare reform at local, state, and federal levels, Angela remains steadfast in her mission to usher in a brighter, more equitable future for all.

## About the Author

*Masters degree*

*Ant & Angie's "Real Good Azz Sandwiches"*

*Anthony and Angela Brown*

*Little Angie*

Maternal grandmother Jane "Madea" Redic

My Mother, me, and my (fathers sister) aunt Helene

Paternal granmother Bessie Freeman

My paternal grandmother Bessie Freeman

Paternal grandfather Herbert Freeman Sr

## About the Author

*My Father Herbert Freeman Jr*

*My dad Herbert Freeman Jr*

*My Godmother Rev. Rosie Lee Wilson*

*My parents Herbert and Odie Mae Freeman*

*Angela*

*Angela*

*Angela*

*Angela*

*Angela*

## About the Author

*Angela*

*Angela*

*Angela*

*Angela*

*Angela*

www.ingramcontent.com/pod-product-compliance
Lightning Source LLC
Chambersburg PA
CBHW070656120526
44590CB00013BA/977